SVINIA IN BLACK AND WHITE

SVINIA
IN BLACK & WHITE

SLOVAK ROMA AND
THEIR NEIGHBOURS

DAVID Z. SCHEFFEL

BROADVIEW ETHNOGRAPHIES & CASE STUDIES

broadview press

Library and Archives Canada Cataloguing in Publication

Scheffel, David, 1955–
    Svinia in black and white : Slovak Roma and their neighbours / David Z. Scheffel.
(Broadview ethnographies & case studies)
Includes bibliographical references and index.
ISBN 1-55111-607-3

    1. Romanies—Slovakia—Svinia.   2. Svinia (Slovakia)—Ethnic relations.
I. Title.   II. Series.

DX222.5.S35 2005   305.891'497043736   C2005-900252-2

Broadview Press, Ltd. is an independent, international publishing house, incorporated in 1985. Broadview believes in shared ownership, both with its employees and with the general public; since the year 2000 Broadview shares have traded publicly on the Toronto Venture Exchange under the symbol BDP.

We welcome any comments and suggestions regarding any aspect of our publications — please feel free to contact us at the addresses below, or at broadview@broadviewpress.com / www.broadviewpress.com

North America
Post Office Box 1243,
Peterborough, Ontario,
Canada K9J 7H5
Tel: (705) 743-8990
Fax: (705) 743-8353
customerservice
@broadviewpress.com

3576 California Road,
Orchard Park, NY
USA 14127

UK, Ireland, and
Continental Europe
NBN International
Estover Road
Plymouth, Devon PL6 7PY
United Kingdom
Tel: +44 (0) 1752 202300
Fax: +44 (0) 1752 202330
Customer Service:
cservs@nbninternational.com
orders@nbninternational.com

Australia and
New Zealand
UNIREPS
University of
New South Wales
Sydney, NSW, 2052
Tel: + 61296 640 999
Fax: + 61296 645 420
info.press@unsw.edu.au

Cover design and typeset by Zack Taylor, www.zacktaylor.com

Broadview Press Ltd. gratefully acknowledges the financial support of the Government of Canada through the Book Publishing Industry Development Program for our publishing activities.

Printed in Canada

CONTENTS

LIST OF TABLES
AND FIGURES

ACKNOWLEDGEMENTS

I am indebted to many people who directly and indirectly contributed to this book. The members of my family, Phoebe, Emile, and Monika, graciously accepted the challenge of a somewhat chaotic existence during our sojourns in Slovakia, and their presence in the field proved of great assistance in my rapport with the Roma. More recently, their remarkable patience gave me the necessary time to bring the long writing process to a successful completion. This book is dedicated to them. In Prešov, my friend and colleague Alexander Mušinka was invaluable in too many respects to enumerate. Without his constant assistance the extended time my family and I spent in Slovakia would have been far less pleasurable and productive. Jaroslav Skupník, Will Guy, and John C. Kennedy very kindly read the manuscript and suggested improvements. Their incisive comments helped me a great deal. Ross Nelson and Jennifer Casorso contributed the maps of Svinia and Slovakia. Gabriela Husarová of the Prešov district archive located files required for the historical sections of the book and circumvented petty regulations that impaired their accessibility. John Paskievich and Joe MacDonald enhanced my insights into the relationship between Roma and ethnic Slovaks by involving me in the production of the National Film Board documentary *The Gypsies of Svinia*. Some of the "native" opinions about the inter-ethnic deadlock that are quoted in the book were originally made in front of John's camera.

The book could not have been written without my participation in the Svinia Project. Ivan Somlai proved an unwavering believer in the feasibility of this humanitarian intervention and my biggest Canadian ally during its execution. David Gifford of the European branch of Habitat For Humanity International and Jim de Vries of Heifer Project International provided much needed support during the early phase of the project. Several officials, who may prefer to remain unnamed, at the Canadian International Development Agency took a considerable risk by approving a scheme that placed the organization in a setting where bureaucratic measurements of success became meaningless. Habitat's eventual departure from Svinia—without having helped build a single house—underlines the exceptionality of CIDA's assistance. The University College of the Cariboo kindly tolerated my long absences from campus and provided some much needed financial support. Generous grants from the Wenner-Gren Foundation for Anthropological Research and the Frank Harry Guggenheim Foundation made a valuable contribution to the quality of my archival research in Slovakia and the Czech Republic.

It speaks for itself that the Roma depicted in this book deserve my deep gratitude. Their frankness, openness, and exuberance eased my entry into their homes and community, and the many friendships that survived my partial failure as a community developer were an important motivation for the writing of this book. Not all my friends and acquaintances in Svinia will agree with all my interpretations and conclusions. But I trust that their magnanimity shall override any misgivings they may have about my depiction of their collective identity.

INTRODUCTION

This book is about a community of Roma—or Gypsies, as some people still call them—in eastern Slovakia. Founded in the late nineteenth century by a handful of migrants, its population has grown over the decades to become one of the largest and most problematic settlements of rural Roma in the entire district. Despite its central European location, it resembles a third-world slum marked by unemployment, internal exploitation, violence, substance abuse, and resignation. Wedged into a village inhabited by ethnic Slovaks whose views of the Roma are openly racist, the dark-skinned squatters on the margins of Svinia are segregated from the surrounding society by physical and social barriers entrenched in local ideology and enforced by rules and conventions reminiscent of apartheid.

Located on the eastern periphery of the European Union, Svinia, together with hundreds of similar settlements inhabited by Slovak Roma, offers insights into topics of global interest and significance. Foremost among them are the much-debated questions of inter-ethnic (in)tolerance, the social exclusion of certain minorities, and the political and cultural context required for modernization to take place. Since the opening up of post-communist Eastern Europe, these questions have increasingly focused on the plight of local Roma whose problematic relations with the majority society have captured the attention of western observers and analysts. In most of the films, books, and articles made and written about the "Gypsies" of Eastern Europe in the last ten years or so, they are depicted as marginal people who have failed to find acceptance in communities with which they have co-existed for hundreds of years (Stewart 1997; Lemon 2000; Guy 2001; Barany 2002; Scheffel 2004b). Yet, although we have been blessed with many fine studies which, in one way or another, examine the causes and consequences of the tensions that in most documented settings prevail between Roma and their neighbours, there is a surprising dearth of detailed ethnographic accounts that supply the social, cultural, and historical context for the emergence and perseverance of local patterns of inter-ethnic inequality and dominance. "What went wrong?" in Svinia is the question that I pursue directly and indirectly in this book, and that I attempt to answer systematically in the concluding chapter. The elucidation of the conditions that prompted the exclusion of Roma from local "civilized" society constitutes the main theme of this book.

It is important to know that I did not select Svinia in any systematic way. My first encounter with it was unplanned and accidental in the true sense of the word. It took place in the spring of 1993 as part of a field trip designed to introduce a group of Canadian anthropology students to post-communist Europe. During our sojourn in the eastern Slovak city of Prešov, I asked the local Romani writer and activist Elena Lacková to explain the situation faced by her people. Instead of lecturing, Lacková took us to what she called a "typical" Romani community. That was my first encounter with Slovak Roma in general and the people of Svinia in particular. Our visit coincided with Slovakia's first year as an independent state, and its leaders were too preoccupied with higher-order political and economic issues to address the multitude of problems faced by the Roma living in hundreds of poverty-stricken settlements located on the very margins of Slovak society. My students and I were shocked by the squalor we witnessed in Svinia, and upon our return to Canada I began to investigate the possibility of initiating a community development project there. A few years later, this idea came to fruition in the form of a loose partnership between my university and several non-governmental organizations. In the spring of 1998, exactly five years after my first visit to Svinia, the Canadian International Development Agency (CIDA)—Canada's largest provider of international aid—agreed to finance a three-year pilot project in Svinia, which brought me back to the community as the director of a multi-faceted "Svinia Project" (see Scheffel 1999). Between September 1998 and June 1999, my family and I resided in Svinia and participated very closely in the affairs of the Roma. Much of the material presented in this book was collected then. It was augmented during our second prolonged visit after CIDA had approved an extension of the project in 2001. Between September 2001 and May 2002 we lived in Prešov, and the expanded mandate of the project gave me a much-needed opportunity to visit and become familiar with other Romani settlements in this region. A third extended sojourn, between January and June 2004, allowed me to carry out supplementary historical research in Prešov's regional and district archives.

Because my involvement with the people of Svinia was triggered by other than scholarly motives, much of the material assembled here carries the imprint of my mission. Unlike the stereotypical anthropologist who attempts to become as unobtrusive as possible in the pursuit of "participant observation," I arrived and worked in "my" community as an agent of change. Together with my co-workers I helped build latrines, designed distribution schemes for charitable donations, set up a daycare, planned the construction of a new settlement, competed with loan sharks through a financial self-help group, and participated in the trials and tribulations of Svinia's first community improvement association. Because I was, at least nominally, in charge of an ambitious project that commanded considerable resources, I was anything but unobtrusive. My presence was felt widely, and many people sought to enlist me as their personal patron and benefactor.

My exceptional status is reflected in the scope and focus of this book. Charged with a practical task that consumed enormous amounts of time and energy, I could not engage in the kind of detached observation and dissection of microscopic minutiae which anthropologists are particularly good at. Although I tried, though not very systematically, I never developed more than a superficial knowledge of the dialect of the Romani language spoken in Svinia. Instead of communicating in their vernacular, I had to depend on Slovak, or rather its local Šariš dialect, which the Roma speak as their second language. Another limitation derived from the fact that I didn't live in the settlement itself, and this clearly affected the depth of my knowledge of local norms and behaviour. On the other hand, by virtue of my position as an aid-giver, I couldn't afford to limit my attention to a handful of informants and their families. On the contrary, I had to get to know everybody, albeit often superficially—and I did. I feel that while I may have failed to appreciate the depth of some local views and habits, I compensated for this loss of ethnographic detail by transcending the usually narrow domain of the anthropologist's informants and extending my observations to the entire community.

The book that has resulted from my engagement with the people of Svinia draws on my experiences as a community developer and presents them in an anthropological format. Its primary purpose is to make available a comprehensive introduction to a type of rural community that has been, so far, hardly touched on in the scholarly literature. Ethnically segregated, economically underdeveloped, demographically vastly different from Slovak villages, and culturally a distinct world encapsulated in their own values and norms, the more than 500 Romani settlements found in Slovakia constitute a veritable *terra incognita*. The home to a large proportion of Slovak Roma, these ethnic enclaves have been associated with poverty, ill health, unemployment, violence, drug abuse, illiteracy, and a host of other problems. But in spite of the negative prominence given to these communities in countless reports of Slovak authorities and foreign agencies (Ringold 2000; Radičová 2001; United Nations Development Program 2002; Vašečka 2002), the settlement as a social formation remains largely unexplored and undescribed.

Since I spent more than ten years visiting and living with the people of Svinia, this book is inevitably more than an academic study. Many of the Roma described here with a degree of detachment are known to me intimately, and some have become friends. I have seen a whole cohort of children grow up, marry, and beget children of their own. Their past is intertwined with the past of my own children, whose lasting impressions of Europe were formed in and around Svinia. The intimacy that I have developed with the people introduced in the following pages brings with it a dilemma of representation. There is a strong tendency in contemporary western anthropology to present an idealized and partial picture of the societies we study in order not to offend our informants, tribal leaders, and ethnic politicians (Scheffel 2000). Were I to follow that model, "my people" would emerge as victims of white racism labouring hard to throw off the shackles of centuries-long oppression, attending adult literacy classes, setting up micro-enterprises, and participating in Habitat for Humanity workshops. Alas, the reality as I saw it couldn't be packaged so neatly, and I felt obliged to dwell on less savoury aspects of local culture, including rampant violence, widespread alcoholism and drug abuse, indifference, and internal exploitation. This concentration on social ills rather than collective triumphs shouldn't obfuscate my sympathy for the people I describe. I have learned to cherish and admire many of them for their ability to conduct seemingly happy and normal lives amidst poverty, grime, oppression, and hopelessness. The perseverance with which they keep the human spirit alive in what must be one of Europe's most inhumane settings is nothing short of remarkable.

The infectious friendliness and exuberance with which the Roma of Svinia impress visitors are the more surprising in view of the tragic history of their community. It is framed by two events that form the background for my *Leitmotiv* question, "what went wrong in Svinia?" The first event was the establishment in 1959 of a modernized settlement used as a vehicle for the integration of advanced Roma into the Slovak-dominated village. Inspired by socialist-era dreams of universal equality and progress, this settlement personified the planned advancement of Czechoslovakia's most backward minority. The integrationist experiment lasted for thirty years. It was aborted in 1989, and its subjects were deported—in the strict sense of the word—back to the muddy camp where they had come from and where they continue to dwell today. The 1989 expulsion—an illustration of what has come to be called "ethnic cleansing"—starkly symbolizes the segregation of Roma from Slovak mainstream society in Svinia and beyond.

At the core of this book, then, is the examination of the failed integration of Roma into one particular rural community. Since ethnic Slovak villagers are the acknowledged gatekeepers of Svinia's mainstream society and culture, they are the ones whose rules are used in determining who gets in and who stays out. Put simply, local Roma have failed the test of civilized behaviour—as defined and administered by their ethnic Slovak neighbours. Because of the profound consequences of this collective "failure," I allocate considerable space to an outline of what may be termed the "cultural deficit" of the Roma. It is in this context that a frank discussion of social ills and various forms of deviance is required, because it is this kind of "pathology" that stands in the way of the integration of local Roma into the normative society beyond the ghetto. I feel compelled to reiterate the culture-specific definition of "civilization." There is no *a priori* reason for valuing the ways of rural ethnic Slovaks more highly than those of their Romani neighbours, and I suspect that in many ways the latter enjoy more happiness than the former. But, as long as ethnic Slovaks maintain the monopoly on economic and political power that they have enjoyed throughout the period under consideration, it will be their rather than the Romani view of the "good life" that shall determine local social boundaries.

Some readers may feel surprised that I haven't made any effort to conceal the true name and location of the community described here. There are two reasons for this departure from what many anthropologists still consider the norm. First of all, the Roma of Svinia have always welcomed strangers in their midst, and there is by now a considerable body of material in the public domain—including a National Film Board of Canada documentary and several websites on the Internet—which describes my personal association with Svinia. Second, because even the little material at our disposal shows remarkable differences between individual settlements, it is important not to pretend that the community described here is a typical settlement that could be encountered anywhere else. Svinia has its own configuration of socio-economic traits, and in the absence of comparative material it is crucial not to jump to unwarranted generalizations. Further research will be necessary before we can begin to understand the diversity of adaptations exhibited by Slovak Roma and the place therein of the community described here.

one

A FRAGMENTED COMMUNITY

On the surface, Svinia is an unremarkable village situated near the east Slovak city of Prešov. With an area of 1,473 hectares and more than 1,300 residents, it belongs to the larger rural municipalities in the district. The centre of the village boasts an attractive Roman Catholic church, a small château converted into a museum of agriculture, a municipal building with an assortment of civic and medical services, an elementary school, and a handful of stores, the busiest of which is linked to a tavern. A cluster of low-slung concrete buildings nearby belongs to the agricultural cooperative which, even more than fifteen years after the demise of socialism, remains the largest local employer. The streets that extend from the village centre are lined with sturdy and well-kept single-family homes. Situated on sizeable lots and clearly demarcated by fences and walls, the houses are surrounded by gardens, fruit trees, and small enclosures for livestock. The residents—and builders—of these dwellings are rooted in Svinia. Most of them have lived here all their lives, and the graveyard shelters the remains of their forebears. The rootedness of these people can be seen in the self-assured manner in which they mark their presence. With measured and deliberate steps they traverse their neighbourhood, seemingly oblivious to any stranger who may cross their path. Elderly men and women relax on benches in the evening sun, exuding the air of self-confident proprietors surveying with pride their possessions. Even the children adopt the same proprietary demeanour as they race their bicycles down the main street and its branches.

But the peace, order, and affluence of the village are not extended to all of its residents. Tucked away on Svinia's northern margin, and barely visible to an unwitting visitor, the Romani ghetto conveys a much less serene impression. More than seven hundred noisy and dirty *cigáni*—as

Figure 1.1. The Slovak Republic

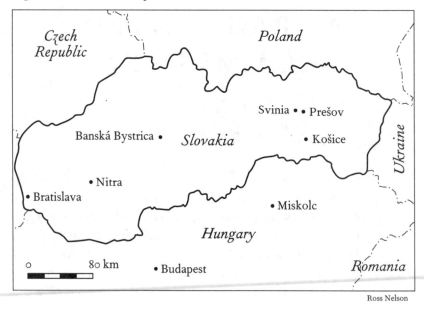

Ross Nelson

they are called locally—make their living here amidst heaps of garbage, confined to an assortment of slum-like dwellings in which no ethnic Slovak would ever live. Marked by race, language, poverty, and powerlessness, the residents of the ghetto constitute a profoundly segregated and in many respects oppressed enclave. The contrast between the ghetto and the village is encapsulated in the local habit of designating ethnic Slovaks as "whites," and ethnic Roma as "blacks."[1]

Officially, Svinia constitutes a single municipality, and all its inhabitants enjoy the same privileges conveyed by Slovak citizenship and local residency. All services, be they related to education, health, social security, housing, or pastoral care, are supposed to be extended according to the democratic principle of universal access. And indeed, public reports and statistical overviews compiled by municipal, regional, and state authorities provide little evidence of the powerful divisions separating "blacks" and "whites" in Svinia and hundreds of similar communities. According to the 1991 national census, the municipality had 1,080 residents, none of whom was officially Romani (*Obce a mestá* 1992:147). The census provides exact enrolment figures for the municipal daycare, but we don't learn that its clients were all "whites," this institution having been effectively closed

Figure 1.2. The Municipality of Svinia

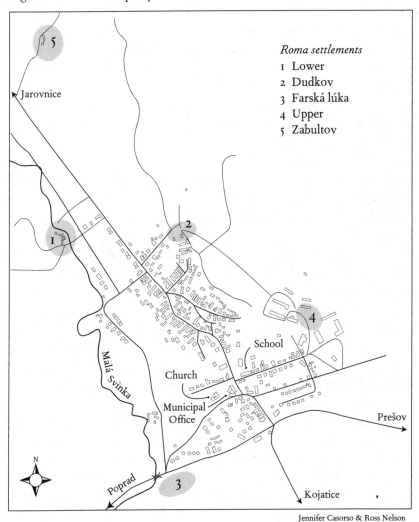

Jennifer Casorso & Ross Nelson

to Romani children. Neither does the information about the elementary school disclose the fact that it was segregated along ethnic lines, and that the Romani segment was barred from many of its functions, including the cafeteria and the after-hours school club. The 2001 census lists 358 Roma—about one half of the actual number—but that is the only reference to Svinia's ethnic bifurcation (Štatistický úrad SR 2001). Let us consider in some detail the local ethnic map as it emerges in the most visible domains of Svinia's public life.

The Setting

In Svinia there is a complete overlap between race and residence. All ethnic Slovaks dwell in the respectable village proper, the *dedina*, while all Roma are confined to the ghetto-like slum on the northern periphery, which is designated as *osada*. The latter term has a connotation of impermanence and instability. Best translated as "settlement," it refers to communities more durable than a camp but less rooted than a village. A cluster of summer cottages becomes an *osada*, as does an isolated hamlet stuck in the middle of nowhere. Unlike a proper village, a Romani settlement lacks genuine foundations. Its history remains obscure, and its boundaries are subject to periodic shifts in response to demands of the villagers. The settlement's marginality is borne out by Svinia's official chronicle, which since 1933 has recorded every local event of significance. While it informs in copious detail about political, economic, and social shifts that transpired in the Slovak part of the community, it wasn't until 1955 that the scribe took official notice of the presence of a sizeable Romani population (*Pamätná kniha*, vol. II:49).

In the 50 years since their first record in the annals of local history, Svinia's Roma have been moved around several times, like helpless pawns in the hands of their more powerful white neighbours, always destined for the least desirable and least visible patch of land. The last move took place on the eve of the 1989 revolution, on April Fools' Day to be exact, consolidating all Roma on the site of the present settlement. It accommodates in excess of 700 people on about two hectares of swampy land that is subject to recurring flooding from the rivulet separating the *osada* from white territory. By contrast, the roughly 650 Slovak villagers are spread out over more than 50 hectares of residential land, and they control an additional 1,400 hectares of forests, fields, and meadows. This eye-catching discrepancy is claimed by the villagers as proof of their intelligence, diligence, and determination to move ahead.

Wherever they venture beyond the confines of the settlement, itself a patchwork of municipal and private land that is yet to be surveyed, the Roma are considered trespassers of one type or other. The fields bordering their residence are controlled by the agricultural cooperative, which uses them to grow crops of various kinds. The extensive forests that stretch beyond the fields used to provide much-needed firewood, but since their privatization in the early 1990s their exploitation by the Roma has become problematic. Even the built-up space of the village proper is heavily racialized. The main street, which links the heart of the village with the road leading to the settlement, provides access to all public institutions, and here the Roma are tolerated to pass. They can move along this corridor on their way to the bus stop, the school, the municipal building, and the stores. The moment, however, they stray from this corridor to one of the side streets lined with family residences, they are likely to arouse suspicion that can lead to verbal and even physical threats. As a rule, private homes are off limit to the Roma. Occasionally, limited communication may take place over the fence, but for a *cigán* to be invited inside a home is highly unusual. The post office, the medical clinic, and the mayor's office—all located within the municipal complex—are accessible to Roma, but several other, ostensibly public, spaces are restricted. For example, the community centre (*kulturny dom*) beside the municipal complex, which is used for family celebrations, dances, and indoor sports events, is open to Roma only in exceptional circumstances determined by the mayor. Even day-time school dances that take place in this facility are restricted to ethnic Slovak students. Their Romani counterparts either go home or end up in a small, dank gym that lacks the capacity and technical equipment of the *kulturny dom*. The same bifurcation extends to Svinia's bar scene. The main tavern, which offers liquor and slot machines in a barren and smoky environment, is open to Roma, and this is the only place where some members of the two ethnic groups exchange more than a few terse words. On the other hand, a more upscale drinking establishment, a bar located in the cellars of a former château, is known for its strictly enforced "whites only" policy.

The People

My observation of the character of Svinia's ethnic Slovaks began in the late summer of 1998 after my family and I had relocated there from our home in Canada. The relationship began under strained circumstances caused by our inability to find accommodation in the village. Although I had located an elderly woman willing to sublet a part of her house, when we arrived on a cold and rainy August day to take possession of our promised home, we were met by a group of the landlady's relatives who began to renegotiate the terms of the agreement. I quickly grasped that we were, in fact, unwanted and that only a ridiculous amount of money would get us into a house where we would be at best grudgingly tolerated. With my family and all our possessions stacked in the small car of a friend, I spent the remainder of the day following up on fresh tips supplied by the mayor via the cellular phone. I don't recall how many bells I rang and how many strained conversations I endured. I do remember very well, though, that the main obstacle in my quest for accommodation was the prospect that we might invite Roma to visit us in our rented premises. At long last we found someone willing to rent us an unused cottage in the back yard, but the demand that I sign an undertaking promising not to allow any Roma to enter our premises seemed so bizarre that we abandoned the frustrating mission and returned to our friends in Prešov empty-handed.

Eventually, we did end up in Svinia, albeit not in the way we had anticipated. Unable to break the ice of local distrust, we decided to move into a room beside the project office, which was located in the old and unused Roman Catholic manse rented from the local parish. It was a good choice. Although we had hardly any privacy for the next ten months during which the old building served as the centre for all kinds of experiments—ranging from an impromptu daycare to sewing and cooking classes, and a distribution centre for charitable donations—we could at least conduct our affairs without any direct interference from our far-from-sympathetic Slovak neighbours.

Having spent close to a year in the very heart of "white" Svinia, I recall only a few occasions on which I managed to involve the locals in a spontaneous conversation. In spite of my more than passable Slovak and daily forays to the store, post office, and municipal building, it proved difficult to progress beyond a civil greeting. Usually, my friendly but secular "good day" triggered the demonstratively Catholic "praised be the Lord Jesus Christ ...," our eyes would meet in a fleeting moment of hesitant contact, and my counterpart would proceed to assume a listless expression that discouraged any further exchange of pleasantries. Even our two children—one of whom attended the local elementary school—didn't manage to break the ice with our neighbours. Six months into our residence, we had made friends with only one family: perhaps not surprisingly that of the former Communist Party chairman and Svinia's only committed atheist.

We consoled ourselves with the knowledge that the far-from-cordial relations with our neighbours most likely weren't caused by a genuinely personal antipathy. As Svinia's chronicle makes clear, the locals simply haven't had much sympathy for any stranger that has landed in their midst. When "the first Jew in 15 years" arrived on the scene in January 1940 to manage the Hungarian noble's estate, the villagers were "very upset and protest[ed] against this" *(Pamätná kniha*, vol. I:35). Two-and-a-half years later, after the unwanted resident had ended his tenure, the chronicler wrote down with obvious satisfaction that "the Jew ... had left our community" (59). I recalled this entry when, in January 2002, a packed village hall erupted in thunderous applause after a local resident with political ambitions had demanded that "all the foundations working with the gypsies pack their bags and leave us alone."

If relations within the village smack of xenophobia, documented attitudes to political events of national importance can best be described as self-serving opportunism. The chronicle provides ample evidence of this. For example, it informs us that in March 1938 a huge crowd gathered to light a bonfire to commemorate the death of Czechoslovakia's founder-president Tomáš G. Masaryk *(Pamätná kniha*, vol. I:20–23). Yet within a few months, the villagers voted 100 per cent in favour of breaking up Czechoslovakia—Masaryk's creation—and dispatched a congratulatory cable to Slovakia's new, proto-fascist, government (28). Several weeks later, 50 residents (Svinia had 84 dwellings at that time) joined to set up a local chapter of the infamous Hlinka Guard—the Slovak equivalent of Mussolini's Fascists and Hitler's Nazis (29). When the country entered the war as Germany's ally, the chronicler exclaimed that "the Slovak nation is fighting for justice alongside the great Germany" (32). The war years are not documented in any detail, largely because someone tore out four pages from the local history book. It was here that the scribe had recorded the names and activities of Svinia's Hlinka Guard members.

The postwar era starts with a new volume, a fresh chronicler, and a new attitude. We learn that the villagers celebrated with happiness and gratitude the arrival of the "heroic Soviet army" that liberated Svinia on 20 January 1945 *(Pamätná kniha*, vol. II:20). Barely a month later, the local branch of the Communist Party was already swelling with 32 members (21) who had begun to inculcate "love for the Soviet Union" and similar socialist values (28). When the first wave of collectivization rippled through the village in the spring of 1953, the war-time chronicler, once an enthusiastic supporter of Slovak fascism, became one of the first members of the agricultural cooperative (33).

Forty years of socialism added more than a few skeletons to the already crowded closet of local history. Rumours abound about the communist-era activities of today's successful entrepreneurs, but, as with the more distant past, rumours and gossip rarely escalate into open confrontations or accusations. The villagers mind their own business. Each family has its own problems with the past—be it the fascist or the communist era—and those are as carefully guarded as the fenced-in family residence. The sharing in this collective burden of history seems to be a major ingredient of local "white" identity.

In addition to being guarded, the villagers are also frugal and calculating in their economic behaviour. My family and I waited in vain for demonstrations of proverbial Slovak hospitality. I saw tokens of it being used opportunistically,[2] but in Svinia's day-to-day affairs, private wealth is used to beget more wealth, and hospitality is reserved for one's own kin. Our closest neighbour and landlord, the parish priest, afforded plenty of opportunity to observe rural capitalism in action. His residence resembled a small estate that supplied the cleric, his aged father, and his housekeeper sister with a steady supply of meat, dairy products, fruits, and vegetables. Although the output of the farm was much greater than the consumption ability of the small household, very little of the bountiful harvest was given away. During our residence, every surplus egg, carrot or apple was either sold or stored in the cavernous cellars beneath the manse. In the fall I observed with a mixture of admiration and incredulity how the octogenarian father gathered every fallen apple and pear that lined the more than 50 trees in the orchard. In the naive assumption that as renters of the premises to which the orchard belonged we had some right to a small share of the harvest, I asked the priest's sister whether my children could pick up a few of the fallen fruits. After some hesitation the woman agreed, but in the same breath she issued a stern warning not to hand out anything to the *cigánata* (little gypsies) who were in the habit of hanging around our residence. In spite of often repeated promises of home-baked cakes and pies, this was the first and last gift we received from our landlords. Although the village overflowed with apples, carrots, potatoes, and squashes of every imaginable kind, only once did a kind farmer give us a bunch of vegetables without expecting a payment.

It is hard to imagine a greater contrast to the meticulous, measured, and taciturn residents of "white" Svinia than the Roma who inhabit its less glamorous periphery. Unlike the stodgy village, the *osada* pulsates with life. As one approaches it along a narrow road that branches off from the main street, one runs into men and women pushing antiquated prams loaded with supplies purchased in the village. Loud, unkempt, and often only partially clad, these people smoke, scream, laugh, and argue with groups of children that accompany them. They are communicative with strangers, and by the time the visitor reaches the settlement, he or she is likely to be surrounded by a lively cluster of curious companions.

If sociability is the first indicator that one has entered a different world, then the settlement's sounds and smells provide further clues. Seven hundred bodies tightly packed into an area the size of roughly two football fields make themselves heard, especially when the majority are children who spend most of the time outdoors. The settlement is built around four concrete two-storey apartment buildings which enclose a kind of village square. Especially in the warm summer months this is where people congregate to socialize, argue, or simply listen to ear-deafening music from speakers placed in open windows. Once a month, during the three days that most local Roma receive welfare and family-support payments, the settlement erupts into one long celebration that diminishes the contrast between day and night. On these occasions, the noise from the settlement can be heard all the way into the village, where it is received with a mixture of anger and envy.

The settlement has its own sound, and it also has its distinctive smell. This too becomes noticeable the moment one arrives. It is a mixture of smoke, body odour, urine, and feces. Since the settlement has no functional bathrooms, young and old urinate and defecate outdoors. Most adults and older children tend to be somewhat circumspect about maintaining a distance between their favourite spot and frequented parts of the community, but small children crouch anywhere they happen to find themselves at the time mother nature calls, and their excrement litters the very core of the settlement, including hallways and stairwells of the apartment buildings. While human waste is the major contributing factor to the stench one perceives in the summer, wood smoke becomes the main culprit during the winter months. Unlike the village where odourless natural gas heats most residences, the settlement depends on firewood for all its heating and cooking. Although Romani workers had dug the trenches for the pipes that supply the village with gas, the municipal council decided not to extend the network all the way to the settlement.

The Numbers

The obvious differences in the living conditions of Svinia's "whites" and "blacks" have a less visible but extremely consequential corollary in the

Table 1.1. Demographic composition of Svinia (in per cent)

Age range	ethnic Roma	ethnic Slovaks
0–14	56	19
15–29	28	24
30–44	12	21
45–59	4	16
60–74	< 1	14
75+	0	6

demographic make-up of the community. The naked eye discerns right away that the village has a much older population than the settlement, but one cannot appreciate the extent of the demographic divide without some historical perspective. This is aided by race-based figures compiled by the municipal administration since 1991.[3] According to these figures, the ethnic structure of Svinia has shifted dramatically during the last decade. While the number of ethnic Slovak residents has barely changed from 664 at the end of 1991 to 666 at the end of 2002, the number of Romani residents has skyrocketed from 447 to 705. Although differential rates of in- and out-migration also have some bearing, by far the most important factor behind the changes reflected in these figures is the vastly different birth and death rates experienced by ethnic Slovaks and ethnic Roma. Between 1991 and 2001, the former experienced 102 births and 90 deaths. Local Roma, on the other hand, recorded 333 births and only 28 deaths. These rates clearly belong to two distinct populations with entirely different demographic parameters and behaviours. This is borne out in the population distribution prevalent in each of the two ethnic clusters at the end of 2001 (see Table 1.1).

It is no exaggeration that the explosive growth of the Romani population constitutes the single most troublesome issue faced by the municipality. Svinia's official chronicle shows that the awareness of an emerging demographic problem goes back at least 30 years when, in 1971, it made a distinction for the first time between the number of children born to ethnic Slovaks and to Roma (*Pamätná kniha*, vol. II:230). But with seven "black" births to eighteen "white" ones, the ratio then was still in favour of ethnic Slovaks. By the time the municipal administration began to systematically analyze annual demographic trends in 1991, the ratio had changed to 24:9 in favour of the Roma, and ten years later it stood at 38:8.

Table 1.2. Ethno-demographic trends in Svinia 1970–2001

Year	ethnic Slovaks		Roma		Slovaks below 15	Roma below 15
1970	765˙	82%˙	165˙	18%˙	266˙	91˙
1980	745˙	73%˙	270˙	27%˙	164˙	149˙
1991	664	60%	447	40%	140˙	246˙
2001	661	49%	685	51%	128	382

˙ reconstruction

The widening of the demographic divide must be attributed to two factors. On the one hand, improvements in health, socialist-era welfare policies, and the failure of the local economy to offer employment to the majority of Romani women created favourable conditions for a dramatic increase in the number of *surviving* Romani children. On the other hand, the socialist economy did encourage the participation of ethnic Slovak women, and this, combined with a massive emigration of young people to urban centres, led to a dramatic decline in the number of white births. Thus, during the latter part of the communist era, local ethnic Slovak women began to function primarily as economic producers, while Romani women took on the role of demographic producers. Table 1.2 captures the demographic trend over the last thirty years.[4]

Inter-ethnic Relations

The explosive growth of the Romani population has had a disastrous impact on the relations between the "blacks" and the "whites." Having lost their numerical superiority, the villagers have sunk deeper and deeper into a siege mentality with the concomitant growth of xenophobic and at times openly racist sentiments. These have been fuelled by the growing perception of the settlement as a slum plagued by extremely serious problems, many of which are directly related to the dramatic population increase since the 1970s. This perception is not without substance. The housing infrastructure available to the Roma has remained at the 1989/90 level, and the 250 residents that have been added to the population since then have been compelled to "set up house" in the primitive and vastly inadequate huts that make the ghetto resemble a third-world shanty town. A severe flood

that hit the settlement in July 1998 carried away most of the flimsy buildings, and the emergency housing provided by the government has hardly
improved the situation. The economic restructuring of the post-communist
era has seen almost all local Roma lose their jobs, with only a lucky few
being able to find new, usually partial, employment. The young generation
has been hit the hardest. A drawn-out economic recession, accompanied
by political instability and a rising tide of racism, has played havoc with
the education system geared toward local Roma. Alarming rates of drug
abuse, early pregnancy, youth crime, truancy, and illiteracy are all at least
in part attributable to the growing gap between the Romani population and
the socio-economic resources at its disposal.

In spite of their numerical preponderance, Svinia's Roma implicitly and
often explicitly acknowledge ethnic Slovaks as the reference group whose
norms and values should regulate local social discourse. This means, in
the first place, that all Roma accept Slovak as the appropriate language
for inter-ethnic communication. They also accept the local usage of being
referred to as *cigáni*, although the term has a derogatory meaning and
has been replaced by *Romovia* (Roma) in official parlance. Habits of local
speech that perpetuate the ethnic asymmetry are deeply ingrained, though,
and nobody takes affront at the tendency of the villagers to restrict the use
of the term *ludži*, which in this context means "people," to their own kind.
Similarly, the "whites" expect to be addressed by the courteous formal
singular pronoun *Vy* (you) while they employ the informal *Ty* (thou),
which smacks of degradation and disrespect when applied to older people,
when speaking with Roma. The linguistic tools that maintain and fortify
the ethnic cleavage include the term *gadjo* (singular) and *gadji* (plural),
which all Roma use when referring to "whites."

The quality of local inter-ethnic relations is reflected in countless beliefs
and stereotypes held by members of each group about their neighbours.
While the Romani views of "whites" tend, on the whole, to be complimentary
and self-effacing, the villagers' assessment of "blacks" is dominated by
overwhelmingly negative and, to a western audience, racist stereotypes. The
material that follows provides an overview of the justifications adduced by
local "whites" for their low regard for, and segregation from, the Roma.[5]

The backbone of local views of the Roma constitutes the assumption of
their inherent inability to live up to basic standards of civilized behaviour.
To the vast majority of villagers, their Romani neighbours constitute an
animalistic society that generates and adheres to customs that negate Slovak

norms of propriety. According to a middle-aged shopkeeper who has daily contact with Romani customers, "They have no discipline, no character. Negative culture. Recently a kid came around, naked, with no pants or anything. What then?" Animalistic nakedness leads to animalistic sexual conduct, and that, in turn, begets mental inferiority as alleged in another interview: "And the way they live, I can't even talk about it, because they have sex within the family, [and then they produce] imbeciles." This accusation is echoed by another informant who claims that "they are imbeciles, pure imbeciles.... Cousins will interbreed, not that foreign gypsies would come in; they keep to themselves, cousins marry, imbeciles are born, imbecile children."

In addition to deviant sexual relations, the Roma are linked to all kinds of other unsavoury practices. One of Svinia's oldest residents, a woman in her 80s who resides next to a busy bus stop, adds these observations:

> They have a place to go to the toilet behind the fire department building. He comes from Prešov, and there he goes; he walks to school, they come from the other end—from the store, and there they go. But I heard one night how a bus driver swore ... "such a stench—goes to the toilet and then hops onto the bus. He just squats and done."

While dirtiness is considered an invariable by-product of the settlement, it is significant that it is presented as a condition chosen and preferred by its residents. Here is the perspective of a middle-aged woman:

> The environment people [of the national government] will say that they can't live like this, but they don't want to have it otherwise; they are taught to live in that unholy mess; they don't know anything else. If they were to live in family homes like we do, they wouldn't know what to do. If you saw those shocking wraps that the babies have to sleep in, it would turn your stomach. The swaddling clothes are almost black. And the clothes, the same. They come lousy to school; it's terrible.

The claim that "gypsies are dirty" is universally believed in. Svinia's mayor, an educated and in many ways enlightened reformer, uses it as an explanation for why his constituents don't like Roma to attend community-wide gatherings: "... there is a problem about cleanliness, [as] nobody wants to be in an enclosed room with somebody dirty and undressed." The same reasoning is employed by the Roman Catholic priest to justify the *de facto* exclusion of Romani parishioners from the weekly mass: "To church—they [the Roma] will come, but only very few.... People pull away from them, you know, they are dirty, and it's difficult that way." In the same vein, Svinia's oldest resident blames the well-known tendency of local bus drivers not to stop for Roma on their alleged body odour: "And then what, the bus comes along, does not want to stop for them, because if they get in, it stinks, and nobody else wants to smell it in the bus."

In addition to a general lack of cleanliness, Roma are associated with unsavoury dietary habits. The most serious accusation in this regard concerns the alleged consumption of dog meat and lard, which is linked, in turn, to thefts of dogs in the village. According to a shopkeeper, "Even the dog they will steal. Mine got stolen twice already. They kill and eat it.... They render the fat and sell 100 grams for 100 crowns. Like butter! It's awful." As the next two accounts show, it is only a small step from reprehensible to threatening behaviour. In the words of one observer, "They have healthy stomachs. They go to the dump, among the garbage, when they are out of money. In Prešov they go around the garbage containers, get old clothes, food, and they ... bring the stuff along, drag in bacteria and infection." The same concern for the collective health of ethnic Slovaks is voiced by an elderly resident who has been repeatedly rapped on the knuckles for letting his dog loose on the main street:

> He goes to the dump to collect all kinds of rags, or some carcasses or what not, and then strews it around,... you can see it here, what need I tell you. You can't do anything with them. If I could let the dog loose in the road here, so they wouldn't come; I don't want them to throw our foodstuffs around here, to drag some disease in.

Most of the villagers seek the root cause for the "negative culture" attributed to local Roma in their alleged passivity, laziness, carelessness, and lack of forethought. Their closest white neighbour puts it this way:

> We don't really need anything from them. They need the whites more. In this region they absolutely don't know how

to start any sort of husbandry, or raise some crops. They were never used to it, neither do they try to start such a lifestyle, to raise their own food or do something for themselves, or start a workshop, absolutely nothing. Maybe elsewhere there are Roma who live among the whites and try to adapt, but ours here have no interest in it whatsoever. They just wait for the monthly social aid payment, when they will live it up for three days, they will lay about the road and in the ditches, the kids lick themselves silly with fancy ice creams, everything from the stores. The feasts last for three days, and then for a month, nothing. While the summer lasts, they scour the gardens and live on prunes ... and on whatever grows in people's gardens. That's how it works.

The widely held belief that Roma are careless and lazy is aptly illustrated by the local controversy surrounding the use of the forests bordering Svinia. Most of them have been privatized and are managed by an association of owners. This body issues permits to interested Roma entitling them to gather dead wood to fuel their stoves. But ever since the introduction of this system, the owners have been charging the Roma with abusing it by chopping down healthy trees and devastating the association's holdings. What infuriates the owners and municipal officials is not so much the perceived cheating as such but rather the wasteful manner in which the trees are cut down. As one young villager puts it, Roma fell a tree "a metre high" because "he won't stoop down for it, he doesn't cut at the base, he is so easy going, it's in their blood. That's how he stands—that's how he cuts."

In one way or another, all the examples of undesirable traits attributed to local Roma serve to justify the villagers' desire for ethnic segregation. Whether on account of their supposed laziness, dirtiness, lack of proper sexual mores, or unsavoury dietary habits, the Roma are not considered equals of ethnic Slovaks, and this is why respectable residents wish to keep them at a distance. As one old man put it, "I would like best if they stayed down in the settlement on their own, and not drag around here all the time."

But instead of staying "where they belong," the Roma seem more and more out of control. On the one hand, the rapid population growth during the last 20 to 30 years has made them far more visible and, as the integrative mechanisms developed in the past began to crumble, increasingly more anonymous. On the other hand, a proliferation of social problems—ranging from alcoholism, drug abuse, and vandalism all the way to theft and violence against villagers—has given rise to unprecedented levels of fear. It is hard to conduct a conversation about inter-ethnic relations without encountering the motif of a wholesale deterioration in recent years. Old-timers who recall the more distant past point out that relations used to be better when the Roma possessed useful skills that made the villagers appreciate them. Here is how Svinia's oldest resident sees the change:

> Back [then] during the time of the Slovak State [1939–1945], they knew how to make wheels, troughs,... and they knew how to do blacksmith's work, shoe the horses; but what they knew they forgot during communism.... The gypsies who knew how to do it have died out, and the present ones do not have those skills any more.... The communists came, all went to do other work, and the skills disappeared. Got buried under a lot of dust. Finished. Nowadays, the gypsies wouldn't know how to handle a horse. He doesn't even know how to sharpen a hoe, so how could he do those things? If they wanted to work, even nowadays they could make themselves useful, because work could be found. But they have no interest.... Since they are getting social aid, they are not forced to do anything. Used to be that a gypsy woman would come to the farmer's wife, helped her with this or that, and would get ... beans, potatoes, or other stuff, for the work.... That is no more now. The only time they show up in the farmyard is to steal something.

As older people point out, the bonds of pre-war solidarity were sustained by the widespread custom of godparenthood, whereby villagers agreed to become godparents to the children of Roma with whom they maintained a working relationship. The patron-client bonds fortified by this ritual association ensured a degree of reciprocity and, in turn, civility unheard of in present-day Svinia. But the view that relations have grown worse is not confined to the older generation. Villagers who are now in their 30s and 40s remember the communist period as being still quite conducive to amicable relations with the Roma. According to one man who went to school during the socialist era, contact at school generated a degree of civility that has since disappeared:

In my days, when the ratio was perhaps 20 whites and 3 or 4 blacks, it was still bearable. They sat in different rows, but, well, even today we are friends, [and] with the ones who went to school with me, we would say "hello" and such.... There we could talk; maybe not friendship, but we took it as normal that they were a little different. For example, the teacher had to explain various things to them differently than to us, but there was no enmity. We just took things as they were.

The very substantial population growth among the Roma, combined with the segregationist trend of the post-communist period, has vastly reduced the chances for amicable inter-ethnic contact. The villagers cannot keep track of "who is who" in the settlement, and as their ability to recognize individuals declines, their tendency to generalize and prejudge increases dramatically. This is well illustrated by the willingness of local whites to invoke what I call the "organic hypothesis" of Romani population growth. This theory holds that Roma, on account of their "natural" lifestyle, are more resistant to disease and injury than the "overcivilized" ethnic Slovaks. A middle-aged woman sums up this view when she postulates that "[t]hey don't even get sick, no epidemics, whites will perish sooner than they. They get no strokes, no AIDS, no heart attacks, nothing." A young man concurs and elaborates with the assertion that "[t]hey also fight among themselves; the newspapers wrote that one threw the axe at his sister-in-law, but she is ill for two weeks and then is fine again. A white would be crippled for life. I don't know what that nation is made of, but they don't suffer any ill effects."

The Roma are believed to use their strong constitution as a simple means to generate income by "breeding" babies. Taking advantage of the government's generous family benefits, the argument goes that Roma are motivated by economic calculation to produce as many children as possible. Here is how a middle-aged woman sees the contrast between Slovak and Romani child-bearing habits:

A white family has one kid, two, three, up to five. And they [Roma] have 10, 15, 25 has one gypsy woman. I think that is a little too many for one family. They can't take care of that many. And then they pull in four times as much money as a white person. And pour it down their throats. Not all, can't say that they are all like that, but the majority.

Perplexed and frightened by the explosive growth of the settlement, most villagers are convinced that its considerable natural increase is further magnified by an influx of Roma from other settlements. This thoroughly erroneous perception—most likely caused by their lack of familiarity with younger Roma—leads to exaggerated assessments of the actual population size of the settlement. Asked whether he knew any of his Romani neighbours, a villager in his early thirties had this much to say:

> Not so many, because lately quite a few strangers moved in. Of our own Roma, the ones who are residents here, there are about five hundred. But without papers we have maybe ... three hundred extra. True enough, they are allowed to visit, but nobody is counting, there are no serious controls, no one knows when he came or when he is planning to leave. Nobody records it, we have now so many that maybe every second or third one is someone I don't recognize—a stranger in other words.

Nowhere does the feeling of helplessness and loss of control come to the foreground more forcefully than in depictions of criminal behaviour attributed to Roma. The most frequently heard accusation holds them responsible for a myriad of thefts reported by the villagers and ranging in magnitude from a dead chicken to clearing entire fields of produce. According to a shopkeeper, "[t]hey steal abnormally. Abnormally. Old ones, young ones, all ages. Even the stores do they break into. In the three years we have been here, the store got broken into four times. Four times! But they send only those less than eighteen years old who cannot be sentenced. The parents!" Svinia's oldest resident agrees and elaborates:

> During the day they eat and sleep, get drugged, and at night they go to steal.... But there you have it, every Sunday, when people go to church, gypsies are all over the village, and when the house is empty, they steal everything. Everything they take away. There is no relief.... I have to stay home all day, can't go to any work, or to the field, or elsewhere, I have to stay home

to keep a lookout. I have a dog, also, a German shepherd, there is no other help. Because they will come into your yard, pick up a stone, throw it at the chickens, kill one, grab it, jump the fence and is off.

The perception of local Roma as thieves waiting for any opportunity to strike at hapless villagers goes hand-in-hand with the conviction that they are inherently violent and that their presence poses an immediate physical threat to the Slovaks. In the words of a middle-aged woman, "Yes, we are afraid. I am afraid, too, scared that they will come to break my windows, beat up my son, worried that I will get a stroke from all this." According to another source, the most vulnerable residents are the elderly, many of whom have become like prisoners in their own homes: "In winter, come four or five o'clock, they are even afraid to turn on the light in the room.... An old woman would be afraid to take the flashlight to go to the outhouse; [she] will go on the pot [instead], afraid that a gypsy is waiting outside. Because they aren't even afraid of the dogs."

In the collective memory of white Svinia several incidents stand out as stark illustrations of the threat that local Roma are believed to pose to the villagers' lives and safety. One such incident occurred in 1985 when a young man was killed by a Romani resident. The villagers' version of the event postulates that, in the words of the mayor, "it started almost innocently, in a pub fight, [then] a chase, in which the whites were unarmed, had no knives like the Roma who used knives and broken bottles. They cut the man's throat, and he bled to death. Another man lost one eye, and the third one's spinal cord was severely damaged."

Some ten years later, in March 1994, another altercation showed that local Roma had allegedly lost their habitual fear of the police. According to the official account in the community chronicle, two police officers entered the settlement to apprehend a suspect on a routine investigation. This time, however, the officers were threatened by a group of Roma who threw stones and mud at them. Even the firing of a warning shot had little effect, and so the police withdrew (*Pamätná kniha*, vol. III:303). A few hours later, reinforcements arrived, and a large number of masked officers in riot gear stormed the settlement, overcame "active resistance" (303), and, after a violent house-to-house search, apprehended the suspect. This episode reinforced the widely held belief that the Roma had grown too aggressive for peaceful conflict-resolution methods. As one white woman puts it, "They need a cop with a nightstick, and [the threat of] jail. There is no other help."

The far-from-complimentary views of local Roma held by their white neighbours should make it clear that most of the inter-ethnic encounters that take place every day are fraught with mistrust and tension. Of course, as always, there are some exceptions to the taboo on consorting with the "gypsies." For the most part, this applies to a handful of villagers of questionable standing who have friendlier relations with at least a few local Roma. The vast majority of the whites, though, abide by the norm of ethnic segregation. This extends not only to banning Roma from their homes but also to refusing to enter the settlement. Even though some are curious about what goes on beyond the creek, they will not visit the forbidden territory for fear of losing standing in the eyes of their neighbours.

There is only a handful of ethnic Slovaks whose periodic forays into the settlement do not lead to an automatic loss of status. These are, without exception, officials of one kind or another. A couple of social workers who work for the district government in Prešov pay infrequent visits to Romani parents whose children reach a state of neglect that the state cannot ignore. Motorized police patrols drop in from time to time to make inquiries about reported crimes or to pick up suspects for interrogation. The mayor may appear once or twice per month. And the Roman Catholic priest visits occasionally to meet with a small cluster of devout Roma or to discuss an upcoming baptism.

Education

The segregationist views held so firmly by the white community are reinforced by the public education system. At the pre-school level the spacious and well-equipped daycare runs at capacity and caters to 32 children ranging in age from three to six years—all of them ethnic Slovaks. Since the regional education authority that oversees the facility cannot legally bar Romani children, the official explanation for their absence is the monthly fee—most of which covers meals—which Romani parents allegedly refuse to pay. The director, however, freely admits what everybody knows anyway: namely, that the moment she enrolled a single Romani child, the facility might just as well close down, because all white parents would pull out their children. Invoking health concerns related to poor hygiene in Romani households, the daycare bars Romani children even from its small outdoor playground. The site, consisting of a few basic see-saws, swings, and metal climbing hoops, is fully fenced and accessible only through a gate that is locked and unlocked by the daycare staff. With our kitchen window overlooking the playground, my family and I witnessed numerous confrontations between trespassing Romani children and white residents who chased them away even at times when the facility was unused. Unable to come up with a reasonable justification, the stern guardians of community standards tried to convince us that the metal equipment could transmit infectious diseases left behind by the *cigánata*.

The same pattern prevails at Svinia's elementary school. Although this is officially an integrated institution, even a superficial glance reveals powerful physical and social barriers that keep ethnic Slovak and Romani students apart. According to official figures, of the 298 students enrolled in the 2001–02 school year, 213 were Roma.[6] But in spite of their absolute numerical majority, the latter are confined to poorly equipped and badly maintained facilities located on the margins of the school grounds. The junior division is still relatively well off with two experimental classrooms that have been refurbished thanks to the support of a private foundation. But the senior grades are confined to a dilapidated small manor house that has not seen a fresh coat of paint for at least 30 years. Boasting crumbling stucco, dingy basement bathrooms, and tiny classrooms equipped with nothing beyond worn chairs, desks, and blackboards, this crowded and noisy facility corresponds to pre-war ideas of a village school.[7] By contrast, the white minority is housed in a modern building equipped with functioning bathrooms, a spacious change room, well-appointed classrooms, a teachers' cabinet, and a computer lab. While its higher level of cleanliness undoubtedly reflects different standards observed in the village and in the settlement, it is not without interest that the school's only cleaning lady is an ethnic Slovak who spends most of her time mopping around the central building. Nor is it irrelevant that the rule on changing footwear normally followed in educational facilities is applied only in the white school—which alone sports a cloakroom. Similarly, the quiet one perceives here is due not only to the better deportment of white students. Unlike the number of Romani students, which almost doubled between 1991 and 2001, the ethnic Slovak enrolment has been declining steadily, giving far more elbow room to the children of the villagers. In this respect, too, the school set-up parallels the contrasts between the spacious village and the crowded settlement.

The ethnic segregation practised by the school is justified by the different success rates of the two blocs of students. The official explanation furnished by the principal and his superiors at the Prešov district education authority points out that virtually all local Romani six-year-olds who enter first grade lack adequate Slovak language skills required for successful participation alongside the better-prepared white students. So, instead of letting them fail and repeat indefinitely, the school channels all Romani grade-one students into a special stream where they receive, at least in theory, the extra attention their situation merits. Alas, although both blocs follow officially the same curriculum, their separation into different buildings and the failure to bring them together in play and extracurricular activities reinforce already existing rifts and deepen the mistrust between members of the two communities. The separation laid out in first grade deepens as the two cohorts of students branch out along different paths in subsequent years. The second grade of the Romani stream is minuscule by comparison with the robust numbers entering school (in 2001–02 it consisted of a single class with 13 students), and the inquirer searching for an explanation is led to yet another section of purely Romani classes. Informally designated as "special school" (*osobitná škola*)—the official terminology applied to this unit is "special classes with the character of a special school"—this division is set up for students with objective cognitive difficulties ascertained by educational psychologists. Here we find the majority of the school's Romani students—147 during the 2001–02 school year—following a simplified curriculum, which, if completed, allows access to a narrow range of "special" vocational schools where students can master the basic skills of brick-laying, house painting, cooking, or sewing.

Unlike the "normal" Romani stream, which comprises a large number of grade-one students and terminates with a small number of second-grade students, the "special" stream runs all the way from grade one to grade nine. This means that virtually all Romani students beyond the second grade find themselves stuck in the special division, which leads, under the best circumstances, to simplified vocational training and, at least in theory, a menial job under the supervision of a fully certified journey-man. Although a number of local Roma have graduated from the special vocational training, none has been able to find work. In theory, again, a highly adaptable Romani student can also be placed in the white division, which opens the way to graduation from normal elementary school and, in truly exceptional circumstances, admission to a regular secondary school.

While each year one finds a handful of such students in the lower grades of the white stream, their presence is always temporary. Sooner or later, they fail to meet the standards of normal school and are expedited to the less stringent special school division. So it happens that to this date not a single Romani student has graduated from Svinia's regular school program. This means, in turn, that no local Rom has ever managed to enter, let alone complete, a normal high school.

The dividing line between ethnic Slovak and Romani students extends beyond the classroom. The school has a club that provides leisure-time activities after regular instruction. Romani students are not encouraged to attend, and most are not even aware of its existence. The school also has a well-equipped cafeteria serving nutritious and subsidized lunches—to white children only. The official explanation for barring Roma from the meal program is the limited capacity of the facility. In reality, though, the cafeteria feeds teachers as well as municipal workers, and these should, if rules were really followed, make place for needy schoolchildren. The root cause for the discriminatory practice lies elsewhere. The parents of white students vehemently object to their children participating in any activity that would bring them into close physical contact with their Romani counterparts. Since the fear of contracting lice, fleas, and contagious diseases provides the dominant and socially acceptable rationale for segregationist sentiments and practices, the collective consumption of food in the school cafeteria assumes a particularly symbolic significance. To my astonishment, during a conversation with the head of the district education authority in October 1998, I was informed that as far as the cafeteria and other potential "meeting grounds" are concerned, freedom of choice for white parents overrides the principle of non-discrimination potentially invoked by Romani parents. This means that if ethnic Slovaks refuse to allow their children to participate in "mixed-race" activities—be these meals, dances, sports, or, for that matter, instruction—the principal is permitted to sanction these preferences by banning such activities altogether.

Religion

Svinia is an almost entirely Roman Catholic community, and the influence of the church extends well beyond its walls. An architecturally significant building dating to the Middle Ages, the church dominates the centre of the village topographically and symbolically. Every Sunday morning, profusive ringing of the bells welcomes throngs of worshippers to the main service of the week. Attendance is so strong that the church fails to accommodate everyone, and groups of villagers remain outside where they listen to the proceedings via a loudspeaker. Many of the people who congregate here each week are former residents of Svinia now living in Prešov, who demonstrate through their weekly returns the desire to maintain membership in the ancestral parish. The mass serves as a prelude to a day-long celebration, which includes the traditional and sumptuous Sunday lunch, followed by drinking and visiting. Each extended family cooks and consumes its own meal, but the drinking and visiting afterwards bring together more distantly related people as well as old school friends and colleagues from work.

An outsider has little chance of participating in these holiday rituals. Living right beside the church, with the parish priest as our landlord, my family and I expected to receive an invitation to attend the service and perhaps even the home celebrations afterwards. We waited in vain. All Souls passed, then Christmas, Epiphany, Easter, and we still felt as distant from the events that unfolded right at our doorstep as we had done at the very onset of our residence. What little contact we had with the worshippers was negative. One Sunday morning soon after our arrival, I found the senior elder knocking on our door, but instead of the anticipated invitation, he admonished us not to hang laundry on the Lord's day. As we found out the next Sunday, the hauling of firewood from our front porch wasn't allowed either. Later, in the midst of an unusually severe winter, the deep snow that covered the parking lot separating our residence from the church occasionally trapped the car of a visitor, and the owners would borrow—without asking—our snow-clearing equipment stored on the front porch. One Sunday, a couple of Romani children who dropped by periodically to help out with chores were busy clearing snow from our front steps when a woman approached them to borrow a snow shovel. I happened to see through the window how the woman tried to free her car from a snowdrift, and I was about to ask the children to help out when I saw her break the shovel. She gathered the pieces, walked the few steps separating her from the house, threw them at the feet of our helpers, and walked away without a word of explanation.

Apart from a handful of particularly devout Catholics who drop in on major holidays, the Roma don't attend the church, and nobody in the village misses them. They claim to feel ostracized and ridiculed by the parishioners, while the latter accuse them of noisy and disrespectful behaviour that clashes with local norms of piety. For most Roma, therefore, participation in organized religion is limited to two universally observed rites of passage: baptism and funeral. Every child born in the settlement is given a proper baptism by the priest. Not to do so makes people fearful of being "like the Jews" and risking ill health and an early death. Unlike ethnic Slovak children who receive the sacrament individually soon after birth, Romani children have to wait until there are a few of them around to justify a collective ceremony. This takes place on an ordinary weekday when the church stands empty. Similarly, Romani funerals take the participants directly from the home of the deceased in the settlement to the cemetery, without the detour to the church customary for the villagers. The priest recites prayers in the settlement and over the grave, but the usual interlude of a church service is left out. All Roma are buried in a separate section of the cemetery—allegedly on account of their incomplete fulfillment of Christian duties.[8]

It would be wrong to conclude that the Roman Catholic Church, as an institution, is not troubled by the profound divisions separating its "white" and "black" parishioners. For several years, a special auxiliary bishop based in Košice has been trying to make the church more responsive to the needs of the Roma, and as I witnessed on several occasions, progress is being made.[9] Even in Svinia, the resident priest tries to minister to the Roma, albeit within constraints set perhaps more by his ethnic Slovak parishioners than by himself. The local recipe for improvement includes pastoral visits to the settlement combined with prayers at a cross erected to commemorate the 1998 flood, and catechism classes taught at a recently completed "pastoral centre" on the outskirts of the settlement. The church plans to offer weekly services here in an attempt to please both sides of its divided constituency. At long last, the Roma are to gain unobstructed access to a church-like facility, but this vision is entirely congruent with the wishes of the white residents, who want to keep the Roma as far from "their" village as possible.

Local Politics

In their effort to reach the masses, Czechoslovakia's communist regime encouraged the installation of simple but effective public announcement systems in every corner of the country. The big loudspeakers, mounted on hydro poles, crackled every day with newscasts, announcements of local interest, and the sounds of uplifting music. The arrangement proved practical, and the communist-era propaganda tool survives in many communities. Svinia is one of them. Every day at noon, the mayor's secretary livens up the air with a medley of folk songs followed by a variety of announcements. Some draw attention to upcoming dances, birthdays, and similar social events. Others convey information about municipal council meetings, elections, and other occasions of political significance. While the fibreglass loudspeakers cover all of the village, not a single one has been installed in the settlement. Here, more than one half of Svinia's population remains untouched by the news conveyed in the daily broadcasts.

This example illustrates the view of the Roma in the context of local politics. Although they are legitimate voters, and although much of what goes on in Svinia these days is of direct concern to them, the Roma are treated as passive objects unworthy of direct involvement in local affairs. Council meetings and other gatherings are not advertised in the settlement, and consequently few Roma show any interest in them. At election times, some candidates for the municipal council may venture into the settlement in search of voters, who may be encouraged to vote the right way with gifts of liquor and cigarettes. The municipal council doesn't have a single Romani member, and the interest of ethnic Slovak councillors in their Romani constituents rarely extends beyond election times.

The concentration of power in the hands of local whites has dire consequences for the settlement. Because of almost universal prejudice against Roma, the ethnic Slovak elite does very little to accommodate their needs. This can be illustrated with several examples from an issue of uppermost concern to local Roma: housing. The settlement has two types of dwellings: as mentioned, the four apartment buildings erected between 1989 and 1990 and roughly 50 huts and other temporary shelters. The apartment buildings are owned by the municipality, which should, in theory, look after their maintenance. Instead, when the shoddily constructed sewer and water pipes began to crumble, leaving residents without access to the most basic hygiene, the mayor "invited" his renters to sign an agreement relieving them of paying rent and absolving the council of its obligation to carry out any maintenance and repairs. Now, only slightly older than ten years, the buildings contravene every conceivable paragraph of the public health code, but their disenfranchised occupants have no hope of compelling the municipality to do anything about it.

Figure 1.3. The lower settlement before the 1998 flood

KCpRO archive

The situation of the hut-dwellers is even more precarious. Even though most of them are duly registered residents of Svinia, their occupation of structures erected illegally on someone else's property turns them into squatters without any legitimate needs. In July 1998, a disastrous freak flood levelled most of the huts, and, exposed to the world thanks to national and international media attention, the hut-dwellers found themselves transferred to emergency shelters provided by the Slovak government. But even the distribution of the aid triggered by the flood was affected by Svinia's bifurcation. Although the Roma bore the brunt of the calamity, the municipal council insisted that ethnic Slovak "victims" in the village—where damage was limited to a few flooded root cellars—be allowed to dip into the relief pot provided by charitable foundations and even several foreign governments. Thus, of the 150,000 Slovak crowns donated by the Slovak Markiza Foundation, 140,000 ended up in the pockets of white villagers, and only 10,000 found their way into the settlement. Worse yet, after the municipal council had purchased second-hand and barely habitable emergency housing units for the flood victims, it used the remainder of the relief funds provided by the national government to put a fresh coat

Figure 1.4. The lower settlement in 2004, with "temporary" emergency housing at the foreground

of asphalt along Svinia's potholed main street, an area that had suffered no damage whatsoever.

The *de facto* division of Svinia into political subjects—the whites—and political objects—the Roma—has an important legal framework. Although the municipal administration lacks authority in the area of citizenship, it controls an essential venue through which the rights of citizenship are exercised locally: the system of residence permits. Like many European countries, Slovakia requires that every resident be registered in a municipality. The registration provides access to municipal and national elections, welfare payments, health care, subsidized housing, and other services. While a municipality cannot arbitrarily cancel a residence permit, it can, under certain circumstances, refuse to issue a residence permit to a newcomer. In Svinia, it would be unthinkable to bar any ethnic Slovak "immigrant" from legal residency. Whether such a person moves here because of marriage, work, or some other reason, he or she is registered swiftly and easily. With Roma, though, the situation is different. In the ten years between 1991 and 2000, the municipality issued residence permits to 99 ethnic Slovaks but to only 17 Roma. This means, for example, that every Romani spouse that marries into Svinia remains excluded from voting in local municipal elections, from obtaining maternity and other social benefits locally, from public works programs available in regions of high unemployment, and from all other services administered by the municipality. Even the exercise of such a fundamental right as voting in parliamentary elections requires that such a person return to the last municipality of his or her legal residence—which may be at the other end of the district. This discriminatory measure undoubtedly helps the municipal council keep the number of Romani voters as low as possible and maintain some control over the size of the settlement, and, above all, sends out a signal to ethnic Slovak voters that it endorses the status quo of white rule.

Despite the bravado with which local Slovak factions manage to exclude the Roma from any positions of power, Svinia, along with many similar communities, lives on borrowed time. The unease that hangs over every discussion conducted by the municipal council about the "gypsy problem" is only partly due to the lack of constructive ideas raised in these debates. The root cause of the unease is the awareness that sooner or later the era of white rule will come to an end, bringing about a future fraught with uncertainty. This changing of the guard will not come about as a result of a violent uprising or some similar cataclysm. Rather, local politicians foresee an entirely democratic changeover triggered by the coming of age of a massive new cohort of Romani voters. As with the race-based birth rates, the mayor keeps precise tabs on the ethnic profile of his voters. And this gives him cause for concern, for the statistics show an unmistakable trend. In the 1998 municipal elections, Svinia had 743 registered voters split roughly 5:2 in favour of ethnic Slovaks. By the fall of 2001, the number had increased to 791, and the ratio had changed to 5:2.5 (524 whites vs. 267 Roma). According to the mayor's calculations, the numbers should be balanced by 2015. And then, provided the Roma learn to vote for their own kind, they could easily defeat the divided ethnic Slovak political spectrum.

Notes

1. Local linguistic usage defines "blacks" and "whites" as categories of colour rather than social status: literally "black ones" and "white ones."

2. Symbols of traditional Slovak hospitality continue to be employed for political purposes. For example, when the Canadian ambassador paid his first visit to Svinia in the fall of 1998, he was welcomed by a schoolgirl dressed in regional costume who presented him with a loaf of bread and

a dish of salt. Naturally, the entire welcoming party consisted of ethnic Slovaks.

3. Although the collection of figures based on ethnic criteria has been illegal since 1990, such figures continue to be gathered by municipal administrations which, in turn, respond to demands from the central government.

4. These numbers are based on data from the 1970 and 1980 national census summarized in the Svinia chronicle, results of the 1991 census (Štatistický úrad SR 1994:128), and my own analysis of figures compiled by the municipal authority.

5. Much of the material was obtained during interviews conducted for the National Film Board of Canada's documentary *The Gypsies of Svinia*.

6. This figure includes 15 Romani students from the nearby settlement of Kojatice.

7. Genuine special schools, staffed with appropriately trained teachers, often present a much better environment. Nearby communities of Jarovnice and Chminianské Jakubovany provide good illustrations of special schools at their best.

8. Even the 1991 national census reflects the religious marginality of Svinia's Romani population. While it identifies 668 Roman Catholics for the village as such, 405 individuals are marked as having "undetermined" religious membership. This number happens to coincide almost exactly with the 406 persons classified as Roma by the census-takers (Štatistický úrad SR 1992). One must be careful, however, not to jump to conclusions about overt discrimination. For example, the church service usually performed on behalf of deceased ethnic Slovaks requires the payment of a fee that the Roma balk at. Similarly, very few Roma are willing to pay for the ostentatious monuments required for the graves located closest to the church.

9. Good overviews of current religious trends among Slovak Roma can be found in Janto (2000) and Kováč and Jurík (2002).

two

INSIDE THE *OSADA*

The People and their Environment

According to local folklore, Romani presence in Svinia goes back to the early years of the twentieth century when the resident Hungarian noble recruited a handful of Roma from nearby Jarovnice to empty the chamber pots in his château. Not everybody agrees on the precise nature of their work, but there is unity on attributing the origins of the settlement to a single couple who got married in the local church, begot more than a dozen children, and thus laid the foundation for a rapidly expanding community. Here is how an elderly villager, born in 1918, recalls the ancestral pair:

> They were called Kaleja. His name was Juraj and hers Hania. Our old priest convinced them to get married. And they did, in church, and we laughed because she didn't say *Juraj* but *Jujar*.... They had nothing. Only straw in their hut, and that's where they lay. There was only one little hut.

Some of the older Roma remember Juraj and Hania as well. One of their surviving grandsons, a man in his early 60s, describes Juraj as being "tall as a soldier" and white as a *gadjo*. This postulated whiteness has convinced some of his descendants that Juraj was in fact a *gadjo*, or ethnic Slovak, who only spoke "gypsy." As we shall see, this twist has some bearing on the self-perception of Juraj's descendants.

Birth and death records, kept continuously since 1896, confirm the arrival of Juraj and Hania, but they provide further interesting details absent from the oral accounts. According to the official Hungarian-language entries, a György Kaleja, estimated to have been between 30 and 40 years of age, and his consort, Anna Holub, did indeed arrive in Svinia around the turn of the century. Their first child to be born here, in 1902, died within a few weeks, but more followed in rapid succession. However, György and Anna were clearly not the only Roma living in Svinia at that time. Another Kaleja from Jarovnice, János, and his wife Barbara Sivak or Matas, seem to have arrived simultaneously. The birth here of their first child in 1901 marks the official beginning of Romani presence in Svinia. Ten years and five more children later, János and Barbara moved on to Brežany—formerly Bujakov—a village south-west of Svinia. It is tempting to speculate that János and György were brothers who had arrived together and split up following the death in 1911 of a György Kaleja senior, who may have been their father. The postulated kinship bond would explain why the only surviving daughter of János and Barbara returned to Svinia in the late 1930s.

If György/Juraj arrived in Svinia with a couple of relatives, so too probably did his wife Anna/Hania. As recorded in Svinia's parish books, between 1902 and 1906 two young women, Barbara and Zuzana, gave birth to three illegitimate children. They shared with Anna/Hania the same family name, Holub, and place of origin, the village of Jakubovany west of Svinia. It is possible that Barbara and Zuzana were Anna's sisters who had attached themselves to her household before branching out on their own in search of eligible young men elsewhere.

In addition to the Kaleja-Holub configuration that constituted the core of Svinia's Romani settlement in the first decade of the twentieth century, two further pairs came, stayed a few years, and then moved on again. One of these consisted of Erzsebet Danuja and her husband György Huszar, identified as "czigany kovacs" or "Gypsy blacksmith." They had three children in Svinia and then departed for an unknown destination. A second Erzsebet, this one married to a Mihaly Cservenyak, arrived with her husband from the nearby village of Kojatice only to return to their former residence two years later.

We can see that the first ten years of Romani presence in Svinia were characterized by a fair amount of traffic. Far from consisting of a single ancestral couple with a bunch of children—as contemporary oral accounts suggest—the early settlement attracted quite a number of migrants. We don't know what may have compelled them to leave behind their former residences, but we do know that they all hailed from villages located within roughly ten kilometres of Svinia, such as Jarovnice, Jakubovany, Chmiňany, and Kojatice. None of them was big by contemporary standards—as late as 1924, only two communities in the districts of Prešov and Sabinov reported more than 100 Roma, and both were towns rather than villages (Nečas 1989:217)—and some, notably Kojatice, were at the same early developmental stage as Svinia.[1]

The early formative era, characterized by instability, gave way to a more settled and stable existence during the 1920s. One of the first reliable censuses of Slovak Roma, carried out in 1924, captured the number, age distribution, and economic profiles of the majority of Romani residents in all eastern Slovak districts (Nečas 1986). This rare tool supplements Svinia's birth and death records in helping us reconstruct the state of the local settlement 20 years after its emergence. Surprisingly, by 1924 the community that numbered at least ten adults during the first decade of its existence had dwindled to a single married couple, three adolescents, and four children (Nečas 1989). Predictably, this was the household of Juraj Kaleja and Hania Holub, the founding ancestors of Svinia's Roma.[2]

Svinia's birth records disclose that Hania bore thirteen children in Svinia between 1902 and 1927. Five of them died in infancy. Of the surviving eight, six—all of them enshrined in the 1924 census—left behind children of their own in Svinia. These six first-generation "natives," all of them dead by now, constitute the parental generation for 26 senior members of the community who are now in their 40s, 50s, and, in a few cases, 60s. The latter are, in turn, the parents of close to 100 younger adults in their 20s, 30s, and early 40s—by far the majority of the settlement's reproductive population. This kinship universe is shown in Figure 2.1.

With the exception of Margita, who moved to Jarovnice prior to the war, Svinia's first generation of native Roma spent most of their lives in their home community. For the first 50 years of its existence, the settlement was located adjacent to the present site, on the bank of the rivulet Malá Sviňka on the northern periphery of the village proper. It consisted of a cluster of primitive huts erected on the property of a good-hearted farmer. The situation changed soon after the end of the war when Józef and Alžbeta split off from the parental site and set up their own colony nearby. The move, which is explained in greater detail in Part 3, took place in the early 1950s, and it had very serious consequences for the future of all local Roma. It split the community into a bifurcated entity consisting of the ancestral lower settlement (*dolná osada)* at the creek and an upwardly mobile upper settlement (*horná osada)*—named so because of its slightly elevated location (see Figure 1.2). While the "creek people"—or *jarkovci,* named after the local term for creek—of the lower settlement pursued a lifestyle that isolated them from their white neighbours, their relatives "up

Figure 2.1. The founders of Svinia's Romani population and the number of their adult descendants living in Svinia

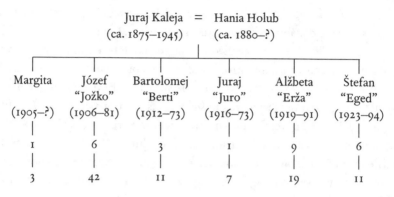

the hill" cultivated a much closer relationship with the villagers. Convinced that they were dealing with innovators capable and willing to assimilate, local authorities initially displayed a measure of generosity toward the migrants. In an unprecedented step, they gave them legal title to the lots they occupied, helped them with the construction of modest but durable dwellings made of concrete blocks, and drilled a well and extended electricity into the new settlement—all luxuries undreamed of by the neglected *jarkovci*. The special status accorded the residents of the upper colony lasted some 30 years—enough to create a deep gulf between the two settlements, but not enough to convince the villagers of the wisdom of the relocation. Responding to a long litany of public complaints about noise, garbage, and unseemly behaviour—as well as pressure from the agricultural cooperative which set up its headquarters right beside the colony—municipal and district authorities eventually decided to abolish the upper settlement and to return its residents to their ancestral site by the creek. Unwarned and unprepared, its inhabitants woke up in the early morning hours of 1 April 1989 to the sound of bulldozers and tractors. They were given a few hours to pack their belongings and to load them onto waiting trucks. Then they watched in horror as bulldozers demolished their homes.

Though reconstituted as a single settlement, the contrast between the *jarkovci* and their relocated relatives has endured. One important reason was the construction of new housing for the returnees. Unlike the "creek people" who continued to live in their primitive huts, the immigrants from the upper colony received new apartments built by local authorities between 1989 and 1991. There are 32 of these apartments, located in four identical two-storey buildings. They correspond to a standard model designed during the socialist era and found in many locations inhabited by Roma. Compared with apartment buildings constructed for ethnic Slovaks, these are "no-frills" units thought to be adapted to the special lifestyle of Roma. As such they are supposed to be sturdier, smaller, and devoid of unnecessary luxuries, such as central heating or natural gas hook-ups. While incomparably more comfortable than the huts of the *jarkovci*, the apartments lost much of their shine soon after their occupants had moved in. The shoddily constructed infrastructure quickly began to crumble, and by the time of my first visit in 1993, the dwellings looked at least 20 years old. Water pumps had broken down, rendering faucets and water closets useless. Sewer pipes had become clogged with garbage deposited by some tenants. Bathrooms had been converted into storage rooms for firewood or emergency accommodation for newlyweds. While the contrast between the apartment buildings (*bytovky*) and the huts (*chatrčky* or *chýže*) endures, the rapid deterioration of the former has diminished it somewhat in recent years.

On account of the explosive population increase characteristic of local Roma, more and more people depend on huts as the only housing available to them. My first detailed census of the apartment-dwellers, taken in May 1996, established 308 persons living in 32 units, which corresponds to an average of almost ten people. Considerable as it is, it pales by comparison with actual rates observed in some of the more crowded units. In the most extreme case I counted 26 occupants in a three-room apartment. Here, an entire family of eight was crammed into an auxiliary room the size of a slightly extended bathroom. Eight years later, the situation has barely changed for the better. Limited by the inadequate size of their dwellings, the occupants of the apartments have only one way out: the huts outside the walls of the relatively comfortable *bytovky*. When an adolescent boy or girl begins to sleep with a partner—this typically happens around the age of fifteen—the parents usually allow the young couple to reside in the family compound, often in the defunct bathroom converted for this purpose. However, as soon as a child appears, the "newlyweds" are put under pressure to vacate these premises, making room for the next sibling and his or her consort, and to set up their own household, invariably in a newly constructed hut. A survey made of the huts in July 1998, shortly before the devastating flood that changed the housing situation considerably, established 311 residents spread out over 60 dwellings. Here, the number of residents ranged from one to twelve, with six being the modal number. The huts fall into two categories. The more durable type, but also the more difficult and time-consuming to build, utilizes adobe-style bricks called *válki*, made from a mixture of soil, straw, and water. The three ingredients are stomped with bare feet before being pressed into wooden moulds in which they are left to dry for a few days. Once the bricks have shrunk a little, they are removed from the moulds and left in a sunny spot to dry further. In their final state, *válki* are used in much the same way as fired bricks except that thick mud substitutes for cement-based mortar. Almost all houses built in Slovak villages before World War II were made in this way, and in Svinia local Roma supplied the *válki*. Postwar developments, though, haven't favoured this durable and exceedingly cheap construction material, which has been replaced with much costlier fired bricks and blocks made of a cement-based compound.

Válki remain in use in some settlements, including nearby Kojatice, but the Roma in Svinia are not fond of them. Claiming that local soil is unsuitable for the production of *válki*, they employ a more primitive technology to build their huts. Here they erect a simple frame made of interlocking thin logs (often merely thick branches) chinked with the same mixture used in the manufacture of *válki*. The frame is then covered with a sloping roof made of scavanged metal sheets nailed to thick branches and elevated above the door to allow rainwater to run off to the back. A single small window covered with a piece of glass or a sheet of plastic lets in just enough light to cook by. Stomped earth provides a primitive floor, which dissolves every time it rains. Because these drafty shelters are difficult to heat, most of them consist of a single room that rarely exceeds ten square metres. The furnishings are sparse: normally one or two beds and an old chest of drawers for clothing and other prized possessions. The huts lack any hygienic facilities, but most are hooked up for electricity by means of illegal and life-threatening wire-taps strung between a hut and the apartment of a relative or friend. The wire-tap supplies enough power for a weak light bulb dangling from the ceiling and, more importantly, a battered television set turned on most of the day. A rusty stove with a makeshift chimney doubles up for heating and cooking.

The striking characteristics of virtually all the huts found in the settlement are their smallness, haphazard construction, and lack of any adornment. Their minimalist architecture provides a strange contrast with much

Figure 2.2. Traditional huts made of *válki* as seen in 1993

more spacious and attractive dwellings found in some other Romani communities nearby. Such homes are usually made of the more durable *válki*, and they are whitewashed and equipped with proper windows, doors, and furnishings. Confronted with these examples, the minimalists of Svinia shrug their shoulders and blame their poverty and inadequate skills.

Although the apartments, at roughly 50 square metres, appear far more spacious and comfortable than the exceedingly primitive huts, they too are marked by a surprisingly low standard of living. While there is hardly one lacking the ubiquitous television set, it is not unusual to see apartments almost devoid of any type of furniture. A stove and a single bed may be all the household equipment owned by a destitute family, and here children may have to sleep on blankets spread over the cold and hard cement floor. In some units broken windows have been replaced with sheets of plastic or cardboard, and occasionally one encounters families who do all their cooking in pots and pans borrowed from relatives.

The deplorable living conditions are at the very top of a long list of complaints voiced by local Roma to every visitor. They point out leaking roofs, smoky stoves, broken windows, unhinged doors "kicked in by brutal police officers," holes in walls chewed by rats "the size of cats," and many more deficiencies. Whatever the shortcomings, blame is laid squarely on

Figure 2.3. Contemporary-style hut built in 2002

the shoulders of the mayor or some other uncaring white official. There can be little doubt that some of the finger-pointing is justified. According to trustworthy informants, the *bytovky* exhibited major shortcomings even before a single family moved in. Many of the apartments lacked doors. Some had stoves but no pipes needed to connect them to central chimneys. Others had pipes but no stoves. Sinks and, in some cases, bathtubs had not been installed properly or at all. Even the far-from-impartial chronicle admits these and other defects (*Pamätná kniha*, vol. III:268).

But if external forces must bear their share of responsibility for the deplorable state of local housing, the residents cannot be exonerated either. Every first-time visitor is invariably taken aback by the amount of litter strewn around the settlement. Wherever one steps, there are layers of refuse consisting of old diapers, dirty rags, bones, feminine napkins, dog and human excrement, pieces of plastic, broken bottles, and a range of other discarded objects, blended into a foul-smelling and ugly melange. Lacking toilets of any kind, local residents face the formidable problem of how to dispose of excrement left behind daily by more than 700 bodies. But what appears problematic to an outsider is not necessarily considered as such by the people themselves. Up to the age of five or six, children are allowed to defecate anywhere they please, including the hut or apartment floor. They may be encouraged to do their business in the stairwell or right outside the hut, absolving the mother of the need to sweep up afterwards, but failure to do so is quietly tolerated. Older children and adults are expected to be more circumspect, and they choose a suitable spot in the bushes that ring one side of the settlement. The excrement left behind in the stairwells, outside the entrances to the *bytovky*, and along the outer edge of the settlement is there to stay. Like all the other litter discarded throughout the community, it won't be disposed of in any way. This is not because of some primordial fear of "displaced matter" (Douglas 1966), but rather because most people aren't bothered by it. The hut-dwellers whose homes are situated right beside the communal cesspools are as unlikely to complain about the smelly and unsightly matter accumulating outside as are the apartment-dwellers who must jump across old and fresh droppings that dot their stairwells.

The nonchalant attitude to excrement is mirrored in most people's treatment of their immediate living environment. When I first arrived in Svinia, I couldn't grasp how even shoddily constructed and improperly equipped apartments could be so run down after a relatively short occupancy. The more time I spent in the settlement, the better I understood that local mores define as perfectly normal conduct that gravely offends the sensibilities of most ethnic Slovaks. It speaks for itself, for example, that firewood is split inside one's home, right beside the stove where it is needed. Whether the floor is covered with stomped earth or new linoleum is irrelevant. The same goes for the disposal of cigarette butts, which tend to be routinely thrown onto the floor and ground into it with the heel. Considering the number of cigarettes smoked in the average household on any given day, the impact is far from negligible, as anything less durable than earth or concrete is bound to be wrecked within a short period of time. Yet ashtrays are dismissed as unnecessary accessories. Many times I watched in horror as a laughing housewife dumped a shovel filled with glowing embers on a linoleum-covered floor while she was rearranging the contents of a smoky stove. Compared with these habits, the custom of discarding potato skins and other by-products of cooking on the floor—to be swept up and thrown outside the door at the end of the day—seems harmless enough, but that too conveys an attitude of carelessness which most rural Slovaks consider highly improper.

The living environment that local Roma have created for themselves reflects a community that attaches little value to the construction and maintenance of good order as defined by the majority society. Few people are interested in keeping up appearances, and this shows not only in their dwellings but also in their deportment and self-presentation. Most of the residents make an unkempt and outright dirty impression. Small children are routinely sent outdoors naked or semi-naked, displaying wild bushy hair covered with lice. Invariably sporting runny noses that nobody wipes off, they play on mounds of trash, throwing dirty diapers at each other or getting a hoot out of setting fire to discarded tires. In really cold weather they are dressed in dirty and torn t-shirts and pants, wearing mismatched shoes that are either too big or too small. When they enter school, children tend to make a cleaner impression on account of teachers who are known to "snitch" about neglectful parents, and upon reaching adolescence they begin to display the same heightened attention to appearance as anywhere else. But once they have found a permanent partner and set up their own household, the adolescents' interest in fashion quickly dissipates, and by the time they reach their early 20s, young adults learn to adopt the same careless attitude characteristic of their parents. Stained and often torn pants, supplemented with a dirty shirt or sweatshirt, constitutes the daily uniform of men. Below-the-knee skirts, often combined with black tights, and colourful blouses comprise the usual apparel of women. While conventions of sexual propriety prohibit the wearing of shorts or mini-skirts (both of which are tolerated in unmarried girls), for older women it is acceptable to move around the house and even venture outside with the upper body clad only in a brassiere.

The entire settlement depends for its water supply on a shallow spring and a couple of wells. As all water must be hand-carried and heated on the stove, baths are infrequent luxuries that many people dispense with altogether. But even less demanding types of cleansing are rarely carried out. Few people perform any type of morning toilet, and toothbrushes are found in only a small number of households. The outcome of this in-attention to personal hygiene is a strong body odour that the villagers find revolting. It provides a convenient excuse for barring Roma from buses, restaurants, and community-wide events.

It could be argued that the "aesthetic deficit" that strikes every outsider upon entering the settlement is an inevitable outcome of the socio-economic conditions that shape the daily lives of local Roma. Indeed, it would be foolish to expect daily baths in a setting where hot water is hard to come by, and one must understand that a mother confined to a mud hut who is responsible for six children cannot maintain the same standard of cleanliness and order as a village woman who raises one or two children in a modern house equipped with labour-saving conveniences. But there is more to this than the undeniable poverty of most local Roma. Another trait that is clearly rooted in the subculture of the settlement, and that at least partly accounts for the desolate state of the community, is a destructive attitude to the environment displayed by adults and children alike. Tell-tale signs of it can be seen in the swampy corners of the settlement where toddlers stone frogs to the amusement of adult passers-by. Once the frog is knocked out, its tormentor steps on the motionless body and slowly adds pressure until the guts spill out. Older children develop a whole range of destructive habits. They pelt windows with rocks, scratch the paint and break off the antennas of cars that happen to visit the settlement, set fires to flammable trash heaps, and attack every technical innovation installed in the community—be it an outdoor pump or a swing set up for their amusement. Unless it is directed against the child's family possessions, this destructive conduct is met with utter indifference by the adults.

The carelessness and outright destructiveness with which the children relate to their environment extends to books and school supplies. Svinia's elementary school teachers don't assign their Romani students any homework because they have learned from experience that most books and papers taken to the settlement end up lost or at least torn up. The same fate befalls pens, pencils, and crayons. As I witnessed on numerous occasions, a frustrated teenager trying unsuccessfully to write a sentence or draw a picture is likely to react in a thoroughly immature manner by angrily breaking the pencil and tossing it into the stove.

The destructive behaviour characteristic of many children and adolescents follows patterns observed in adults. Instead of learning how to mend minor tears or sew on a button, women routinely dispose of torn shirts and blouses that could be easily repaired. Such clothing may be used as kindling or is simply tossed outside. Much of the garbage one finds strewn around the settlement consists of discarded apparel. Men too demonstrate little concern for material objects. An angry man often vents his frustration by inflicting damage on his surroundings. He takes an axe and breaks down a door that somehow "stands in his way." Or he grabs a heavy club and smashes a large window to pieces. Or he swings a sledge hammer at a concrete sidewalk until it is broken up. Other destructive acts are carried out without any emotional overtones. On several occasions I witnessed huge grassfires burning out of control in an abandoned orchard on the outskirts of the village. Each time the fire required the intervention of

Svinia's voluntary fire department—equipped with an antiquated pumper truck operated by three men—and a score of villagers armed with shovels. Their Romani neighbours stood at a distance and made no attempt to assist the fire-fighting effort. After all, they confided, the blaze had been started by people from the settlement in an effort to improve access to the forest above the orchard.

Another act of wanton destructiveness keeps being played out at Svinia's small garbage dump. Characteristically located near the settlement, it is run by an entrepreneur allowed to dispose of organic waste—mostly spoiled fruits and vegetables trucked in from Prešov's supermarkets—in a facility resembling a huge compost. Naturally, every shipment of half-rotten bananas and oranges triggers a minor invasion of people from the settlement eager to carry away some free snacks. This wasn't anything the leaseholder objected to, and he in fact tried to assist the pickers by having the loads of fruit dumped as accessibly as possible. What he did object to was the fact that some of the visitors always thanked him by setting the empty crates on fire. In spite of repeated pleading the fires kept being set, and at long last the entrepreneur closed off the dump and placed a German shepherd at the gate to enforce the new status. The next day the dog was dead, and the fires flared up again.

The carelessness and destructiveness described here as contributing factors in the desolate state of Svinia's settlement must not be seen as characteristics of rural Roma in general. While trash strewn around indiscriminately can be found in many settlements, there are communities where this problem doesn't exist, or at least not to the extent found in Svinia. Similarly, one only needs to venture a few kilometres outside Svinia, for instance to nearby Chmiňany, to see no-frills apartment buildings identical to the ones built in Svinia that are in much better shape. There, the taps still dispense water, the toilets do flush, and the stairwells are not littered with feces. Farther down the road, in Fričovce, we find multiple-room houses made of *válki*, nicely painted and well equipped, inhabited by Roma whose lifestyle differs little from that of the surrounding villagers. Here, the ability to *construct* outpaces the tendency to *destroy*. But even in Svinia itself, there are individuals who stand out from the bleak environment of the settlement. A handful of adults and their children appear much cleaner, better groomed, and better dressed than the majority. Most of them inhabit apartments that reinforce the impression made by their occupants. Here one finds carpets on the floor, lace curtains in the living-room, Slovak-style cabinets with china dolls and framed photographs of relatives. There are ashtrays on a coffee table, a washing machine in the kitchen, and a tub in the bathroom that still serves the original purpose. Although small, this home-grown elite constitutes an essential ingredient of the local community, which is discussed in some detail further below.

Making a Living

Throughout the century of its existence, the settlement in Svinia has always depended on the surrounding majority for the livelihood of its members. But the nature of the dependence has undergone some interesting modifications. The economic adaptation that evolved among local Roma during the first half of the twentieth century was a mixture of outright reliance on the charity of their white neighbours and the provision of services that fulfilled some of their needs. Understandably in view of the low esteem in which the Roma are held, the element of begging is played up in Slovak accounts of the early years of the settlement. One of the old-timers has this to say about the economic strategies pursued by Juraj and Hania:

> They were good gypsies. He just sat underneath their hut [he kept sitting all the time; such a strong man....], and she went around begging.... And we would give her flour, potatoes, ... and she had such a jug full of small holes, and she filled the holes with straw, and so she carried whatever milk we gave her. She didn't have anything that wouldn't leak.... And people would give her, here some sour milk, and here some regular milk, and that's what they lived on [He just lay in the hut, and when someone died, he got the old rags, because what else would he have worn?]. They had nothing, but they didn't steal. Nothing. They lived off whatever she got through begging.

This account doesn't differ much from the recollections shared by older Roma. Of particular significance are the memories of the children of Józef Kaleja, the upwardly mobile founder of the upper settlement. In spite of Józef's relative affluence, his children recall living in abject poverty and depending on the villagers for all their clothing. In the words of the lineage "matriarch," a woman born in 1948, this situation prevailed well into the

1950s: "There was no money, we had just enough to purchase produce, but for other things we depended on our neighbours, like clothing. My mother took great care of this clothing given to us by neighbours, so that it would last."

The dependence, though, wasn't total. Interestingly, each of the three adult men associated with the settlement during the first decade of its existence—György Kaleja, János Kaleja, and György Huszár—is described in the parish records as a "gypsy blacksmith." This designation is defended by Juraj's oldest surviving grandson, born in 1937, who claims that his grandfather shoed the villagers' horses. While some ethnic Slovak old-timers dismiss this postulate with derision, others concede that Juraj was a man of exceptional strength who knew how to make strong nails and durable chains. Curiously, although the parish records extended the term "gypsy blacksmith" to each of the male newcomers in the formative years of the Svinia settlement, it was used only once, never to be repeated again. Thus while Juraj managed to receive this designation in the first entry of 1903, the next time a notice was made of his profession, in 1922, all he earned was a dismissive *dubko*, a term reserved for Roma of lowly origins. The next entry, made a year later, called him simply *cigán*, and when his last child was born in 1927, Juraj was listed as a mere *nádenník*, which translates as unskilled, manual labourer. Czechoslovakia's 1924 "Gypsy register" identified him as *šarka*, that is, village servant. This apparent loss of status may have had its roots in the inability of rural Roma to keep abreast of technological changes wrought by the postwar industrialization of eastern Slovakia.

Another skill for which Juraj is remembered by Roma and *gadji* alike is the manufacture of *válki*. While in his case it may have been a somewhat sporadic activity, Juraj's sons developed this skill to perfection and became acknowledged masters of their trade. This applies in the first instance to Štefan (nicknamed Eged), the immediate ancestor of most of today's *jarkovci*. The activities associated with this occupation are described by one of his sons:

> Someone needed to build a wall, so he [father] did that; here they made a cellar, they had no cash, ... so people would bring flour, potatoes, milk, everything possible was given as payment for work.... [Mother] also worked, she fetched the soil.... I remember how they used to work.... They travelled far away. Someone came with horses, cows, back then there

were no cars, and called on people interested in working. They knew that he [father] worked well, so they would give him a glass [of liquor], he drank, and wanted no more. And mother also worked. She had a mould, they made *válki*, placed them in a row, and when they had dried, they put them aside. And all that had to be transported away.... [Father had a wagon and a cow, and] the cow stomped on the soil, [and] to make it moist and mixed with straw, they shovelled the soil on a heap, and the cow stomped it down. All of that was made here.

While the manufacture of the *válki* took place in the settlement, the local market was limited, and Štefan had to accept assignments in neighbouring villages. As many of the jobs required considerable investments of time, the entire family was rarely together. While the father laboured in some distant location, mother and children tried to make themselves useful in Svinia itself. Here is another excerpt from the son's recollections:

If [father] returned for a week, that was long. He would go away for weeks and even months. He was never home with the children. He worked constantly.... [In the meantime, back in the settlement, mother] put the children on her back every morning and ventured into the village in search of work.... And people would feed us, and we carried straw [and performed other chores]. We worked until midnight. [Then] the farmer came and brought a can of milk, some cheese, butter and bread—we had it all the time. Flour they also gave us. We went wherever there was any work.

The transportation of *válki* from the place of their manufacture to the construction site in another village took place in a cart drawn by a cow, and it appears that Štefan possessed both. So did his upwardly mobile brother Józef, but the latter branched out into the transportation business. It seems that he maintained a partnership with a villager who owned a horse, and this increased the size of his territory and the income derived from this activity.

In view of the complete absence of any type of livestock in the settlement today, it is surprising to learn that this hasn't always been the case. After the breakup of the community, the *jarkovci* of the lower settlement seem to have acquired a whole range of livestock that they kept as recently as the late 1960s. Here is how Štefan's son remembers his parental household during his childhood years: "They fared better than nowadays. They had everything: cows, swine, they kept everything. Today—nothing. They even had goats, everything, milk. More than the whites.... They had everything; [they] kept a cow, goats, sheep. They had enough milk. They had a horse." Since this speaker is inclined to exaggeration, his assessment should be taken with a considerable grain of salt. Štefan is known to have worked occasionally as a herdsman for the villagers, and it cannot be ruled out that at least some of the animals described here may have belonged to local farmers rather than the Roma. But other informants confirm that some livestock used to be owned by the "creek people"—certainly goats and an occasional cow.

The manufacture of *válki* was a seasonal activity, which stopped with the onset of cold weather in the fall. At this point some men took up another commercial activity: music. By all accounts, local Roma have always been good at music, but only a few could use it to supplement their incomes. Although this is vehemently denied by the people in the settlement, older villagers claim that the Roma in the nearby community of Chmiňany were better musicians who could perform the traditional czardas as well as the more cosmopolitan polka. Accordingly, the villagers used to hire musicians from Chmiňany for big dances held on major holidays, while local Roma had to take satisfaction with more modest occasions requiring less skillful performers.

The mixed economy described here corresponds with the larger pattern prevalent in pre-war eastern Slovakia. With the exception of a handful of sought-after professional musicians, found only in large towns and cities, the majority of local Roma eked out a modest living through the exchange of their labour for foodstuffs and whatever other available surplus—such as used clothing—provided by neighbouring villagers (Horváthová 1964; Nečas 1986). This economic adapation was characterized by an almost complete absence of money, which precluded the acquisition of land or livestock on a scale even remotely comparable to white villagers. Although the socialist system, introduced in 1948, began to modify the traditional subsistence economy through the provision of old-age pensions and new forms of work, it wasn't until the late 1960s that the traditional pattern gave way to a cash economy based on permanent employment provided by the state. Several factors were of great importance here. The socialist

Figure 2.4. Romani musicians at a village wedding in the 1970s

KCpRO Archive

regime introduced legislation that required most adult members of society to be gainfully employed, and in order to realize this goal, local authorities were expected to create new jobs for the Roma. In Svinia, these jobs were primarily in construction and in the newly formed agricultural cooperative which, since the 1950s, had replaced private farming. Older Romani men recall with pride the contribution they made to the many edifices of socialism erected in the village between the 1960s and 1980s. They helped build the new school, the municipal building, the "house of culture," and the collective farm with its sprawling stables, garages, and large administration complex. The construction boom of the socialist era was propelled by a definite bias in favour of "big is beautiful," which in turn encouraged the use of concrete and other cement-based products on a grand scale. And as new construction materials and designs found their way into Svinia, new notions of progress began to dismiss the traditional *válki* as an inadequate vestige of the past. As more and more villagers chose the "global" concrete blocks over the local *válki*—a transition completed during the 1960s—the Romani manufacturers of the old-fashioned bricks had no choice but to seek new forms of employment.

Factory-produced construction materials doomed not only the home-spun cottage industry in the settlement. Its downfall also deprived local Roma of the grain—a key ingredient in the traditional barter economy—that they needed as winter fodder for their livestock. As grain production became increasingly monopolized by the collective farm, and as traditional opportunities for its acquisition by the Roma declined, so did, according to old-timers among the *jarkovci*, their ability to keep livestock.

The new socialist economy doesn't seem to have created significant opportunities for local Roma to upgrade their skills. Unlike their Slovak neighbours who climbed to positions of responsibility in the collective farm (Svinia's largest employer), Romani workers went on feeding pigs, shovelling manure, digging irrigation ditches, and mixing cement, the kind of manual work they used to perform in the pre-socialist economy as well. Some men passed through special vocational training that increased their qualifications and allowed them to work as auxiliary brick-layers or painters. But even this type of upgrading remained based on the premise that only white workers could be trusted with supervisory responsibilities. I will return to this in the section devoted to Svinia's experience with mod-ernization.

The collapse of socialism following Czechoslovakia's 1989 "Velvet Revolution" had a quick and devastating effect on the employment of local Roma. As state-owned companies either collapsed or transformed into privately run enterprises, Romani employees were the first ones to lose their jobs. No longer protected by affirmative-action-style legislation, exposed to a rapidly rising level of publicly expressed prejudice and racism, and lacking the technical skills required by the new, profit-driven economy, all of Svinia's Roma lost their jobs within a year or two. The all-out unemployment that ensued has prevailed until now, and there is little hope that it might change for the better in the near future. But while the socialist-era job guarantees are a thing of the past, much of the previous regime's welfare system remains intact. And this is what keeps the Roma of Svinia alive.

According to the best estimates available, as many as 80 per cent of Slovak Roma depend directly on welfare payments provided by the state (International Organization for Migration 2000:50). In Svinia, welfare pay-ments have become a crucial component of every family income, but it is important to differentiate between the various categories of the labyrinthine system. The social benefits provided by the state reflect the unequal needs of a range of recipients. In the first instance, those unable to find gainful employment because of disability or unwillingness to work receive "social support" (*dávka sociálnej pomoci*)—a monthly stipend the size of which is adjusted according to the reason for the recipient's dependence on the state. Claimed to be sufficient for someone to live on, in 2003 the allowance amounted to 3,300 Slovak crowns, which was around $100 US. This sum can be increased or reduced depending on family circumstances and the recipient's length of dependence. In order to keep the basic stipend from declining, the beneficiary must accept placement in a public works scheme financed by the state, which gives municipalities with high levels of unemployment access to cheap manual labour. The program runs for three months in a year, enough to convince officials that the participants are motivated to work, and in Svinia it's the only kind of quasi-employment available to Roma. Under the supervision of a white foreman, they dig ditches, clean streets, and pick up autumn leaves from graves in the cemetery.

Technically separate from "welfare," but perceived by the Roma as part and parcel of the same system, are family allowances that are supposed to offset the cost of raising children. Every mother of a child under the age of three who remains at home is entitled to a monthly stipend of 2,740 crowns—around $90 US—as compensation for lost income. This mother's allowance (*materské*) is in addition to a "baby bonus" (*detské prídavky*), which commences at birth with 640 crowns and rises proportionally to the age of the child.

Contrary to popular Slovak belief that Romani "welfare bums" are showered with money by a naive and over-protective government, the system as it is executed in practice incorporates many safeguards and qualifiers that make it possible to reduce payments to clients considered unworthy for one reason or another (Radičová 2001). But the administration of the system is based on an erratic patchwork of legal principles interpreted not always systematically by distant civil servants who have little knowledge of their clients and their needs. So it happens that while some families derive a respectable income from the various payments, there are individuals and even families that can barely survive on minuscule handouts. The variance is not always the consequence of different levels of need but often of one's ability to navigate a Kafkaesque maze of sometimes contradictory rules, and to negotiate favourable terms with a government official in Prešov. For those who have mastered the basic principles, and who are willing to investigate and use various appeal procedures, the social assistance system does provide enough of an income to take care of their basic needs. This is borne out by my 1999 survey of 88 local families, ranging in size from a single individual all the way up to twelve members. I found that 27 per cent of the families subsisted on less than 4,000 crowns; 43 per cent had an income between 4,000 and 10,000 crowns; and the remaining 30 per cent received in excess of 10,000 crowns per month. Although 10,000 crowns converts officially to only $350 US, the local buying power of such an amount is about twice that much. And since most families spend next to nothing on housing, health care, education, holidays, and entertainment, 10,000 crowns is adequate to cover the essential expenses of even a fairly large family. It is more than twice the legal minimum wage—4,400 per month—and it is almost equal to the country's average income. On the other hand, a radical welfare reform introduced in January 2004 in preparation for Slovakia's entry into the European Union has reduced the incomes of many local families by up to 40 per cent, and it is possible that the relative generosity of the Slovak welfare system will soon become a thing of the past.

While it would be far-fetched to accept the villagers' accusation that Roma bear children as a way of making a living, it is undoubtedly true that most local Roma are acutely aware of the financial benefits associated with children. And this means that in some cases decisions are made that seek to maximize that benefit. Let us consider the example of teenage pregnancies. In Svinia it is far from exceptional for girls to bear their first child at the age of 15 or 16. It would be an exaggeration to suggest that such early births are financially motivated, but it is acceptable to suggest that the general acceptance of early pregnancies derives partly from the expectation of financial benefits. After all, a teenage daughter who normally "brings in" slightly over 1,000 crowns in child bonuses suddenly becomes "worth" more than triple that amount. Since she is a minor, both her mother's allowance and baby bonus end up with her parents who can in this way postpone the inevitable reduction in family income caused by the maturation and departure of their children. Since education beyond the elementary school level isn't considered a viable option by the vast majority of local Roma, and since adolescents have absolutely no chance of finding any kind of paid permanent employment, early pregnancy can be seen as a relatively rewarding step that brings about more financial security than any other locally accessible alternative.

Figure 2.5. Young Romani mothers at the Svinia maternity clinic

Because social assistance payments, or *dávki* as they are known collo-quially, constitute the backbone of the settlement economy, they assume tremendous practical as well as symbolic importance. The social calendar of the settlement revolves around the dates when *dávki* are handed out at Svinia's post office. Normally this happens once a month, and it is a proc-ess that takes up to three days as the alphabetically sorted cheques are assigned to legitimate recipients and then cashed on the spot. Like payday anywhere, the date becomes a benchmark for financially demanding events and activities. Baptisms, weddings, public dances, and any other celebra-tion that costs money are scheduled to fall on a day close to the magic date. Naturally, the timing of payday also influences local commercial activities. Normally, a large share of the cash disbursed at the post office is spent right away as the recipient stops at the various stores that line Svinia's main street and stocks up on frozen chickens, sausages, flour, oil, vodka, and other necessities of daily life. The volume of the purchases made on this day is such that it requires the participation of several family members. The stuff is loaded into child carriages or push carts normally used for hauling fire-wood and wheeled into the settlement. There, some people make further purchases from motorized peddlers of chickens, clothing, potatoes, and other wares who drop in once per month at the time of *dávki*.

The week following *dávki* is a time of happiness and relaxation. As everybody has enough money, people indulge in their favourite delicacies, some go to Prešov to look for new clothing or to reclaim pawned television sets, and some go on vodka-drinking binges that make them incoherent for several days in a row. But this "feast" portion of the monthly cycle comes to an end very quickly, and as most families begin to run out of money, the settlement enters the much longer "fast" period that lasts for the next three to four weeks and may be dubbed the "post-*dávki* depression." The transition can be best seen in the food people consume. Suddenly, the chickens and ribs cooked daily during the short few days following payday give way to the less glamorous *haluški*—a potato-based pasta dish resembling *gnocchi*—and, eventually, the *chapatti*-like thin pancakes called *marikle*, which are made from a thin mixture of flour and water. And as meat dishes give way to watery gruels and tasteless pancakes, vodka—the liqour of choice for most men and quite a few women, too—also begins to dry up. At this point some of the less discriminating drinkers, especially among the *jarkovci*, resort to a deadly home-brew, called *kamfor*, consisting of pure alcohol mixed with water and sugar. Others, weary of the coma-like condition induced by *kamfor*, are compelled to abstain from or at least dramatically reduce the desired level of alcohol consumption. And as the supply of money dries up further, it begins to affect the availability of even coffee and cigarettes—two substances to which the vast majority of local adults are hopelessly addicted. At this point, people begin to appear listless, tired, and irritable. They stay indoors, watch television or sleep excessively, and avoid the company of others.

The acute shortage of cash that most local Roma claim to experience more or less permanently is caused by several factors. As we have already seen, their incomes are not significantly out of step with Slovak economic realities, and even though local family size is well above the national norm, their one-dimensional lifestyle absolves them of the need to spend almost anything in sectors that consume a considerable portion of the income of the average Slovak family. On the other hand, the settlement as such is at a distinct disadvantage in not allowing its residents to grow any of the food they consume. Unlike the neighbouring villagers whose gardens and fields provide much of their daily diet, the Roma raise no livestock and grow no potatoes or vegetables to supplement theirs. All their food must be purchased in stores and paid for with hard cash.

There are other differences with wide-ranging financial implications. As we have already seen, the villagers accuse the Roma of wasting their money on frivolities instead of stocking up on the basics required for a balanced diet. And, indeed, even a cursory survey of local shopping habits reveals purchases of vast quantities of overpriced frozen chickens, huge packages of sausage, bundles of expensive bananas, imported chocolate bars, and other luxury foods that no budget-conscious villager would think of buying. Some Roma admit that the "feast and famine" cycle of their lives is partly caused by their expensive consumption habits. These are moulded early on as too many young mothers come to depend on the extremely expensive infant formula. Although most children are raised on mother's milk during their first two years—and at times well beyond that—in instances where a mother experiences difficulties with breastfeeding, she is more likely to start the money-draining infant formula routine than to seek help for her problems or to look for less costly alternatives. Then, after a child makes the transition to solid foods, it is put on a steady diet of starchy *rožki*—white breakfast rolls sold in every Slovak store—supplemented with fruit yogurt. Local Romani children consume enormous quantities of *rožki* throughout the day. They receive them for breakfast, they take them to school, and usually they end up munching on one whenever they go shopping with their parents. Alas, these rolls are not only short on nutritional value, but they are also relatively expensive. Yet many Romani mothers refuse to replace them with the nutritious, tasty, and cheap rye bread that is the staple of choice of most Slovaks. Similarly, the whites consider commercial fruit yogurt to be too expensive, and stores stock them mainly for their Romani customers. A more nutritious and certainly much cheaper alternative would be the locally produced quark (*tvaroh*) favoured by the villagers but rarely touched by the Roma.

The preference for expensive foodstuffs is embedded in local taste and its relationship to the dominant society. Much of that relationship is shaped by television. Most first-time visitors to the settlement experience a mild shock upon seeing satellite dishes perched on top of primitive shacks or attached to the walls of run-down apartment buildings. Virtually every household is equipped with a television set, and a growing number have access to a satellite universe of dozens and even hundreds of channels. Although most of it is delivered in languages which the viewers cannot understand, this distorted window on the world is heavily commercialized, and as such it has a noticeable effect on local consumption patterns. For

Figure 2.6. *Rožki* for breakfast in a Romani household

example, the much-advertised but expensive *Danone* yogurt is preferred to its cheaper competitor made in a small town 15 kilometres down the road. Similarly, the outrageously overpriced *Pamperski* have virtually eliminated the use of cotton diapers. And brand-name mobile telephones are beginning to make inroads into the more affluent pockets of the settlement.

There is another reason for the consumption pattern of local Roma, and this one arises out of the work ethic particular to the settlement. This is an important topic to which I will return in some detail further on. In the context that interests us here, let it suffice to observe that most adults consider physical work a necessary but by no means pleasurable by-product of daily life. Unlike white villagers with their multitude of practical pastimes—such as gardening, cooking, baking, preserving, sewing, building, and a whole range of home-improvement activities—most local Roma prefer a sedentary lifestyle centred around talking, eating, television-watching, and sleeping. And this type of lifestyle favours consumption patterns that are convenient and not demanding on one's time. For a parent, it is easier to hand out *rožki* and plastic cups of yogurt in front of the store, thus encouraging children to eat their breakfast "on the run," so to speak, than to slice a massive loaf of bread, put something on or between the slices, heat milk for a gruel, and gather and prepare the dishes needed for a Slovak-style breakfast. In the same vein, it is more convenient to spend a hundred crowns on a small frozen chicken—an extravagance avoided by the villagers—than to raise one's own, or to plant potatoes and cultivate them all the way to a successful harvest. Herein lies a crucial difference separating the domestic economy of the Roma from that of their white neighbours. That the main reason behind this is cultural rather than environmental—such as the lack of a land base suitable for cultivation—is borne out by the minimal extent to which local Roma even try to imitate the frugal and self-sufficient villagers in cost-cutting methods easily within anybody's reach. At harvest time, most locally grown fruits and vegetables can be purchased cheaply directly from the farmers and then dried or canned without much cost. Most Slovak rural (and many urban) families with any degree of self-respect prepare dozens of jars filled with jams, preserves, compotes, and pickled vegetables of a wide variety. In the settlement, by contrast, nobody engages in this kind of activity, and nobody appears interested in taking it up. Other cost-cutting methods, such as baking bread or preparing *tvaroh*, are similarly entirely absent.

The area surrounding the settlement is blessed with wild foods, such as a large assortment of edible mushrooms, several species of nuts, rose-hips, and berries. All of these can be used to supplement one's diet or to earn some money by selling them to commercial buyers. Many Romani families eat and pick mushrooms, and certain varieties that ripen in the fall are gathered by children and offered for sale to the villagers. But nobody in the settlement ventures beyond this modest use of free local resources. Mushrooms are neither dried nor pickled, and none of the other natural products attracts anybody's interest. Yet people comment on the annual "intrusion" of Romani women from nearby Jarovnice who gather a bountiful harvest of wild rosehips each fall in the immediate vicinity of the settlement. Most of the rosehips, used in the manufacture of excellent natural teas, end up with commercial buyers in Prešov. When pressed to explain why local Roma fail to participate in these activities, people tend to shrug their shoulders and state laconically that these things don't interest them.

Nevertheless, most families need to supplement their income derived from *dávki* somehow, and there are several ways in which they do this. Although the economic bonds linking the two ethnic hemispheres have grown rather brittle in recent years, a few villagers can still be counted on to maintain some degree of commercial contact with the Roma. Thus the children who sell mushrooms in the fall know not to waste their time by

Figure 2.7. Pedlars of brooms in white Svinia

ringing every doorbell in the village. Instead, they call only on a handful of "friendly" whites, such as the priest, one of the store owners, and a couple of teachers. The same strategy is followed by a young maker of brooms who peddles them in Svinia and a neighbouring village. Occasionally, someone from the settlement may land a small job weeding or digging a vegetable patch, but such work is usually paid for in kind rather than cash. The only reasonably rewarding job available from the villagers is offered by a local entrepreneur who employs a small crew of manual labourers that he then hires out to perform various short-term tasks. Working through a middleman, a boy of 17, in the settlement, he has access to up to 30 young men and adolescents willing to dig potatoes in local fields or trenches on construction sites in Prešov. The pay is between 150 and 300 crowns per day—up to $10 US—depending on the location and nature of the work to be performed. One core member of this "chain gang" confided in me that he had been participating in this scheme since he was 12 years old. He also claimed that the school principal collaborated with the contractor and falsified attendance records of students absent from school because of their involvement.

While most villagers agree that local Roma are good at heavy manual work, they quickly add that this applies only to young men, because adults past their late 20s tend to grow lazy. They do, though, admit that there is one type of useful activity in which all Roma excel, and that is scavenging in the widest sense of the word. We have already seen that the arrival of Roma in Svinia is linked in local folklore with their willingness to clean the chamber pots of white nobility. Subsequent years reinforced this early motif with numerous accounts that portray the newcomers as pickers and users of all kinds of stuff discarded by the villagers. Old rags, the clothes of deceased people, furniture and household equipment broken beyond repair, parts of slaughtered animals not fit for human consumption, and, above all, carrion, all figure prominently in the list of discarded articles associated historically with the *cigáni*. Today, a villager looking for a way to dispose of an old piece of furniture, an old-fashioned television set, or outdated stereo equipment tries to unload it in the settlement before turning anywhere else. Similarly, a farmer about to slaughter a pig will send word—often through a storekeeper—to a client in the settlement, encouraging him to pick up body parts not consumed by the villagers, specifically intestines that some Roma employ in their cooking. None of this "surplus" is given away, and the prices charged range all the way from 10,000 crowns for a used wall unit to 30 crowns for a bag filled with intestines.

The practice of collecting carcasses is welcomed not only by individual farmers but also by Svinia's agricultural cooperative. Without this service, deceased animals would have to be burned or otherwise disposed of at the owner's expense. Thanks to the Roma, the carcass is hauled away promptly and is even paid for. The buyer, in turn, turns a profit as he receives a large amount of meat at a very modest price. How profitable this activity can be may be seen from the following example. One of Svinia's more notorious carcass collectors received word that the agricultural cooperative wanted to dispose of a dead calf that had strangulated itself. I accompanied the man on his way to the collective farm. Without much ado, he paid 300 crowns, slung the animal across his shoulders, and proceeded back to the settlement. There he expertly skinned and butchered the calf outside his hut. The meat was divided among his brothers, who would later reciprocate in kind, and the hide was carefully scraped clean and dried. Next day we drove to a small meat plant in a neighbouring village where the hide was weighed in at five kilograms, cleaned further, salted, and stored for future sale to a shoe factory. My companion received 150 crowns, which reduced his original investment by one half. Given that 150 crowns will buy less than two kilograms of beef in any of the local stores, this was a thoroughly successful venture.

Figure 2.8. Scavenging for left-over potatoes in ethnic Slovaks' fields

In addition to the semi-formalized disposal of surplus goods and animals that requires some kind of payment on the part of the taker, there are other forms of scavenging that involve no investment at all. Every morning, one can see a small number of children rummage through white Svinia's trash bins in search of useable clothing and shoes. A much larger crowd, which includes adults, converges on the local dump after every delivery of spoiled fruit and vegetables from Prešov's supermarkets. And then there is the perhaps most lucrative form of garbage picking monopolized by a handful of families that trace their ancestry to Juraj Kaleja junior. Some members of this cluster, which, as I show further below, possess a separate collective identity, spend the better part of the spring and summer in a makeshift camp adjacent to Prešov's principal garbage disposal site. Here they search for copper wires, car batteries, and discarded engine parts containing aluminum, nickel, and copper components. The salvaged metal parts are then carted to scrap metal dealers in Prešov, where they are sold at the going rate. This is a fairly lucrative business in which a diligent and lucky picker can earn a few thousand crowns per month.

Most of the economic activities described so far as supplementing the various forms of social assistance provided by the state are pursued by a relatively small segment of the local underclass. It consists, above all, of

Figure 2.9. Garbage pickers in their summer shelter at the Prešov dump

the "creek people" and other families closely associated with them. By contrast, the settlement also has a small, upwardly mobile middle class, whose members engage in far more lucrative economic strategies, which are usually rooted in a merciless exploitation of needy neighbours and even relatives. The most rewarding of these ways is usury or loan-sharking. Locally known as *úžera* (Slovak) or *interes* (Romani), it takes advantage of the feast-and-famine consumption pattern that prevails in the settlement. Plagued by periodic shortages of cash, and unable to borrow from banks or villagers, most local Roma sooner or later turn to loan sharks in their midst in order to make essential purchases. The money-lender (*úžernik*) provides the requested funds, but he or she expects a *monthly* return of up to twice the amount of the initial loan, payable on the following *dávki* date. This means that a loan of 1,000 crowns must be paid back with 2,000 crowns, and, if one is unable to erase it, the amount doubles again the next month, and so on.

Being illegal, usury is hardly an easy topic for investigation or detached analysis. Reliable figures are impossible to come by as both lenders and borrowers try to quash the likelihood of police probes or even convictions. Caught between their financial needs and the limited means by which these can be fulfilled, even the greatest victims of *úžera* have an interest in its continued existence. Still, it is beyond dispute that most of these illicit transactions are controlled by a handful of big loan sharks with a sprinkling of smaller ones on the periphery of the local social spectrum. The identity of the lenders is established easily enough even without the cooperation of their victims: they can be seen standing outside the post office on the days of the welfare payments, waiting for their clients to cash their cheques, only to claim their share, or at least a substantial portion thereof, before the money is exchanged for goods at a local store. But because the profits gained through usury are so staggering, few people who find themselves with a surplus of cash can resist its lure. This means that although the circle of "professional" lenders is small, there are always opportunistic "amateurs" waiting on the sidelines to turn a quick and easy profit.

But it is not only cash that begets cash in the settlement. Considering that local Roma are relative newcomers to the world of money, it is truly amazing to observe the skill and speed with which they have learned to bestow a cash value on a wide range of sought-after goods and services. Since legal electricity is available only to the tenants of the apartment buildings, the less fortunate hut-dwellers make do with wiretaps that allow them to divert electricity from the apartments of relatives. The price they must pay is much higher than the equivalent of their actual consumption, and failure to do so leads to immediate "disconnection." Similarly, the few lucky residents who have a telephone line in their apartments earn a decent income by overcharging their less fortunate neigbours for making use of it. The going rate for a local call is one hundred crowns, which is at least twenty times the actual cost. Even emergency calls to the Prešov-based ambulance service are flatly refused without the payment of the customary fee. Less substantial amounts are charged for the use of washing machines, wheelbarrows, and a wide variety of tools. In the nearby settlement of Hermanovce, a local "entrepreneur" sells water from his well.

It is important to keep in mind that while the exploitation of local means for profit-making may be taken up by anybody who happens to be in a suitable position for doing so, its intensity and refinement increase with social status. This means that while someone from among the low-class "creek people" is quite able and willing to charge his neighbour for the use of a cellular telephone, this may happen only once or twice before the battery is depleted and the telephone sold, exceedingly cheaply, to a more calculating exploiter drawn from the ranks of the local elite. We shall have occasion to examine the composition of this elite in the next section. Here, it is enough to point out that it is the members of the elite who have learned to maximize, rather than simply use, the entrepreneurial potential that exists within the settlement. To use Max Weber's famous distinction between rational and traditional modes of behaviour, it is tempting to suggest that the elite has developed a (more) rational framework for optimizing economic opportunities, while the majority of the residents remain stuck in (more) traditional ways of making a living.

The two ideal types of economic adaptation are based on different approaches to time as a factor in economic activities. In the conduct displayed by the majority, time is perceived as a hostile force that works against people. As days and weeks go by, people have less and less cash, they are driven to the loan sharks, and their debts grow bigger and more difficult to settle. Perpetually fearful of the future, the majority live for the moment and thus allow the small elite to exploit it. For the latter have learned to take advantage of local opportunities by thinking about and planning for the future. The best illustration of this aptitude is the very institution of usury, based as it is on the lender's ability to have large reserves of cash at precisely the time when everybody else is totally depleted of it. But there are other examples. The most powerful local "clan" of money-lenders spends the two weeks preceding the *dávki* making preparations for the three or four days on which most people have enough cash to truly waste it. This entails purchasing vast quantities of bootleg vodka and beer—acquired from dubious sources through business contacts in Prešov and neighbouring settlements—and setting up an indoor or outdoor disco with live music provided by the money-lenders' own band. Having received their welfare money, local residents are then invited to spend it at the loan sharks' dance, which comes complete with entrance fees and cheap liquor. Of course, nobody knows that the oversized vodka sold at 300 crowns a bottle had been purchased for a fraction of this amount. A less crass example involves a well-known money-lender who makes and sells wreaths for decorating graves. Unlike her neighbour, the broom-maker, who manufactures and peddles his wares at times when few people have any money to spend, this calculating woman limits her activity to a couple of weeks preceding All Souls' Day, because she knows that even the poorest family adorns its members' graves with wreaths in anticipation of this important holiday. She also knows not to waste energy trying to cater to the villagers, because they are likely to purchase their wreaths more cheaply in Prešov. Instead, she concentrates on her Romani neighbours, who have little choice but to buy her overpriced products. The wreath-maker's husband, in turn, a gifted and skillful fellow born in the Czech lands and disdainful of local *cigáni*, makes his own contribution to the household income. Well known for his diligence, reliability, and dexterity, this man has maintained a good rapport with the collective farm where he used to be employed. Thanks to his connections, he enjoys some valuable perks. He is the first one to be hired for seasonal work and the last one to be laid off. And he gets a chance to purchase, more or less at cost, piglets from the cooperative's swine nursery. These he takes home, fattens them up in a shed built for this purpose, and once they reach a respectable size, he slaughters the pigs and sells the meat to his neighbours.

There are other examples that bear witness to the rationally pursued economic goals of the local elite. The settlement's two successful livestock operations are both conducted by prominent money-lenders. The men raise chickens during the summer months and turn a handsome profit selling close to a hundred eggs per day. Another well-known usurer grows the settlement's only vegetable garden, which supplies his kitchen with potatoes, carrots, and radishes. But perhaps the best illustration of the careful planning that goes into economic activities pursued by the elite comes from a recent innovation hatched by the eldest son of Svinia's most powerful *úžernik*. Cognizant of the profits made by Prešov taxi drivers who transport people and goods between the city and the settlement, the man decided to set up his own taxi service. First, he purchased a used Škoda—the settlement's first automobile—and then he set about mounting the most formidable obstacle: the need to obtain a driver's licence. He explained to me that taking and paying for lessons and exams constituted a poor investment due to the very real risk of failing the test and having to repeat it. Instead, he chose the foolproof method of bribing a police official willing to "sell" him the licence for 8,000 crowns. The transaction unfolded according to his expectations and to his complete satisfaction.

As we shall see imminently, the presence in the settlement of a wealthy and powerful elite of money-lenders and rational exploiters of their less fortunate neighbours is a very important component in the social and political dynamics played out within the community. While some factions blame the money-lenders for all the ills that plague local Roma, there are other members of the "under-class" who look up to the proto-capitalists as potential leaders and patrons. However, they all tend to exaggerate the wealth enjoyed by the loan sharks. This is especially so in the case of the most influential local *úžernik*, a woman in her 50s and the undisputed head of the cluster of families that traces its ancestry to the upwardly mobile Józef Kaleja—one of the founders of the upper settlement. Several tales make the rounds attributing almost legendary riches to this woman nicknamed *Velryba* (whale). One of the latest ones claims that while she was escaping the great flood of July 1998, *Velryba* stumbled and divulged 80,000 crowns concealed in her brassiere. The mystique of her wealth is so powerful that it hasn't failed to impress local villagers either. When this woman celebrated her 50th birthday in 1998, Svinia was abuzz with rumours of the expenses incurred in preparing the festivities. The cakes alone were assessed at 2,000 crowns, and the video recording made by a professional from Prešov was rumoured to have cost the astronomical amount of 10,000 crowns. Interestingly enough, the object of all this speculation denies any involvement in usury and related practices and attributes her comfortable status to her ability to make rational economic decisions. Here is her thoroughly Weberian assessment of the situation:

> They say that I am rich. No. I subsist solely on the cash that I receive as part of family benefits, and which I save instead of making purchases.... I get 3,000 crowns in pension payments, 2,000 of which I spend, and 1,000 I put aside. In addition, I receive 2,700 worth of food coupons, and that's enough for me.... They [the jealous members of the under-class] take it all at once, and then they have nothing more and suffer hunger. I take 500 crowns, and that lasts for a week. Next week—another 500 crowns. And so it goes, step by step.... And I tell them [to do the same]. But no, they need bottles [of liquor], because without bottles they can't live. And what will their children eat?... If I did this, I would have nothing. Today, liquor costs 200 crowns. 200 crowns make a good lunch. They don't think; don't think at all. They don't know how to save.... I told [my boyfriend]: "My golden boy, if I received as much money as you, then I would be a millionaire by now." After all, he gets between 15,000 and 16,000 all in all. And within a week he has nothing? If I received 15,000, I would put 10,000 into my bank account.

Sex and Procreation

If money is the settlement's foremost concern, then sex and its consequences follow very closely on the list of local preoccupations. Sexuality
and its expression have several important dimensions, all of which tran-
scend individual interests. There is adolescent, experimental sex, which
constitutes one of the benchmarks of adulthood. There is adulterous sex
with the potential for conflict and violence. There is the procreative sex of
teenage girls intent on increasing their family income. There is the criminal sex of rapes and assaults. And there is the political sex that cements
informal marital alliances between groups of families. Each and every one
provides a window on the community and its value system.

Given the cramped living quarters of local Roma, it is inevitable that
sexual activity cannot remain a private matter between two individuals.
Many households have more than one sexually active couple, and each
intimate encounter is likely to be noticed by other residents. This is
especially the case during the winter when sex must, by necessity, take
place indoors. It is, therefore, not surprising that even young children are
aware of the mechanics of intercourse, and that some incorporate it into
their games. What remains hidden at home is readily available on television
screens. Many families have access to satellite channels that carry erotic
content, and it is normal for children to be exposed to such at a very young
age.

Growing up in an environment saturated with sexual images and
conversations, a child enters puberty well aware of its consequences. This
is particularly true for girls whose visible maturation invites comments
and actions that reinforce the social significance of the physical changes.
As soon as a girl begins to show breasts, she is likely to receive thinly
veiled invitations from young, and sometimes not so young, men looking
for a quick encounter in the bushes above the settlement. At school, she
may be grabbed by boys waiting outside the girls' toilet, and some older
women are in the habit of jokingly squeezing young girls' breasts as a way
of testing their preparation for motherhood. What happens next is at least
partly determined by the girl herself and her parents. If she comes from
a family considered respectable, the girl will likely be closely guarded
and not allowed to frequent events, such as dances in other settlements,
where she may be led into temptation. If she obeys and acts accordingly,
the girl will earn a reputation matching that of her family, and she will

most likely stay out of harm's way until she is ready to enter a durable union resembling marriage. On the other hand, if the girl lacks the parental authority and self-discipline required to preserve her virginity, she will don tight jeans or revealing mini-skirts, apply excessive make-up, and seek out encounters with men during unsupervised visits to other settlements. Such a girl quickly earns a reputation as an easy prey, and she is likely to end up pregnant long before choosing a partner for life.

Regardless of their social status, most local girls are pregnant by the time they turn sixteen. But the circumstances differ, and so do the consequences. In order to do justice to the diverse factors at play, let us examine in some detail a number of case studies from the contemporary cohort of adolescents.

I will start with Jana, a girl from what could be termed a lower-middle-class family. Born in 1986, she grew up to become an intelligent non-conformist who quickly became bored by the settlement and the prospects it offered. By the time she reached the age of 14, Jana already had a reputation for being an easy target for boys. One day, she attended a small party where alcohol was served, and, having become drunk, Jana had voluntary or involuntary—depending on the source—sex with a number of boys, including one of her first cousins. This experience fortified her resolve to escape Svinia. She began to stay with relatives in Prešov, and her frequent absences from school led to truancy charges and deductions from her mother's welfare payments. Eventually, Jana, by now 15, returned to Svinia, accompanied by a sixteen-year-old partner from a nearby settlement. Her mother accepted the boy as Jana's consort, and the two were allowed to stay with her family. The young man, however, turned out to be abusive, and after he had tried to seduce Jana's twelve-year-old sister, he was thrown out and forced to return to his community. Jana, by now pregnant, stayed behind and resumed her attendance at school.

Jana's sister-in-law, Slavka, affords another illustration. Born in 1982, Slavka grew up in a small and respectable family. Her mother kept a close watch on her conduct and activities, but even so the girl developed a reputation for being fond of boys. Still, her mother's vigilance limited Slavka's opportunities for intimate encounters. Finally, having reached the age of 17, Slavka was allowed to attend a large public dance in Jarovnice—on the condition that she would spend the night with her aunt there. At the dance, Slavka became attracted to a young man whom she eventually followed to his house. According to her account, she was then raped by this man and ten of his friends. Back in Svinia, Slavka's mother pressed charges, which resulted in the conviction of the main culprit. Nine months later, Slavka gave birth to a child. In spite of her status as a single mother, she found a partner in Svinia: Jana's older brother Pepo. Alas, soon after the two adolescents had moved in together, Pepo was convicted of a rape and forced to serve a prison term. Although she denies it, Slavka is claimed to have developed an illicit affair with a married man. Recently, she gave birth to a second child, and she is waiting for Pepo to return from prison and acknowledge his paternity.

While Slavka is eager to keep up the appearance of respectability, some of her friends are not the least concerned about public opinion. An especially striking case concerns four sisters, ranging in age from 14 to 20. Raised in a large family by a passive and sickly father and a permissive and opportunistic mother, the four young women display an exceedingly utilitarian attitude to sex and its consequences. Encouraged by her mother, the oldest girl became impregnated at the age of 16 by a superficial acquaintance from Jarovnice in order to raise the family income. As the mother and daughter put it laughingly, the man's sole task was to "make a belly" (*urobit' brucho* in Slovak). A second child followed soon after, boosting the income further. Her younger sister, 17 at that time, chose to become pregnant for the same reason. The two remaining sisters expect to follow in the footsteps of their older siblings. None of the four shows any interest in developing a durable bond with a man, and the identity of the "impregnator" is of little concern to them. They view having children as a local career option that optimizes their limited talents.

The economic dimension of procreation can be detected in quite a few other cases. Sofia, a young mother of two born in 1984, became pregnant for the first time at the age of 15 following a sexual encounter with her fourteen-year-old second cousin. Neither Sofia, who displays clear signs of mental retardation, nor her partner, who is a drug addict, was fit for parenthood. Both children are, therefore, raised by Sofia's mother-in-law who receives, in turn, the lion's share of Sofia's not inconsiderable social benefits. More than that, Sofia, who resides with her "husband" in an extremely primitive hut, spends most of her time in the household of her mother-in-law, where she performs the work of a servant. A similar situation prevails in one of the settlement's elite families. Presided over by an influential money-lender, the family's reputation has been tarnished by the liaison of one of its female members with a young man of low status.

Unable to prevent the birth of an unwanted child, the family patriarch integrated its father into his household not as a full-fledged son-in-law, but rather as a servant who hauls firewood, weeds the family vegetable patch, and stands by for any menial task.

These few examples should make it clear that most first-time mothers give birth under somewhat nebulous circumstances. In some instances, sexual aggression provides the vehicle for a young girl's first and necessarily traumatic pregnancy. In other instances, youthful passion, usually incited by alcohol, triggers the fateful event, which may be masked later on as a rape in order to protect the girl's reputation. There are cases of "one-night stands" on a relative's couch in Prešov or Jarovnice. And there are liaisons between innocent-looking fourteen-year-olds and married men 20 years their senior with a well-earned reputation for sexual predation. Given the invariably young age of the girl and the haphazard circumstances of her sexual initiation and first pregnancy, the first birth becomes a chaotic affair. Not only is the mother emotionally and often physically unprepared, but there may be uncertainty about the father's identity or at least about his future involvement in the lives of the child and its mother. There may be criminal charges pending, blood tests to establish legal proof of paternity, court cases to enforce child support payments, and a plethora of other formalities necessitated by the mother's status of a minor.

It is surprising that this chaotic beginning leads to any degree of stability, but in many cases it does. Most young mothers eventually end up in a common-law partnership with a quasi-husband, who is not necessarily the first child's father, and together they create the conditions required for the procreation and sustenance of further offspring. But the couple, being young, inexperienced, and poor, remain heavily dependent on their parents. This dependence influences the settlement's residence pattern. Although most young couples are likely to establish their own quarters after an initial sojourn with the family of one of the partners, they usually choose a location in close proximity to the parental household. This allows the newly-weds continued access to items in short supply, such as washing machines, coffee grinders, or even cutlery and dishes. Conversely, this dependence sets the precondition for some parents' exploitation of their adult children.

Svinia's Roma do not profess a preference for patrilocal or matrilocal residence, and one finds all kinds of arrangements made in response to local conditions. Depending on the size of her parental family and the quarters it occupies, a young woman may spend the first year or two of her common-law marriage in her parents' household or in the household of her husband. Practical circumstances outweigh all other considerations. Similar reasons determine whether a bride joins her spouse in his community, or whether the husband moves to hers. But in spite of the flexibility that the locals display in their residential choices, it is clear that some remarkable shifts have taken place over the last three decades or so. Anecdotal evidence provided by middle-aged informants indicates that a far higher proportion of newly-weds remain in Svinia nowadays than used to be the case a generation ago. One woman in her early 50s, for example, has seen most of her 13 siblings leave the parental community in order to join their spouses elsewhere. By contrast, only one of her own 12 married children has left Svinia for another settlement. Analysis of the marital choices made by local Roma shows that 75 per cent of the children born here between the 1930s and the early 1970s had at least one parent who hailed from elsewhere, whereas that ratio fell to 25 per cent during subsequent years. This dramatic shift doesn't mean that young people no longer leave Svinia for spouses in other settlements—some continue to do so—but it does mean that of those who remain behind, which is the vast majority, far fewer end up with spouses from outside the community than used to be the case with their parents and grandparents.

I don't know how to explain this remarkable shift toward settlement endogamy. The people who are responsible for it don't indicate any significant changes in their preferences, and the most plausible conclusion one can draw in the absence of evidence pointing in a different direction is to correlate the shift with the dramatic increase in Svinia's population size, which translates into a corresponding growth of the local marriage universe. Unlike their parents and grandparents who lived in a small community that imposed strict limits on their choice of partners, the people who have reached maturity in more recent years have faced a much expanded pool of potential local partners, enabling them to make a selection within their own settlement.

The result of this shift has been a decrease in the amount of traffic between Svinia and other Romani communities. Every marriage with a resident of another settlement brings about increased contact between the two communities. Relatives and friends travel to and fro as they attend baptisms, birthday parties, funerals, and other important events. They learn from one another about economic opportunities, political developments, local educational initiatives, and a multitude of other issues. When such contacts decline, local residents become increasingly isolated from the outside world, and stagnation sets in. I will return to this further below, but first let me mention another remarkable transformation that has accompanied the trend toward settlement endogamy. The shift from choosing mostly spouses from other settlements to marrying predominantly one's own neighbours has gone hand in hand with a remarkable increase in the rate of unions between relatives. It is certain that common-law marriages involving close relatives did exist among Svinia's first- and second- generation Roma. Indeed, there is strong evidence that the common-law spouse of Bartolomej (1912–73), one of Juraj and Hania's sons and the founder of one of the lineages of *jarkovci*, was his biological niece. And of Hania and Juraj's 27 grandchildren who remained in Svinia and found partners there, seven chose first cousins or first cousins once removed. But this rate of roughly 25 per cent pales in comparison with the situation among the third- and fourth-generation: people who have reached maturity during the last 30 years or so and who have remained in their ancestral settlement. Of the 159 persons in this category, 101 (or close to 65 per cent) opted for a biologically related partner. Roughly one half of these unions involves close cousins—first and once removed—while the other half consists of more distant degrees of consanguinity.

The rising frequency of consanguineous marriages is undoubtedly related to the aforementioned tendency toward settlement endogamy. Given the limited influx of "new blood" from the outside, it is inevitable that third- and fourth-generation locals face a shrinking pool of unrelated contemporaries. Interestingly, local Roma profess avoidance of cousin marriage, and few of those who have broken this norm will disclose it voluntarily. Confronted with genealogical evidence, most will shrug their shoulders and declare pragmatically that affection overrides conventions. On the other hand, many people have such a vague grasp of their own ancestry that they cannot establish the identities of all four grandparents. This means that more distantly linked spouses, such as second or third cousins, are often not even aware of their relationship.[3]

Most of the reproductively active couples in Svinia live in a common-law relationship, which few have plans to formalize by means of legal marriage. Indeed, during all the years of my involvement in Svinia, I was aware of only two weddings. Normally, where two young people decide to become engaged in an ongoing relationship, one of them moves into the household of the other, and they begin to live together publicly. As far as the community is concerned, this signifies their determination to stay together and raise a family. In spite of their informal beginnings, such common-law unions are surprisingly stable. Like anywhere else, Svinia has its share of notorious adulterers, and this generates a great deal of conflict which, as I show below, can have a devastating impact on the families involved. But the majority of local couples seem to be satisfied, and their partnerships endure until old age.

Permanent unions of the type described here are expected to generate offspring, and, with the exception of one or two infertile couples, they all do. Children are regarded as an essential by-product of one's maturity, and this is why abortions, even in pregnancies resulting from sexual assaults, are frowned on. The same goes for contraceptives. Pregnancy follows pregnancy, and today's young women seem to be as prolific as their mothers and grandmothers. However, an increasing number of older women are willing to engage in some form of birth control once they reach their early 30s. Tired and worn out, they look for ways to slow down or even stop the reproductive cycle. Because the husband often doesn't condone this step, the woman usually looks for a type of contraception that her partner doesn't need to be aware of. The most popular technique employed in Svinia is the intra-uterine device, or DANA as it is known locally. This device is fitted and implanted routinely at a hospital in Prešov. While exact figures attesting to its use are hard to come by, it seems that the number of women interested in this or some other contraceptive is rising.

The Family and the Community

Most people who enter a foreign community have a tendency to look for a leader or spokesman, and first-time visitors to the Svinia settlement are usually pointed in the direction of a man in his late 40s who claims the title of *vajda*. Traditionally associated with delegated authority conferred by the municipal council or some other institution of the majority society onto a local man of some standing, the position of *vajda* no longer exists today as a formal office recognized by outside society. In settlements where the title retains some degree of authority, it is bestowed internally and usually quite informally onto someone who is held in respect and who is trusted to speak on behalf of the community before the municipal council, the police, and similar agents of authority. But even there, the *vajda* has no formal power and isn't necessarily recognized by the entire settlement. In Svinia, the man who introduces himself as the local *vajda* is an outsider who married *Velryba*'s sister and thus gained a certain degree of prestige on account of his affiliation with the most powerful money-lenders. Beyond that, the only authority he enjoys derives from his ability to convince foreign visitors to treat him as a "community representative."

Local Roma are deeply suspicious of every man or woman who attempts to act as a community-wide leader or spokesperson. Mercilessly anarchic in their dismissal of any imposed authority within the settlement, its residents cut down everyone who tries to dominate the hopelessly fragmented political scene. The protesters are driven by strongly held notions of egalitarianism that don't tolerate the emergence of formally sanctioned political elites. Persons who are believed to aspire to such positions are accused of presumptuousness or, literally, self-elevation (*povyšovanie* in Slovak), which carries with itself the threat of the degradation or, again literally, lowering (*poniženie* in Slovak) of others. Local Roma are exceedingly sensitive to conduct that smacks of arrogance, and most of them avoid situations and encounters that entail a power imbalance. They refuse, as they put it, to be "ordered around" (*rozkazovat* in Slovak).

In some ways the political structure of the settlement resembles the "headless" tribal societies designated by anthropologists as *acephalous* (Middleton and Tait 1958). Lacking any higher-level political institutions, local Roma constitute a good example of a "kinship polity"—a social universe governed by rules from the realm of kinship. This means that relations within the family—in the widest possible sense—are relatively well-defined while relations outside the family are brittle and subject to conflict.

In Svinia, the centre of all social, political, and economic affairs is the household (*kher*). In accordance with the developmental cycle that each family runs through as it grows and matures, a household typically begins as a small nuclear family, and then, as its children turn older and beget offspring of their own, it may accommodate one or two additional nuclear families before they split off and establish households of their own. Ideally, the latter are located in close proximity to the parental household, and these intimately related residential units constitute the core of every person's social universe. Their members are expected to cooperate, assist one another, and provide various forms of support. Local Roma identify this formation as *familija* or *fajta*, terms that correspond roughly with the anthropological notion of "extended family." In theory, it consists of one's parents, children, and siblings. But in practice, the boundary is elastic and differs from person to person. Depending on one's individual circumstances and sentiments, one may extend the solidarity that is expected to prevail within this kinship universe to all of one's siblings or only to some. One may incorporate a single aunt, uncle or cousin. And one can even expel a shameful father or child. A good illustration of local kinship dynamics is accorded by the secession 50 years ago of Józef and Alžbeta from their ancestral settlement. The single kindred that had prevailed until then gave way to two, with grave consequences still felt today.

While the composition of the family is flexible, relations within it are governed by rules that every member is supposed to respect. These are grounded in a patriarchal model of authority that assigns decision-making powers to the *pater familias* and delegates women to a subservient status of child-rearers and homemakers. The *vajda*—an expert on local notions of ideal behaviour—volunteered this sketch of the division of labour that should prevail between men and women:

> Men should be at work, and women should be with the children, keep them in line, so that our kids grow up properly.... Because we [men] protect the women. We don't want them to go to work. We want them at home, so that the man would earn money, and ... have her look after the kid, make sure the kid goes to school, is clean, and so on. And the man's duty is to go to work, and to earn money.... [W]e won't let them go to work, ... because a woman is a delicate creation, and a man is hard, for hard work, no matter what work, if there is something heavy to lift, if she bends for it, she will stay stooped; a man won't. A woman is something ... like Our Lady Mary. And a man, on the other hand, is like a bulldozer. When he goes, he goes. And the woman should be like a flower, a rose, so she doesn't grow old and get wrinkles.

It is questionable whether this ideal ever approached reality in Svinia. As we have seen, even the ancestral pair of Juraj and Hania departed from it, with Hania doing most of the work and her husband sitting in the hut, to the consternation of the villagers. The ideal may have prevailed for a while during the communist era when most Romani men did indeed have paid work, but nowadays, following the massive job loss of the last decade,

it is women, in their position of child-bearers and child-rearers, who sur-
pass men as principal breadwinners. Clearly aware of their importance
as "wage" earners, many women insist on being in control of the family
purse, especially when they live with men who tend to indulge in alcohol.
The women one encounters in the settlement, young and old alike, are, for
the most part, more assertive, active, and generally alive than the men. Far
from being under the patriarchal thumb of their husbands, women are the
driving force behind many families.

It is possible that the dominant position of women is a long-standing
tradition that hasn't changed dramatically in recent years. But the hopeless
employment situation faced by all men since the end of the communist era
has eroded the patriarchal ideal even further, creating a growing contradiction between the theory and practice of local gender relations. On the one
hand, the patriarchal ideal continues to be affirmed in the socialization of
children, where boys are treated with greater respect and attention than
girls. Yet, on the other hand, the moment an adolescent girl has borne her
first child, she gains a degree of financial security that no boy of the same
age can match. Some men, especially the younger ones, seem to accept the
weakening of their position, and they have learned to accept new responsibilities within the household. Unlike former times, when men were at work
all day long and women did all the shopping and child care, nowadays it
is fairly common to see younger men carrying shopping bags and pushing strollers. But there are other men who deeply resent their perceived
emasculation and refuse to accept the new socio-economic reality. Some of
them turn to alcohol and become oblivious to their families. Others resort
to violence and take out their frustrations on their spouses and children.

Spousal violence is well known to occur in the settlement. But its extent,
intensity, and underlying causes are difficult to gauge in the absence of a
thorough investigation. The situation is complicated by the local ethos that
accepts a certain degree of domestic violence as inevitable and, some might
say, desirable. According to many local Roma (men as well as women), an
occasional slap exchanged between spouses, especially when induced by
excessive alcohol consumption, is no ground for panic. As explained by the
vajda,

> Those are certain customs of this community. [And] a slap in
> the face given out of love is for love and good life. That's how
> it is. Like in the White school. If you don't listen, the teacher

will slap you, not for wanting to beat you, but to make you learn. And our way is similar.... The White man wouldn't do it, because he doesn't cherish the woman so much, but we do respect our women. Whether I slap her face or not, we are still on good terms. With you [whites], it's different. If you slapped her face, five minutes, divorce.... [Here] some women ask for it; if you don't beat them up, they won't live with you. I have known cases like that.

During my stay in Svinia, several women were victims of violence that clearly exceeded the norm described by the *vajda*. One of them, a friendly and quiet woman in her mid-40s married to an exceptionally aggressive man, suffered so much abuse that she abandoned her large family and sought refuge with her sister in Jarovnice. Eventually, though, she returned to tend to her incurably ill tormentor, who died soon afterwards. The stated reason for the abuse was jealousy, a condition that surfaces in many accounts of domestic violence. The extreme to which a jealous spouse may be driven is illustrated by the suicide of an elderly woman convinced of the infidelity of her husband. Although there was no proof of any wrong-doing, this extreme step triggered a sequence of events with further tragic consequences. The alleged seductress at the centre of this affair, a woman in her early 50s whom I shall call Renáta, had aroused the suspicion of her husband who then began to search for evidence of her infidelity. Although he didn't find it in the settlement itself, the trace led him to an unmarried middle-aged man in a neighbouring village. Here is the husband's account of what happened after he had followed Renáta to the house of her suspected lover:

Yes, I saw that they went to the kitchen, they embraced, kissed, and entered the house.... And I go inside, because the door to the kitchen was open. I go inside and see that there is nobody in the kitchen. And I see that the doors to all rooms are open. I peek around one and see that she had him in her hand, she worked on him, and she was naked, and so was he. Then he lay on the floor, they had a towel thrown there, and she lay down too. Then he lay on top of her and she worked. They wanted to finish, but I jumped inside and shouted: "Blessed be the Lord Jesus Christ!" She jumped up and cried that she was innocent, that he had made her do it and had promised to pay for it.... [Later] she told me to my face that it wasn't true. And she said that she would go to church and swear to her innocence.... It was on a Sunday after the mass. Nobody was there, but the church was open.... And I tell her, "get undressed, take it all off here, get on your knees and go all the way to the altar." She stripped, and I say to her, "kneel down." So she kneeled down and pulled herself all the way to the altar. "Do you swear? Place your thumbs onto the altar if you do." And she told me, "I cannot swear, or I would die." This was enough for me, why should I force her any further? "Go and get dressed," I told her. She got dressed, and father [who witnessed it all] said, "don't beat her."

This ended the marriage, and the two went their separate ways. Today, almost 30 years later, the former spouses remain in the same settlement, but when their paths cross they pretend not to see each other.

Given the limited mobility of local Roma, serious marital conflict can only rarely be softened by the temporary or permanent departure of one of the partners. Usually, the situation goes on and escalates to a point where the entire family becomes embroiled in a never-ending chain of serious expressions of ill will. An extreme situation is described by one of Renáta's daughters whose recollection of the causes underlying the conflict clearly contradicts her father's account:

My first memories are of the time when I was small, and how my father came back from prison and, I am ashamed to say, made her [mother] another baby. We were already 14 or 15 [children]. Then he left mother, and she had to take care of all of us. She didn't get any money, and so she had to go around begging. She had to look after our food. And she had to make sure that we went to school. All of this was on her shoulders. Then, when father returned from jail, he tortured her, beat her, and was jealous of her even though mother wasn't in-terested in other men. He beat her for nothing, picked up a knife and stuck it in her leg. He hit her head with a hammer, I remember that, I was thirteen then. She fell down like a pig and lost consciousness. He didn't feel any compassion for her and couldn't care less whether she would survive.... When I was fifteen, father was at home—he no longer sat in jail—and he would send us children to the forest [to fetch firewood], and mother to go around begging. We would come home, split the wood, and he would sit in the tavern, drinking. When mother came home—it froze outside—her hair was all frozen, and [she carried] a rucksack on her back with things. We looked at her, and we felt terribly sorry for her, because without her we wouldn't have survived. [One day] when mother returned home, she didn't even have time to take off the rucksack, he approached her, grabbed her hair, and began beating her like a man. Then I confronted him: "Why are you beating her? Don't you see how much she suffers?" I tried to explain, but he hit me so hard that I fell down.... Then my younger brother, Miro, who was fourteen then, also let himself be heard that he didn't like what father was doing. Well, and then they started to fight—father and son.... And father called his brother, and the two of them went against the boy.... And father pulled his knife, and then his brother grabbed a pitchfork, ... and when Miro saw how they were getting ready, ... he pulled out a long chain and beat [his uncle]—not on his head but on his legs, so that he wouldn't stab him with the pitchfork.

This degree of intra-family violence is exceptional, but when it occurs, the community tolerates it as something reprehensible yet unavoidable. And it's not only men who resort to it. The mother of Renáta's husband, for example, served a prison term for seriously stabbing her own brother—in retaliation for his own stabbing of her husband earlier. Even where domestic violence doesn't reach this kind of intensity, the home environment is hardly an oasis of peace and tranquillity. Children are clearly loved by their parents, and affection is displayed openly as babies are kissed, cuddled, and carried around by mothers and fathers alike. But as they grow older, the amount of attention they receive diminishes rapidly, and hugs and kisses are traded for scolding, threats, and slaps. With large families and cramped quarters, conflict is never far away. Screams, outbursts of anger, and beatings are facts of life that most children learn to take for granted. Inside and outside the home, they quickly learn that if you are kicked, you kick back unless you want to end up lying on the ground.

There are several clusters of closely related families linked through three, four, and even more siblings who get along very well, and whose members seem to comprise one large extended household where children wander freely from one hut or apartment to the next while their parents carry on many of their daily tasks collectively. This kind of ideal kin solidarity is particularly striking among the low-class "creek people" who all reside in the same area and who seem to take genuine pleasure in each other's company. On the other hand, there are adult brothers who hardly ever speak to one another, even though they live in the same apartment building. Some may be merely indifferent about their close kinsmen, while others harbour decidedly hostile feelings. Most of the families are some-where in-between these two extremes. Their members profess ideals of family cohesion, but when the opportunity arises, parents are quite capable of over-charging their mature children on some goods or services—such as the "sale" of electricity—and children reciprocate by allowing aged parents to live in poverty while they themselves may be relatively well off. Indeed, family members often conceal their financial situation from one another in order to guard themselves against unwelcome requests for loans. I witnessed situations where a man would spit into the face of his married daughter because she had refused to buy him a bottle of vodka, and I also had to watch a middle-aged woman slap her father's face during an argument over money. In another demonstration of parental selfishness, a middle-aged couple appropriated funds given to their teenage daughter to help with expenses arising out of the funeral of her prematurely born child.

If severe conflict between closely related people bound by an ethos of solidarity is of frequent occurrence, it assumes catastrophic proportions outside the realm of kinship. According to the ideologically tinted introduction to Romani values provided by the *vajda*, this shouldn't be the case, because "Roma like each other, and that is why we are also nice to each other, not indifferent [but] friendly, and if one of ours comes, he doesn't need to knock on the door like you [whites] do, ... but with us he just opens the door and walks in any time. He will get food, drink, and everything." There are times, especially during the few days following *dávki*, when the entire settlement resembles one big happy family. Ear-deafening music, groups of adults and children whirling around and clapping to the tunes of a fast csardas, bottles of beer passing from hand to hand and mouth to mouth, and a seemingly random selection of revellers who come and go as they please, create an atmosphere that appears to confirm the *vajda*'s dictum that "Roma like each other." But upon closer inspection one discovers that each party is encircled by an invisible border that is rarely crossed by uninvited guests. Far from drawing a random crowd, most celebrations are far from open. Whether fairly formal occasions, such as baptisms and weddings, or more haphazardly organized events, such as birthdays, the festivities that take place in the settlement draw a precisely selected crowd. True enough, nobody makes up a guest list or issues formal invitations. But because everyone has a clear grasp of the community's web of relationships, such formalities are unnecessary. Fearful of public humiliation (*poniženie*), unwelcome guests simply stay away. Extended into everyday life, the observance of local rules of etiquette makes it, indeed, redundant to knock on someone's door. But the doors remain open only because everyone, including children, stays away from the dwellings of people who are outside one's social circle. To do otherwise is considered trespassing.

Far from genuinely liking each other, local Roma find it very difficult to get along with their neighbours. And although they complain about the exclusionary territoriality of the villagers, they engage in similar practices within their own community. Just as it is unthinkable for a *cigán* to enter the courtyard of a villager without arousing apprehension, so it is also highly inappropriate for a member of the low-class *jarkovci* to visit one of the apartment buildings. Not to observe this unwritten rule invites rude comments and even outright accusations of criminal designs. Even immediate neighbours are often suspected of kleptomaniac tendencies, and the heavy chains and padlocks that secure every door bear testimony to the mistrust that prevails here. I was taught a revealing lesson in community priorities when some of the recipients of brand-new latrines donated by the project that I directed decided to take them apart and use the premium lumber for fences instead. Just like in white Svinia, the "landlords" then placed menacing dogs into the enclosures.

The clear demarcations of "us" vs. "them" go hand in hand with an intense scrutiny of possible gains made by one's neighbours. Just how competitive local Roma are was shown in the aftermath of the devastating flood of 1998. As national and international aid organizations rushed to assist the people of Svinia to rebuild their shattered lives, the victims screamed and fought over every bed, mattress, blanket, and cooking pot delivered by outside benefactors. I watched in horror as dozens of men, women, and children besieged the truckloads of "cargo," each of them attempting to

Figure 2.10. Low-class *jarkovci* in front of their hut

carry off as rich a booty as possible. In most cases, the donations by far outstripped the sparce household equipment destroyed by the flood, and yet very few people seemed satisfied with their share of the aid package. What disturbed them was not some genuine shortage of donated goods but rather the perception that other people were getting more than they were felt to deserve.

Just as all local residents are aware of the web of relationships that envelops the entire community, so they are also attuned to a sense of balance that is maintained by the social order. People know where they belong on the local status scale, and actions that compromise it, such as the distribution of free goods to undeserving community members, trigger conflict. The lowest-status people are all descendants of the four siblings—Margit, Bartolomej, Juraj, and Štefan—who remained on the ancestral lower site after the exodus of Józef and Alžbeta. Although they are often lumped together as a single collectivity of *jarkovci*, there are, in fact, several sub-groups, each with its own residential area, lineage, and collective identity. The two major clusters that stand out here are *Pokutovci*, named after a son of Juraj, and *Kalejovci*, the descendants of the other three siblings. They share a reputation for unsavoury consumption and sexual practices, they monopolize the activities related to garbage-picking and carcass-disposal, and they maintain friendly relations—cemented by marital and economic alliances—with the nearby settlement of Chminianské Jakubovany, whose residents are loathed on account of their indulgence in dog meat. At the other end of the social spectrum is a smaller grouping of families that comprise the settlement's elite or "upper-class." These trace their ancestry to the two founders of the upper settlement, Józef and Alžbeta, and their respective spouses who both hailed from high-status communities. Here we find the most prominent loan sharks and opinion-leaders. But while the kinship universe enveloping the descendants of these two siblings comprises dozens of individuals, only a few of them have managed to rise to the top of the local ranking system. This is because elite status is conferred not only by ascribed factors, such as affiliation with certain ancestors, but also, and even more importantly, by personal qualities and talents. People associated with the progressive upper settlement and its founders but lacking the additional personal attributes required for social mobility find themselves confined to a position in-between the elite and the underclass. Constituting the local equivalent of the middle class, this large grouping consists of people whose social status is subject to fluctuations in response to economic developments, affinal relations, and micro-political alliances.

Although affiliation with the upper settlement is a precondition for elite status, its two core determinants are wealth and cultural refinement. Whereas wealth is largely the result of the kind of internal exploitation de-scribed earlier, its accumulation is seen as being linked to an advanced pat-tern of thinking that goes hand in hand with cultural refinement. Imitating ethnic Slovaks, Roma refer to the attainment of this higher cultural level

Figure 2.11. Middle-class respectability in one of the apartments

as *kulturnost'*, a term that can loosely be translated as "the state of being cultured." This condition plays a very important part in the local inter-ethnic discourse. As we have seen, the villagers attribute the poor state of affairs in the settlement to its residents' lack of cultivation or, as they put it, *bezkulturnost*. This view is shared by the Romani elite whose members blame the lowly status of their less fortunate neighbours on poor manners (*mores* in Romani) and general cultural degeneration. Accordingly, they have adopted the common Slovak habit of referring to Roma dismissively as *cigáni*. Whenever they need to find a culprit for this or that shortcoming, they are wont to castigate the uncultured behaviour of the *cigáni* in their midst.

The chasm that separates the elite from the under-class is sustained by symbols that go beyond the mimicry of Slovak views about the attainment and loss of culture. Local Roma, especially those aspiring to upper-class status, draw a distinction between clean (*maluša* in Romani; literally "white" or "light") and unclean (*melale*, literally "black") people. The former must maintain proper hygiene (including, for example, the use of latrines, but also cutlery), they should dress neatly, and they must abstain from foodstuffs considered impure, such as meat derived from dogs and horses. In order to uphold their elevated status, *maluša* people shouldn't

Figure 2.12. A cinder-block duplex inhabited by local entrepreneurs

eat together with *melale* people, and, above all, they should marry only their own kind. These purity rules impose limits not only on patterns of interaction within the settlement, but also on associations with the inhabitants of other communities. Unlike the *melale* "creek people" with their long-standing alliance with Roma from the dog-eating community of Chminianské Jakubovany, the status-conscious members of the upper class avoid contact, especially of the sexual kind, with residents of this and similar settlements. Some even refer to these people as *dubki* or *degeše*: two equivalent terms meaning "dog-eaters" and "degenerates."[4]

The uneasy equilibrium that prevails among the various segments of the community is maintained by informal means, and in the absence of a recognized leader or arbiter, conflict is frequent and often violent. In its most innocuous form it leads to verbal duels between two individuals who seek to call public attention to some perceived injustice. Such a duel begins with an encounter in the settlement's central square, which leads to a loud exchange of insults. The screams attract an audience, and as a crowd of spectators assembles, the two combatants escalate the intensity of the encounter. This means not only an increase in the volume of the accusations, but also the addition of ritualized bodily expressions of anger, which include wrinkling the nose, pounding the chest, and slapping one's hands for emphasis. At this point the duel assumes such intensity that physical aggression seems inevitable. But the next step of physical violence doesn't always follow. Certainly when the combatants are women, they are likely to abort the confrontation before a genuine fight breaks out. Men, on the other hand, are less likely to get involved in a public conflict, but once they do, it often does escalate into a physical confrontation. The more bellicose men carry knives (*nožiki*), which are meant to protect them from assailants, and when a fight erupts it doesn't take long before both parties brandish a knife. Depending on the nature of the conflict, the assembled crowd may try to neutralize the skirmish or, if its cause extends beyond a single family, it may join it. In the latter case an all-out fight (*bitka*) ensues, which has serious consequences for the entire community. While nobody seems to have ever been killed, these confrontations can inflict far from benign injuries that may require medical attention. Head wounds, stabbings, and partially severed fingers testify to the intensity of these encounters.

Although the public expression of conflict isn't confined to a single faction or cluster of families, it is evident that its frequency and depth are influenced by one's standing in the community. Someone with little prestige and few supporters isn't likely to attract much of an audience, and such a person's grievance will most certainly not escalate into a *bitka*. On the other hand, the public airing of a perceived injury by a member of the elite will not only accord a more interesting spectacle; it also promises to attract support from family members and clients, and thus to transform a private grievance into a community-wide confrontation. Indeed, it would appear that the most vocal public expressions of displeasure are to some extent considered a prerogative of the members of the core elite. It is their way of calling attention to perceived shifts in the local balance of power, and of trying to intimidate and humiliate those who "don't know their place."

It has already been shown that what I call the "balance of power" benefits the local elite in its attempt to perpetuate the various exploitative mechanisms that it controls. In order to maintain their privileged position, the major money-lenders must have ways to compel their debtors into making periodic payments. This is not easy in view of the rapid accumulation of debt caused by the exorbitant interest rates, and it is here that outright coercion is sometimes resorted to. Here is a sampling of short eyewitness accounts of the violent methods resorted to by the money-lenders:

> For example, take Velryba or her sister [both prominent money-
> lenders].... They know that they can intimidate [the "creek
> people"]. They know that they will submit without raising a
> hand.... And so, when someone refuses to give money to C.
> [Velryba's sister], she threatens "why don't you pay up? if you
> don't, you will get it." And comes her daughter ..., and slap,
> one or two. An old woman treated like that by a snotty nose of
> thirty, she comes to her and pulls her by her hair like a dog....
> All these girls of C., when they see that someone refuses to pay
> their mother, it's not C. but them who start the fight.... And
> these poor people, they must pay up even if they don't want to,
> because they are afraid.... [Same methods are resorted to by
> another loan-shark] ... if someone doesn't pay, he beats him to
> a pulp, and if he doesn't do it himself, his sons will.

The reference to grown-up daughters and sons acting as lieutenants
of major loan sharks points out an essential dimension of local kinship
solidarity. Close relatives are supposed to provide tangible physical
support, if necessary by force, and though not all do, most will live
up to that expectation most of the time. This means that the clusters of
closely related families are regarded not merely as a source of emotional
and material support, but also as units of defence and offence in times of
exacerbated conflict. I witnessed deliberations resembling those of a war
council where local "big men" used their fingers to determine the strength
of their own and their opponents' troops. The more brothers and grown
sons you can count on, the greater the fighting power of one's *familija*. In
some instances, as we have already seen, mature daughters with a fighting
disposition can become valuable substitutes for missing sons.

The numerical factor—and the reputation of individual family members
for being good fighters—is an important ingredient of the settlement's
balance of power. While the Velryba "clan" surpasses all other families
in terms of economic and cultural capital, it nevertheless doesn't enjoy
uncontested monopoly on power, because there are other factions that
outperform it in terms of fighting prowess. The several major clusters
of related families that dominate social and political life in the settlement
are thus engaged in a perpetual competition for influence and authority, a
state resembling a "cold war," which prevents the eruption of large-scale
violence.

This situation puts small families and migrants from other communities at a serious disadvantage. Even though they may gain powerful allies through marriage or friendship, such associations are imperfect substitutes for real kinship. The self-appointed *vajda* provides a case in point. Although he cuts an impressive figure on account of his cosmopolitan background and affinal connection with Velryba's family, he nevertheless feels vulnerable knowing that the support he enjoys is far from solid. This realization makes him reluctant to play up the *vajda* card more self-assuredly or to get personally involved in his wife's money-lending activities. Other immigrants, who lack the *vajda*'s erudition and family connections, feel easily intimidated and largely disenfranchised. They rarely venture beyond the confines of their own territory, and if they dare make themselves heard in public, they always remain aware of the danger of being shouted down on account of their peripheral status.

Due to the high level of animosity and conflict that affects relations between local residents, the settlement isn't perceived as a homey community to which people develop strong attachments. Shunned by the villagers and exploited by the loan sharks, many residents stay put in small kinship-based pockets of relative safety where they dream of escaping to Prešov or a higher-status settlement where daily life is deemed more rewarding and less fraught with conflict. During the socialist era, a friendlier political and economic climate permitted emigration not only to Prešov but beyond Slovakia to the more promising industrial centres of Moravia and Bohemia. It is evident that such exit strategies were taken advantage of by some members of the local population. Today, these avenues are blocked to such an extent that even nearby Prešov has come to be thought of as an unattainable destination for all but the wealthiest members of the elite. The significant reduction in mobility during the post-socialist period has starkly limited the gamut of traditional conflict-avoidance strategies.

Deviance, Handicaps, and Pathology

We have seen several times by now that commentators outside as well as inside the settlement attribute many social ills and problems to specific traits of local residents. For most of the ethnic Slovak villagers, "their" *cigáni* are simply stupid, dishonest, lazy, and violent. What sounds like typical racist slurs is repeated by the settlement elite in an effort to substantiate and justify internal boundaries between the rich (*barvale*) and the poor (*čorore*).

Thus the cultured loan sharks bemoan what they perceive as a lack of *mores* displayed by the "gypsies" and use it to justify the racism of the villagers as well as their own growing distance from the "untouchables" that surround them. More surprisingly, perhaps, the same racist stereotypes are encoun- tered in conversations with many members of the underclass, who agree with the whites and their own Romani patrons that the local community and people are somehow inherently dysfunctional and pathological. Is this a textbook example of the internalization of colonial stereotypes, or does it reflect empirical facts observed and accepted by both groups? This is a dif- ficult question to answer as it raises important ethical and methodological issues. Nevertheless, notions of degeneration, pathology, and dysfunction- ality receive such widespread support in both ethnic camps that an exami- nation of this theme is certainly called for.

Perhaps the best place to start is with Svinia's sole ethnic Slovak "gone native": a man in his early 50s who arrived in the settlement some 30 years ago, moved in with a Romani woman, learned the local dialect to perfec- tion, and founded the first *mestizo* lineage. This man, who resembles a modern-day Robinson Crusoe in appearance and conduct, has this to say about his Romani neighbours and relatives:

> They are all cocksuckers, zeroes, losers. Here is not a single decent person.... They are all imbeciles.... They have all gone to school. Nine years in grade one without repeating once. Why do these children go to school and when they leave eight or nine years later, they don't know how to read a watch? Why do they go there?... Look, I have my own spoon. I hang it up there [on the wall]. I have my own clock. I hang it up there. Everyone comes and asks what time it is. When I get drunk and forget to wind up the clock, it's all lost the next morning. They won't even go to school. That's the system here.

The reference to imbecility and illiteracy introduces a much-repeated theme of the lack of formal literacy as one of the root causes of local dys- functionality and pathology. Telltale signs of illiteracy are easy to find. Although most children attending Svinia's elementary school master the rudiments of reading, writing, and counting, there are girls and boys in their early teens who don't know how to sign their names, add up single- digit numerals, or even determine their exact age. These gaps grow wider once adolescents leave school—by law they must remain until the age of 16—and spend all their time in the impoverished milieu of the settlement. Young recruits called up for compulsory military service are routinely discharged on the grounds of illiteracy or substandard results of intelligence tests.[5] Men in their early 20s are incapable of understanding the concept of right angle, let alone using metres and centimetres as units of measurement. Among middle-aged Roma the situation is generally better, since they went to school during the socialist era when formal education appears to have left more palpable traces. But even here we find only a handful of men and women capable of drafting a simple letter on their own. Some are unable to sign their names, and surprisingly many cannot recall the year of their birth.

The climate of illiteracy clearly diminishes local children's chances at succeeding in the formalistic environment of the school that they all attend. It has become fashionable in recent years to target the "negative discrimination" underlying the segregation of Romani students into "special" schools where they encounter a simplified curriculum often delivered by less-than-enthusiastic teachers (Ringold 2000:41). But the critics of these institutions often fail to recognize the magnitude of the cognitive deficit experienced by children from a marginal community such as the Svinia settlement. Raised in families where reading and writing are practised sporadically if at all, such children cannot keep pace with their more sophisticated counterparts from the village. Occasionally, an exceptional Romani student manages to bridge the gap, and in such instances the inability of the administration to ensure successful integration into the normal school becomes an unmitigated tragedy. But these singular cases shouldn't obscure the very real cognitive handicaps preventing the participation of most Romani students in the regular curriculum.

What exactly are these "cognitive handicaps"? Curious to know how professional educators view and respond to "retarded" Romani students, I asked an elderly and experienced teacher to write down her key observations. It should be pointed out that this kind and gentle woman possessed not only a wealth of experience but also a generous character that endeared her to her Romani students and their parents in the settlement. Here is what she reported:

> I have the great advantage that all my [current] Romani pupils are relatively fluent in the Slovak language and know how to

express themselves quite well, albeit not grammatically correctly. I devote much time to the development of language
through the recitation of riddles and sayings, dramatization of
stories, singing of songs, and so on.... The children [always]
begin with great interest and determination, but they grow
tired quickly. They have difficulty with concentration, and they
require constant encouragement and frequent changes of work
format and controls of attained results. Faced with a new task,
they can't proceed independently. New knowledge is acquired
very painfully. It is important to repeat the same things endless-
ly. When we arrive at a new insight, we repeat the same thing
over and over again.... While normal children acquire already
at pre-school age certain concepts, such as "above," "below,"
"before," "after," "less," "more"..., they need help mastering
them. They confuse letters, even those as dissimilar as "m" and
"o." The linking of letters into words takes very long.... So does
the transition from a point, a line, a wave to the composition of
letters.... What helps? Encouragement, corrections, guidance.
Each pupil alone could keep a teacher busy during four instruc-
tional hours.... I pay particular attention to the development
of manual skills, because I realize that in practical life they will
depend on manual labour.... We work with simple materials
which we shape into simple objects that have some practical use.
These objects are taken home by the students.... It is necessary
to add that they are not particularly handy. Even the use of glue
and scissors requires constant supervision.

All these observations correlate with my own experiences. Indeed, I
began to pay attention to cognitive factors partly in consequence of my
own encounter with Romani students at the Svinia elementary school.
Having convinced the principal to set up an afternoon enrichment program
for particularly gifted children, I ended up teaching rudimentary English
several hours per week. This experience gave me some insights into the
challenges faced not only by the students but also by the teachers of the
"special" program. On the one hand, even my best students needed weeks
to memorize a few simple phrases such as "how are you?," "what is your
name?," and "my name is...." We repeated them one by one; we repeated
them in unison; and we repeated them separately as well as together.

Yet all my techniques could not bridge the wide gap between desire and realization. The children simply couldn't memorize these few basic phrases. On the other hand, I confronted not only a group of exceptionally slow learners, but also a horde of extremely unruly and restless children who grew easily tired of even nominal mental exertion. Holding their attention for more than a few minutes proved beyond my pedagogical abilities, and I eventually abandoned this effort—but not without recognizing that the regular teachers lack such an easy way out.

The unruliness of the children is apparent not only during their school attendance. Most first-time visitors to the settlement tend to be charmed by the spontaneity and effusive friendliness of its children. As one enters the ghetto, small children congregate immediately to form an impromptu welcoming party that accompanies the visitor into the heart of the community. Starved for attention and bored by the monotony of daily life, children compete with one another trying to capture the stranger's attention. The contrast with white Svinia is overwhelming. There, children have learned to imitate adults, and they exude an air of disapproval or at least disinterest. But the Romani cordiality comes with a price. Once a visitor has been classified as approachable and friendly, it becomes very difficult to shake off the little urchins. Especially if one arrives by car—an immediate object of curiosity—and happens to respond to outstretched hands with small gifts of candy or spare change, the welcoming committee may transform itself into a screaming and demanding mob that threatens to suffocate the stranger. Unwilling and at times unable to listen to pleas or verbal threats, the mob responds only to aggressive screams followed by hard slaps meted out by a local adult.

The frenzy and unbridled curiosity with which children welcome diversions have resulted in numerous complaints from the villagers. Svinia's agricultural cooperative cultivates a large field in the hillside above the settlement, and this necessitates the passing of heavy farm machinery along a narrow road that skirts the settlement. Some 15 years ago, a combine severed the arm and the leg of a boy who was playing in the field. Since then, the tractors, trucks, and combines traversing the road that links the village with the settlement have been a source of irritation for Romani parents fearful for the lives of their children. Yet they do surprisingly little to keep the children under control. Seeing this as a welcome thrill, boys wait for a truck or combine to approach the bottom of the hill where the driver slows down in order to shift into a lower gear, and then they jump onto the vehicle in the expectation of a joy ride. Unable to convince the parents to respond in some constructive way, the drivers have "solved" the problem by passing the settlement as quickly as possible, which in turn increases the risk of injury to the many toddlers who play along the road. Ambulance drivers responding to medical emergencies have been known to stop at some distance from the settlement in order to avoid the obstructions created by undisciplined children. The same factor is cited by the municipal council as the reason behind its reluctance to allow Roma use of the spacious and well-equipped community centre in the heart of the village.

Although some Romani adults—notably the militant *vajda*—blame their children's unruly behaviour on allegedly unmotivated and lazy Slovak teachers, there is widespread agreement that this is an escalating problem with adverse consequences for the entire community. Not everybody endorses the opinion of the "creek people" that it was the aggressiveness and lack of discipline of children that led to the closure of the upper settlement. And not too many Roma feel sympathy toward the villagers whose fruit trees are attacked daily by mobs of children on their way to and from school. But there is hardly a dissenting voice when it comes to discussing the damage caused by children and adolescents within the settlement itself. There is consensus that too many young people are dangerously out of control.

The settlement experiences a great deal of theft and vandalism, the blame for which is laid on the shoulders of criminally inclined or simply destructive children and adolescents. Hardly a week passes without a household being robbed of something valuable and the theft being attributed to an underage culprit. Not a day goes by without an act of wanton vandalism against public or private property. The thefts rarely involve money or really valuable household equipment—such as televisions, radios, or VCRs; for this the community is simply too small and the removal and resale of such objects too difficult. What tends to get stolen are less conspicuous articles such as tools, loose boards, plates, bed sheets, and blankets. Vandalism, on the other hand, targets every imaginable installation and innovation. Its perpetrators break windows, slash tires, and destroy gardens. When a manual pump was attached to a water well in the centre of the settlement, it survived only two days. All that remained after the second night was a useless metal pipe rising from the ground. The construction of a daycare centre provided another target for vandals. Windows were smashed, playground equipment was removed or destroyed, and even the picket fence enclosing the complex disappeared within a short period of time. Most of the chickens raised by local innovators in an effort to encourage livestock production were stolen a couple of weeks into the experiment—and this in spite of massive chainlink fences and barbed wire around the fortress-like chicken coops. Most of the heavy garbage cans introduced in an effort to improve public hygiene would also have disappeared had they not been promptly secured with padlocked chains.

Local Roma blame children and adolescents for these acts of vandalism. Within this group exists a smaller circle of highly problematic youths whose destructive behaviour is magnified and perhaps caused by drug use. Nobody knows the exact extent of local drug use, but at least 25 youngsters are self-declared addicts. All are male, and most between the ages of 14 and 18. Some drug users are, however, as young as ten and as old as 30. Without exception, the drug of choice is a widely available paint thinner known as Toluen, which can be purchased in most hardware stores. The liquid is used to soak a piece of cloth that is then enclosed in a small plastic bag. The bag is concealed inside one's jacket—a garment worn by local addicts even on hot summer days—and one gets "high" by inhaling the vapours emanating from it. According to the users, prolonged use of Toluen leads to visions, increased assertiveness, and a heightened sense of well-being. Concerned parents hold the drug accountable for sleep disorders and aggressiveness. Many of the users profess a desire to wean themselves of the substance, and some have, in fact, spent time in drug rehabilitation centres run by the government. So far, though, all have resumed the habit after their return to the settlement. Information provided by local health-care workers indicates that prolonged use of Toluen leads to brain damage and permanent dependence.

Although there are claims that a popular hair dye, known locally as "Hofman's drops," became a widely used drug-like substance in some settlements during the 1970s and early 1980s (Lacková 1999), local Roma see Toluen as the first "hard" drug to have appeared in their community. They regard its spread with alarm, especially as there is strong evidence that the number of users is multiplying rapidly. But Toluen is not, of course, the only addictive substance used in the settlement. A large number of the population regularly consume alcohol, and many are heavy drinkers. In contrast to their white neighbours—most of whom are hardly abstainers themselves—the Roma include a sizeable number of women who drink heavily and regularly. Even women who indulge only occasionally may get completely drunk at parties and binges that follow the monthly "payday."

Figure 2.13. Adolescent boys getting high on Toluen

Unlike Toluen, with which the older generation has no direct experience, alcohol is an integral and approved part of local culture. Most people enjoy beer as well as vodka or rum and a sweet apple wine known colloquially as *čučo*. When money runs out, hardened alcoholics may resort to after-shave and similar alcohol-based products, which are referred to collectively as *kamfor.*

The second socially sanctioned and nearly universally used drug is tobacco. Unlike alcohol, which a few people abstain from, smoking is a habit indulged in by almost everyone above the age of fifteen or so. Women and men smoke outdoors, indoors, at home, while visiting their neighbours, and the habit is so ingrained in one's conduct that most households don't even possess ashtrays. A lit cigarette becomes an extension of one's body, and it follows the body wherever it ventures and whatever it does. Ashes are discarded wherever the smoker happens to sit, stand, or lie. The "tobacco culture" is so entrenched here that it has generated its own myths about the magical qualities of smoking. One of them reverses western beliefs about the health effects of tobacco use. Here is the *vajda*'s rendition of it:

> I am surprised that they are prohibiting smoking, because smoking is good in one way [now] that people live in cities a lot, and as factories release [harmful] particulars, or cars release it, ... it means that this metal, ... if you smoke a cigarette, the metal can get inside you, [but] it could also be prevented, because if the metal falls into the smoke, as you smoke, you can blow it out.... Sometimes a cigarette aids expectoration. If you have a cough, and have a smoke in the morning, ... you would spit out something like yolk, or puss, something like that.

Asked about the reasons for smoking and drinking, most local Roma reply that these habits increase their enjoyment of life. Living as they do in an unpleasant environment and being exposed to constant shortages, strife, and hardship, alcohol and tobacco are seen as necessary antidotes to the poison of daily life.

Sex plays a similar role. As in the surrounding society, the expression of sexuality is regulated more carefully than the indulgence in alcohol and tobacco, and we find the same definitions of dangerous and prohibited sexual practices. Incest, relations between adults and children, sexual violence, bestiality, adultery, prostitution, and homosexuality are all considered aberrations that local Roma condemn. In practice, though, deviation from some of these norms may not be met by anything more disapproving than raised eyebrows and backroom gossip. Mention has already been made of the nonchalant attitude to unions between first cousins—a widespread habit that is clearly in violation of the local definition of the incest taboo. And there are other illustrations of illicit forms of sexuality that seem to surface from time to time without causing much indignation. Two of the men belonging to the "creek people" are known to have been engaged in lengthy liaisons with a number of their underage daughters. Another member of this group is said to indulge in bestiality. I received a detailed account of an encounter, witnessed by several neighbours, during which this man allegedly had sex with a bitch outside his hut, and due to the swelling of his penis, he became stuck to the dog. His neighbours apparently had to help out by dousing him with cold water—to the amusement of bystanders. Another member of the "creek people," a woman in her early 40s, is believed to prostitute herself—with the knowledge and cooperation of her husband.

There are well-documented examples of other kinds of sexual deviance that can be verified more easily. Homosexuality is a case in point. Although it is derided as an abnormality, those who practise it are accepted without any undue intereference in their lives. The settlement has two openly gay men and three openly lesbian women, with a sprinkling of others who present themselves as bisexuals. One of the gay men is a slightly deranged adolescent who puts on discarded high-heeled women's shoes and acts as a transvestite—to everybody's amusement. The lesbian trio includes a young cohabiting couple, and a single woman in her early 40s who lives with an adolescent girl believed to be more than a room-mate. The middle-aged woman blames her homosexuality on prisons where she spent more than 15 years of her life. Highly unusual for an older woman, she never wears skirts or dresses and plays guitar in public, an activity and an instrument normally reserved for men.

One type of deviant behaviour that clearly occurs in the settlement but is difficult to verify and quantify is sexual assault. Although rapes and attempted rapes undoubtedly do take place, local residents tend to be skeptical about the background of some accusations. This is especially so when the alleged victim belongs to a group of "loose girls" who walk around in provocatively short skirts and seek out the company of aggressive boys and men of ill repute. Since most of the reported assaults take place at dances and parties—often in neighbouring settlements—after the victim becomes inebriated, many people dismiss such attacks as fabrications intended to mask unwanted pregnancies. There is some justification for the skepticism, as confirmed by cases where the alleged rapist surfaced later to claim paternity of an illegitimate child and to marry his victim. I became privy to one such case after witnessing a public scene during which the mother of a 15-year-old girl screamed at the top of her lungs that her daughter had been raped by a much older man. The girl stood by, and her ripped blouse and soiled mini-skirt were pointed out as prime evidence of the alleged assault. Yet most of the bystanders laughed and dismissed the accusation as a settling of scores between two hostile families. The mother was believed to have roughened up her daughter herself in order to make the story more believable. This opinion was shared by the police who refused to press charges after interviewing both parties. A little later, rumours began to circulate about an affair between the "victim" and her much older—and married—"attacker," which predated the alleged assault. The conclusion took place roughly a year later when the wife and five children of the "attacker" moved out, and their place was taken by the adolescent "victim."

Sexual relations between adolescent girls and married adult men provide an illustration of overtly sanctioned conduct that is practised, accepted, and at times even encouraged. Typically, such an affair begins as a short-lived infatuation between a girl just embarking on sexual experimentation and an older man who, on account of his looks, wealth, or social status enjoys the position of a dominant, or "alpha," male. Such a relationship may last only a few weeks—though long enough to result in an unwanted pregnancy—or it may go on for months and even longer. In rare cases, such as the one described above, the young lover may eventually replace the alpha male's wife and legitimize her new position with offspring. When the boyfriend is seen as a really good "catch"—especially if he belongs to the local elite of big money-lenders—such a resolution may be actively encouraged by the girl's parents. Under more conventional circumstances, an unwanted pregnancy is masked by the girl's marriage to a younger suitor who may or may not be aware of his first child's real paternity.

The girl-man liaisons found in Svinia are a manifestation of the early onset of sexual activity among local adolescents. Unable to pursue other pastimes, such as organized sports, academic studies, drama, or simply what we call "hobbies," the settlement's teenagers develop an early interest in sexuality and the whole gamut of behaviours associated with it. Some of it may be channelled into emotionally satisfying relationships, but there is also a great deal of fascination with unsavoury sexual practices and imagery. How deeply this has penetrated the youth subculture can be surmised from the fact that when adolescents are asked to recite riddles, rhymes, or ditties that they share with their contemporaries, one finds a surprising number of compositions revolving around incestuous sex, menstrual discharges, and sexual encounters between humans and animals. Two of these contemporary "poems," translated from their original version in mixed Romani and Slovak, exemplify this genre:

> *Abaro* [fellow, man], *abaro*, the whore [*kurva*] is going for a walk; she has big tits, [and] she bleeds from her pussy [*piča*];

hand me a [feminine] napkin—I won't give you one, because I
am afraid of your vagina [*pišot*].

We are a big family; father is a deviant, sister is a whore, her
big brother is a drug addict; her little brother is stuffing drugs
into her; mother is in church—devouring cocks [*kokoty*].

Turning to examples of medical pathology, the very demographic
distribution of local Roma, discussed earlier, is indicative of a population
that succumbs to death at an early age. The outstanding cause of early
death is a wide assortment of diseases that seem to strike the Roma more
often and with graver consequences than their ethnic Slovak neighbours.
Thanks to a thorough survey conducted among 352 children as part of the
Svinia Project in the fall of 2001, we can draw some reliable conclusions
about the health situation of children between infancy and adolescence.
The picture that emerges from this study is one of a sickly population in
need of an unusually high degree of medical attention. Only one third
of local children had never been hospitalized, and only a small minority,
roughly ten per cent, had not required the services of a physician for an
acute or chronic ailment. The most common reasons for seeking medical
assistance are, in descending order, respiratory ailments (such as bronchitis
and pneumonia), acute diarrhea, fevers, hepatitis, and ear infections.
Among chronic disorders, most serious cases include grave vision problems
(17 children), heart disease (9 children), epilepsy (7 children), hearing
problems (7 children), and hernia (7 children). It should be emphasized
that these findings are based on evidence obtained from parents and are,
therefore, likely to be subject to a degree of under-reporting.

In addition to this assortment of physical ailments, several children also
suffer from severe mental retardation. At least six exhibit extreme forms of
mental and physical debility that seriously impede their ability to move and
to interact with their environment. Three of these are confined to special
institutions. Five further children have less serious neurological disorders
that interfere with their speech and comprehension but not with their motor
development. This milder form of retardation can be encountered among
at least five adults as well. They are all defined as mentally slow by their
community, and three of them are deaf and mute on top of that.

Mentally and physically retarded children are generally cared for rather
well. Their parents try to adhere to routines prescribed by medical specialists,

including check-ups and appointments with physiotherapists. For people without automobiles, this is not an easy task as it requires periodic trips on crowded buses that are not equipped for the transportation of people with disabilities. Special dietary and pharmacological regimens impose further hardships. Yet most people are unwilling to confine children with special needs to institutions—an option that is free of charge and readily available. The reluctance to part with seriously impaired children is in most instances undoubtedly due to parental love, which doesn't discriminate against sickly offspring. But in a minority of cases, financial considerations play a role as well. The caregivers of physically and mentally impaired children are entitled to a special monthly pension on top of the regular child bonus, and in some families it is this reward that motivates the retention of seriously handicapped children or attempts at having them returned from institutions where they were placed at birth. In one such instance I was privy to the deliberations of a middle-aged couple who were about to demand the return of their ten-year-old daughter from an institution for severely impaired children. Although the couple lived with five dependent children in a small room leased from one of the apartment-dwellers, they seriously considered adding their handicapped daughter who required specialized care—including intravenous feeding—which by far exceeded the possibilities offered by their living arrangements.

Cases such as this strengthen the conviction of many ethnic Slovaks that Roma abuse the generous provisions of the national health and welfare system. A belief that circulates in the ranks of health-care workers who have direct contact with Roma holds that pregnant women pay up to 500 crowns to sufferers of infectious diseases such as hepatitis or tuberculosis for the "privilege" of inhaling their breath in the hope of giving birth to a handicapped child! Such extreme beliefs are undoubtedly far-fetched and hardly reflective of the situation as it prevails in most Romani communities. But, as with many caricatures, even this stereotype holds a kernel of truth. This we encounter in the encouragement of sexual unions involving seriously retarded individuals in the expectation that their offspring would also be retarded and thus "earn" an appropriate pension. I witnessed one such case in Svinia. It involved an 18-year old severely retarded woman who lived in the household of her aunt. This arrangement alone made a not insignificant contribution to the aunt's income. She decided, however, that even greater benefits could be had from children born to her ward, and to this end she requested the cooperation of a young male relative who subsequently impregnated the niece without any intentions of striking up a durable relationship. The child that followed became a ward of the aunt—with all the expected financial benefits.

Instances where mental disability is not only exploited, in the form of legitimate pensions, but deliberately perpetuated in as unabashed a manner as in this case are undoubtedly rare. Far more numerous are cases of benign tolerance where parents do nothing to prevent the reproduction of children who are defined as mentally retarded by the surrounding community, rather than by some abstract measurement wielded by the majority society. The settlement has several young women who fall into this category and who are more likely than others to become pregnant without the likelihood of this leading to a durable union with a man. Although the parents of these women are aware of ways to minimize unwanted pregnancies—such as by implanting an intra-uterine device—they profess a complete lack of interest in such a course of action. A variety of factors, ranging from indifference to the expectation of financial benefits, is behind this reluctance.

It goes without saying that the disastrous physical and social infrastructure of the settlement plays a very significant role in the range, frequency, and intensity of the local disease pattern. Drafty, cold, and crowded quarters, drinking water of questionable quality, exceedingly poor hygiene, inadequate knowledge of physiological processes, and the absence of any first-aid facilities in the settlement are all factors that have an obviously adverse effect on the health of local residents. Anybody with an even cursory exposure to this community cannot but feel deep sympathy for the plight of the mothers of sick children who spend long hours waiting for a bus to take them to the pediatric clinic in a neighbouring village, where they must await their turn among dozens of other patients, and then return to another bus stop for the trip back to Svinia—and all this while carrying a crying baby and clutching the hand of another sick toddler or two. Having chauffeured many families on their search for medical assistance—be it a clinic, a pharmacy, or the hospital in Prešov—I am painfully aware of the challenges rural Roma face in their interaction with the medical establishment and of the many obstacles erected by the majority society. Bus drivers who refuse to stop for a group of sick children, inflexible bus schedules, rude nurses and physicians, and hostile strangers all make a difficult situation even worse. But the situation becomes disastrous because external impediments are compounded by internal causes of ill health, which can be traced to voluntary lifestyle choices. Everybody will be struck, for example, by the skimpiness of the attire of children playing outdoors in sub-zero temperatures. Untied sneakers, often with partly detached soles, no socks, light pants full of holes and torn shirts are as uniformly worn during the hot summer season as during the very cold winter. Hats and gloves are a rare sight—not on account of some kind of financial barrier, but because Roma sporting such *gadje* inventions become an object of ridicule. The same explanation, incidentally, clarifies why not a single resident wears glasses. This is not due to exceptionally good eyesight, but rather because of cultural norms that dismiss eyeglasses as unbecoming. The two children whose parents dared to violate this taboo have had their glasses smashed to pieces by their comrades.

Internal factors are primarily responsible for a wide range of accidents that afflict local Roma. Children are particularly vulnerable, because their parents lack the energy or will required to supervise them adequately in the chaotic environment of the settlement. I recall an exceptionally ugly accident involving a boy of two whose entire leg and groin were so badly burnt in an accident that the skin was peeling off in long strips. We drove him to the children's hospital in Prešov, where he underwent a difficult skin-grafting operation that left him alive but seriously disfigured. A day later I was asked to help out with another young boy who had almost lost his middle finger during a fight between his mother and a hostile man. The finger, partly severed by a hatchet wielded by the attacker, had been wrapped up with dirty rags soaked with blood. This boy, too, required emergency surgery. Dog bites, burns resulting from scalding water or woodstoves, and cuts self-inflicted by children playing with knives are all relatively minor, but frequent, injuries.

While some of the many calamities are attributable to the unusual risks that arise in large families confined to inadequate quarters, some of the worst cases of parental neglect can be found in small households headed by young couples or single mothers whose daily routines consist of little else than sleeping, smoking, and watching television while the children are under the care of a sister or mother. These women and men carry to an extreme a trait that is firmly embedded in the settlement subculture: indifference. Indifference seems to appear at puberty when lively, playful, and alert children turn into reticent, dour, and at times passive teenagers. This change in attitude—more pronounced in girls than boys—is strikingly noticeable when adolescents begin to respond to questions with a shrug, a listless facial expression, and the telltale rhetorical question "Do I care?" While most individuals outgrow this premature stage at which disengagement is considered a sign of free will and independence, almost every adult seems to retain the capacity to respond to certain situations in this "idiom of indifference." It is usually encountered when people are reminded of problems that they'd rather forget. So, for example, a young mother having a smoke and watching a soap opera on television employs this idiom to shrug off any responsibility for her son who is playing outside with a sharp knife. A 15-year-old girl, asked about her plans after leaving school may reply in the same vein. More tragically, after becoming pregnant, she will likely resort to the same formula of indifference when told that her smoking and drinking might have disastrous consequences for her offspring.

One of the greater shocks experienced during my first extended stay in Svinia occurred one day when I ran into the settlement to raise alarm about a brush fire that was burning out of control on a hillside above the village, and one of the senior "creek people" shrugged his shoulders, muttered "do I care?," and walked off to attend to some more important business. Showing indifference provides an acceptable way of avoiding responsibility—especially when the problem extends beyond one's immediate family. Instead of giving a hand where it is needed, the disengaged individual pretends not to see a problem or simply walks away from it. But what is acceptable in the settlement becomes less acceptable in the village and beyond. The failure of the "gypsies" to come out and help their neighbours put out a fire reinforces the local stereotype of Roma as lazy parasites with no sense of social responsibility.

If indifference constitutes one extreme of the local pattern of culture, fear occupies the other. Fear is expressed for a wide variety of reasons. A traditional source derives from supernatural dangers associated with the spirit of a deceased person known as *mulo*. Because it is believed that *mulo* may haunt the living, the clothing, personal effects, and often even the furniture of a deceased person are destroyed in an effort to reduce the range of hiding places for the *mulo*. A related phenomenon is encountered in beliefs surrounding the *striga*, which is a witch-like female held responsible for certain misfortunes, including specific ailments. A third traditional source of supernatural danger is known as *pokeriben*, or unclean force, which is reminiscent of the evil eye. Unlike the *mulo* complex, which coexists quite effortlessly with the local brand of Roman Catholicism, *pokeriben* is seen as a pagan belief to which devout Christians shouldn't subscribe—but never-theless do. It appears that some people place a comb or scissors underneath their pillow in order to ward off the unclean force during the unguarded period of sleep. But a more widespread defence against the evil eye is *jagalo pani*: a charm that requires the removal of nine glowing red coals from the stove, their immersion in water, and subsequently the drinking of some of the water and the sprinkling of its remainder around the room. The same precautions are employed widely in the early stage of an illness.

A more profane source of fear stems from the widespread tendency to exaggerate the harmful consequences of slightly extraordinary natural phenomena, such as a heavy snowfall or an unusual constellation of stars. Just how much significance is attached to these things became apparent during my first winter in Svinia, in February 1999. Eastern Slovakia was then in the grip of exceptionally low temperatures accompanied by heavy snowfalls. One morning, after the snow cover had reached about one me-tre, several Romani children appeared at our house and begged me to come to the settlement immediately. On the way there they explained that people were in a state of panic on account of the snow that kept falling, which they feared would eventually bury them alive. Given the poor state of their housing, this was not an unreasonable fear, for it had happened before that the flimsy roofs on the huts had collapsed under the weight of wet snow. But once we reached the settlement, I learned that the real cause of the alarm had nothing to do with collapsing roofs. A multitude of people kept running between the huts and the well, carrying buckets, pots, and jars filled with water. They explained that if the snow kept falling much longer, they would be unable to replenish their supply of water, facing a certain death. My assurances that they had access to plenty of water in the mounds of snow everywhere made little impression. Every household maintained a generous supply of water until the snowfall subsided.

These and similar episodes alerted me to the extraordinary significance local Roma attach to slightly uncommon events. Only two weeks after the snowfall drama, some people became alarmed again by a bright star that seemed to appear one night out of nowhere. For sure this signified that the end of the world was imminent! That expectation solidified as television stations began to show footage of the conflict in Kosovo, triggering fears of fighter planes appearing in the sky above Svinia and dropping bombs on the settlement.

Music, Dogs, and Celebrations

Unlike most Slovak rural communities where full-time employment and the care of gardens, livestock, and the family home keep villagers busy, the settlement presents a picture of idleness. Sure enough, the residents must collect firewood, cook, do the laundry, and look after the basic needs of small children. But because of the absence of regular paid work, gardens, livestock, and substantial homes, as well as the casual manner in which many people attend to the inevitable daily chores, there is considerably more leisure time than what is the norm in the Slovak countryside. While their white neighbours rush to catch the early-morning bus to Prešov, the settlement remains sound asleep. Parents wake up when their children go to school around eight o'clock, but many are too drowsy to prepare a breakfast or send along a snack. Most children arrive in school hungry, and they remain so until their return.

The community begins to function around nine. As people wake up, they turn on television, brew a cup of strong coffee, light a cigarette, and slowly embark on their morning chores. Men generally depart for the nearby forest where they gather firewood, while women, accompanied by young children, go shopping. The first meal of the day is often consumed in front of a store, and it is rarely more elaborate than a roll of white bread and a fruit yogurt scooped out with fingers. A cooked lunch is usually served after the return of the older children from school. Many adults like to sleep afterwards while their children, not burdened by homework or excessive domestic responsibilities, venture outdoors to play with friends. The games they engage in don't differ markedly from those of their white counterparts except that the groups they play in are usually larger. Toddlers push each other in strollers, chase after a ball, or throw rocks into the muddy creek. Older boys construct slings or small bows and arrows with which they try to shoot down birds, or they play a popular game that resembles squash and is played with home-made wooden paddles. Girls are fond of hopscotch, hide-and-seek, and similar universal games. If the weather is bad, children retreat home where they watch television or sleep.

Adults spend most of their free time visiting relatives, where they smoke, drink strong coffee, play cards, and exchange local news. Television is an extremely popular source of entertainment, and a television set is found in all but the poorest households. As mentioned, satellite dishes have become widespread in recent years, and this facilitates the reception of a multitude of channels in several languages. While most of the daily fare is scanned without much engagement, two types of programs enjoy widespread popularity. Spanish and Italian soap operas, dubbed in Slovak, are watched almost universally by adults and children alike. Latino productions appeal more than domestic ones because of their exaggerated drama and the exotic beauty of the actors and actresses. Some characters become so popular that adolescent girls compose songs about them, and their names may be used as nicknames for local people. The second type of program watched widely, particularly by men, is erotic films.

The only pastime that overshadows television as a medium of universal enjoyment is the performance of music. Music is everywhere: it is broadcast from cassette and, increasingly, CD players placed in open windows and turned up to the highest volume. Beamed into the "village square" between the apartment buildings, the music inspires toddlers and pre-adolescents to gyrate and swing in time with the tune. And it is performed live by impromptu bands and young and old soloists. Wherever and however music is performed, it touches and moves people. They sing, clap, dance, and laugh. More than anything else, music offers relief from worries and conflicts, and it connects individuals who normally stand apart. Together with kinship and the Romani language, music is a most powerful bonding agent of local solidarity.

Music as it is understood locally consists of songs that are usually, though not always, performed with instrumental accompaniment. With a few minor exceptions, all songs are sung in Romani, and they belong to one of three distinct genres. The first category is known collectively as "old songs" (*phurikane gil'a*), and it is subdivided into "slow songs" (*halgató*) or "sad songs" (*čorikane gil'a*) and "dance songs" (*czardasʐa*). The "slow songs" are for the most part laments that bemoan the loss of a loved one, the hunger of a child born into poverty, or the oppression of Roma by the majority society. These traditional tunes, nowadays very much in decline, are rarely accompanied by musical instruments (see Belišová 2002). Old-fashioned "dance songs" or *csardasʐa*, on the other hand, are fast tunes that are supposed to make people come alive and be merry, and they are always underscored with instruments. Although they continue to be performed much more often than the laments, young people prefer to dance to the modern tunes of what may broadly be called "contemporary Gypsy pop." Like the genuine folk songs in the first category of *phurikane gil'a*, contemporary pop also represents music composed and performed in a restricted territory, that of eastern Slovak Romani communities, where it is spread and modified by performers from individual settlements. But unlike its predecessor, "Gypsy pop" relies heavily on western disco tunes and its instruments. Electric guitars, synthesizers, drums, and amplifiers are its necessary accompaniment. Finally, the third, and in many ways most interesting, music style combines elements of both. As yet without an agreed-upon name, this genre comprises contemporary compositions that preserve the lament-like tradition of the *halgató* but combine it with contemporary themes and musical accompaniment. Anybody—women, men, and adolescents—can compose a song in this style, and the themes are accordingly diverse, ranging from the celebration of a soap-opera hero all the way to commentaries on Slovak politics. Truthful, however, to its kinship with the *halgató* style, much of this genre preserves the traditional preoccupation with lamentable motifs. Natural calamities, poverty, oppression, premature death, and, increasingly, drug abuse are the topics most often reflected in these contemporary laments.[6] Like the *halgató* compositions after which they are modelled, these modern renditions spread quickly beyond the community in which they originated. So it happens that songs composed in Svinia can be heard in neighbouring settlements, Prešov, and beyond. As they diffuse throughout the eastern Slovak "culture area," they undergo small and large modifications in accordance with the preferences of local performers and the social conditions prevalent in their communities.

While everybody in Svinia loves music, subtle demarcations influence its production. Early on, children learn to internalize the gender-specific division of labour that holds that vocal music is a predominantly female prerogative, while instrumental music is almost exclusively reserved for men. Girls, encouraged to sing not only at home but also in public, burst into spontaneous song whenever they hear a catchy tune. It isn't unusual to see groups of girls walk home from school and belt out some popular song—to the consternation of white passersby. I shall never forget the sunny morning when our whole family awoke to the Romani rendition of Céline Dion's *Titanic* theme song, performed beautifully by a group of girls whom my wife had befriended and who became frequent visitors in our home. It happened to be Easter Saturday, and the Roman Catholic priest stopped on his way to church and admonished the girls not to sing on a day when Christ's crucifixion was being commemorated.

While girls' craving for musical expression is channelled into singing, boys are encouraged to master an instrument. But instrumental music is a less egalitarian activity than singing, because it presupposes not only talent but also instruments that can be expensive to purchase and repair. This is especially the case with the modern electronic equipment required by "Gypsy pop," which remains outside the range of all but the wealthiest young men. Several older men are well known for their mastery of traditional instruments—such as the violin, accordion, clarinet, and guitar—but only a few play regularly nowadays because of limited access to their instrument of choice. Particularly instructive, and sad, is the plight of the undoubtedly most gifted local musician: Janko, a man in his late 30s whose speech impediment is compensated for by an extraordinary musical talent. Unable to express himself properly in words, this man plays the guitar with exceptional virtuosity. Without any formal training, let alone the ability to read notes, this self-taught master can pick up any tune and render it flawlessly in a wide range of styles. Alas, this virtuoso doesn't possess a guitar, because every time he gets one, it ends up in a pawn shop in order to nurture his indulgence in Toluen and vodka. There are several more good guitar players, including the lesbian woman mentioned earlier, but none compares with Janko, who, sadly, spends most of his time stretched out in a drunken stupor on a soiled bed in his dingy apartment.

The number of men well versed in the use of traditional instruments is declining. One older man plays the accordion very well, but he cannot afford to buy his own instrument, and so he performs only sporadically on one that belongs to the inventory of white Svinia's "house of culture." Several men in their 40s and 50s are good violin players, but their instruments have been either destroyed or lost, and they show no interest in getting new ones. I think that they have come to the conclusion that the days of traditional music, as they define it, are numbered. This decline can be illustrated with an interesting example. It was only in the spring of 2001, exactly eight years after my first contact with the people of Svinia, that I realized to my great astonishment that one of the settlement's oldest and most colourful men is a remarkably skilled violin maker. Although I had talked to this man many times before, it was only after I had noticed three hand-made violins hanging on the wall of his barren kitchen that he volunteered some insight into this unusual "pastime." Few people know about this man's talents, and those who do find it of little interest. This indifference seems to have rubbed off on the craftsman himself, who sees his activity as the futile pursuit of a dying skill.

This view is certainly shared by most young men, whose taste inclines towards Gypsy pop and its electronic apparatus. Since the purchase of appropriate instruments and the assorted gadgetry is beyond the means of most, the performance of this popular type of music has become the prerogative of a small circle of affluent individuals. At its core is a well-equipped band that consists of young men affiliated with the Velryba group of money-lenders. The band plays an essential role in the economic transactions of this family, for it is the centrepiece of the exploitative dances staged around the monthly "payday." There is considerable interest in extending the band's impact and earning power by organizing large-scale discos that would attract hundreds of visitors from neighbouring settlements. The main stumbling block is the lack of a suitable venue. The only facility large enough for this type of activity is the "house of culture," but the mayor has steadfastly refused to grant permission for such events in the expectation of chaos and mayhem.

The association with music has always raised the status of families and even entire settlements (Lacková 1999), and this certainly holds for Svinia's upwardly mobile loan sharks. Controlling the settlement's only organized band of semi-professional musicians helps maintain the boundary against the fallen and de-skilled *cigáni*. But in spite of the economic and social capital entangled in the performance of music, there remains an underlying agreement that music cannot be reduced to a tool for personal enrichment, or, to use the language of capitalism, "commercialized." Like the sun, air, or water, music is considered essential for human well-being, and as such it cannot be privatized. The numerous songs composed by local musicians are immediately released into the public domain, copied and modified, and sooner or later their composer is forgotten. And the members of Svinia's band, so commercially minded during their paid performances, never fail to show up at funerals where they lead the procession, playing the favourite tunes of the deceased, without the slightest expectation of remuneration. It is through music that the soul of the dead is placated and laid to rest, and the provision of such an essential service is considered an act of basic human decency that transcends economic motives.

The description of hobbies and pastimes would be incomplete without mentioning the local affection for dogs. It was only in the aftermath of the great flood of July 1998 that I began to appreciate the depth of this sentiment. As I surveyed the half-destroyed settlement and visited dozens of residents confined to temporary shelters, I kept hearing laments over the fate of the dogs. In a probably overzealous measure taken ostensibly to avert the threat of rabies, public health authorities had rounded up all dogs kept in the settlement and had them destroyed. For a surprising number of Roma, this was the greatest loss attributed to the flood. They kept reminiscing about the special qualities of their favourite pets, including the contribution made by some to the rescue of drowning children. The teary eyes and tenderness with which these accounts were told underlined the widely felt sense of loss. Asked to explain the special status of their canine friends, a local dog-lover had this to say:

> It is as if you raised a child. For example, you have a puppy, you take interest in it, you feed it, and it grows, and you feed it still, and it comes everywhere with you like a child, like a child. And someone else comes along and kills it. What are you going to do?... A dog is not a child. But it is love. Everyone should keep something.... We had in one year, we counted 98 dogs in one year. We in our family.... You wouldn't believe the dogs we had. [One] was so intelligent that it made you weep. I used to talk to her as if she were human. She would come to me and play, bite me gently, and so on.... My best dog [ever] was a hunting dog given to us by a *gadjo* woman.... Her name was Tina. She was so understanding that it made me weep.... Hunters lured her away. I saw it with my own eyes how they stole the dog.... Hunters. And my brother, how old he is, and he wept for her. They took her, and even the dog cried and squealed. And I went to tell the mayor, and the mayor chased me away with police....

The dogs that inhabit the settlement come from a variety of sources. Some are purchased cheaply from an animal shelter in Prešov. Some are bought from ethnic Slovaks in Svinia and neighbouring villages. Some are traded with other Roma in the settlement. And some are stolen. Whatever their origin, most dogs are put through basic training that in large measure determines the dog's destiny. Animals that respond well and possess certain desirable traits, such as obedience, alertness, and a measure of aggressiveness, are kept as guard dogs or simply companions. Occasionally, a particularly well-trained dog may even be bought by a white client. On the other hand, animals that turn out to be disobedient, excessively

Figure 2.14. Young dog lovers in Chminianské Jakubovany

aggressive, or otherwise displeasing are sold to the nearby community of Chminianské Jakubovany. This is the only settlement far and wide where dogs are routinely and openly eaten.

Driven by curiosity, I visited Chminianské Jakubovany on several occasions between 1999 and 2001 in search of insights into the local "dog complex." In order to preserve the exploratory flavour of my discoveries, I reproduce them without any modification from the field notes documenting these visits:

> We pulled up at an affluent looking house by the road, inhabited by a friend [of my companions from Svinia]. A fierce looking fellow who lives with his brother and their respective families in a large compound littered with dogs and their remains.... I was shown a metal pot filled with raw dog meat parts, salted and spiked with cloves of garlic, sitting in a shallow creek, cooling and fermenting for a week or so. I noticed that wherever I step, there are remnants of dogs lying around: a severed paw still covered with hide, and a small skull being some of them. Dogs are everywhere, and children showed off several puppies which they are clearly very fond of.... I was

told that all dogs taste the same, and no distinction is made between young, old, male or female. Main consideration is given to size and the amount of fat.... They explained without any hesitation that they do, indeed, eat dogs and prepare dog lard which is eaten on a slice of bread or smeared on the chest as a remedy against pulminary disorders. This lard is called *žiroš* in Romani or *mast'* [salve] in Slovak. They sell it for around 600 crowns per litre. Dog meat is called *rukonalomas.* Children and adults alike described with laughter how excellent dog meat is in gulash or schnitzels. They prefer it to all other kinds of meat. Dogs destined for the pot are usually purchased from other settlements or Whites for relatively modest amounts.... A mid-sized dog supplies enough meat to last for 3–4 days, and 3–4 litres of lard.... Generally speaking, only "bad" dogs are eaten. Good ones (nice-looking and well-behaved) are raised as pets and trained. Some of these cost thousands of crowns and may be sold at a profit though the dog-keeping enterprise is not viewed as a commercial venture. People simply like dogs—just as the Roma in Svinia.... Later pulled up by another man who, together with his wife, claimed to sell lots of lard to outsiders who come and buy the stuff in dozens of litres at once. This group includes a professor from Prague. The woman also described the healing properties of *žiroš* which she holds responsible for her excellent health in spite of heavy smoking. Small sickly children are said to be wrapped up in cloth soaked in the stuff for several days in a row. Adults receive it on a sheet of thin paper applied to their chest. The preferred method, though, is eating.

Eventually, I was allowed to witness the slaughter of a dog, which, unlike the mere consumption of dog meat, is accompanied by some precautions on account of its association with cruelty in the eyes of the majority society. I was warned that film- or video-recordings were out of the question. Ordinary photographs were allowed—at 100 crowns per picture and on the condition that they wouldn't be shared with journalists. Here is my sketch of the procedure:

The dog, a mangy German shepherd, was killed with two blows to its head with the dull edge of an axe. Then, while the carcass rested on its side, the throat was slit and the blood let out. One hind paw was severed, a chain wound around the leg bone, and the carcass pulled up and suspended from a beam. Then the rest of the blood was allowed to drain. Dog blood is not used. The butcher sharpened his knife and carefully skinned the carcass before chopping off the head. Cutting open the chest cavity, the innards were allowed to spill out. They are discarded. Incidentally, local dogs eat dog meat, but only if they had been raised on it. Otherwise, they won't touch it. [The butcher] suggested afterwards that we go together, in my car, to visit his suppliers from whom he buys dogs. The usual price is 50–100 crowns for regular, small dogs. More is paid for larger ones. Only adult men are allowed to slay dogs. Women wouldn't even attempt it.

In spite of rumours about the unsavoury dietary practices of the "creek people," a public slaughter such as the one I witnessed in Chminianské Jakubovany would be impossible in Svinia. While some members of the elite claim that dog-eating was widely practised by the *jarkovci* prior to the merger of the two settlements, and that it has been merely driven underground by the civilizing influence of the upper-class, the "creek people" themselves vehemently deny any involvement in a habit that would justify the imposition of the highly derogatory label of *degeše*. But many members of the settlement's under-class have intimate kinship bonds with Chminianské Jakubovany, and it is indisputable that they possess more than a passing familiarity with the canine subculture of their cousins and in-laws.

In addition to the largely unstructured and idiosyncratically observed pastimes and customs described so far, the Roma of Svinia adhere to six more or less obligatory ritual events that originate in the majority society. Three of these—baptism, marriage, and burial—are rites of passage; the remaining three are calendric rites associated with Christmas, Easter, and All Souls.

The three rites of passage are faithfully modelled on customs and rituals observed by ethnic Slovaks. This is hardly surprising given the prominence played in their execution by the Roman Catholic church. The imitative character is the strongest in baptism. Every child born in the settlement is baptized, and this is due not only to the exhortations of the parish priest, but also to the popular fear that the soul of an unbaptized individual cannot find rest after death. The Roma explain that children deprived of the seal of Christendom become "like the Jews" and that in addition to the expected consequences for their spiritual state, they also face increased risks of ill health. All this accounts for the determination—unparalleled in any other domain—with which Romani parents seek to follow this dictate of the majority society.

Unlike ethnic Slovak newborns who are baptized promptly after their appearance, Romani children must wait until there are at least six or more candidates who are then dealt with in a collective ceremony. It is up to the priest to appoint a suitable time, which means that these collective baptisms always take place in an empty church, witnessed solely by the parents and godparents of the children. In a touchingly faithful imitation of their absent patrons, the Romani participants go to great lengths to make the setting as Slovak as possible. Parents and godparents don formal attire borrowed or purchased for this occasion. The children themselves are dressed in a special white baptismal shift blessed by the priest, and the godfather is expected to supply a long, decorated baptismal candle which, together with the shift, becomes an important keepsake of the child. These standardized and surprisingly expensive baptismal paraphernalia are purchased from one of the local stores. The festive meal served afterwards at the parents' home is usually an exceptionally sedate occasion during which guests partake of the Slovak equivalent of cucumber sandwiches and de-alcoholized punch, catered by a local store.

Weddings are also imitations of white practices. In view of the strong local preference for common-law unions, very few cohabiting couples bother to formalize their arrangement, but those who do insist on a formal white gown for the bride and an up-to-date suit for the groom. Because a church wedding requires active participation in the parish, the few couples that seek official confirmation of their status do so in front of the mayor rather than the priest. The ceremony unfolds in a large meeting room of the municipal office, and it is skillfully directed by the mayor and his administrative assistants. It begins with the customary wedding march from *Lohengrin*—beamed from a 1960s record player—and concludes with the exchange of rings and solemn secular blessings. If the mayor feels particularly generous, he may throw in a bottle or two of Slovak champagne, served in tall crystal glasses that add a touch of class to the whole affair. Afterwards, the newlyweds and their guests return to the settlement for a formal banquet consisting of catered canapés and a multi-layered white cake baked by a Slovak specialist.

Unlike baptism and marriage—two rites of passage which display a preoccupation with ethnic Slovak models and a surprising absence of idiosyncratic local elements—funerals are mixed affairs that draw on Slovak as well as Romani traditions. The corpse is washed, dressed formally, and then laid out on a table or a sheet of plywood supported by chairs. The coffin is usually purchased from a white firm and paid for with money that most people keep aside to cover their funeral expenses. The coffin remains uncovered, and it is surrounded by a small crowd of wailing female relatives. Word is sent out to the parish priest and deacon, who then select a site in the cemetery and instruct male relatives of the deceased where to dig a grave. By the time the priest arrives for the burial, the dead person's belongings have all been removed in order to encourage the soul to leave its former abode. This may involve at times even the removal of the roof. The priest recites the customary prayers over the open coffin, which is then closed and carried outside. By now, the vicinity of the home teems with dozens or even hundreds of people assembled for the procession to the cemetery. Every funeral attracts visitors from surrounding settlements and beyond. Adults and children alike arrive by bus or on foot, and many carry plastic wreaths purchased in local stores. Close relatives all wear special black shirts customary at Slovak funerals. The procession is led by an altar boy carrying a cross, followed by musicians who play the favourite tunes of the deceased. After reaching the cemetery, the priest says more prayers, the coffin is lowered into the grave, and the band continues to play while friends and relatives throw earth onto the coffin. A wooden cross is erected at the gravesite, and the plastic wreaths brought along are placed at its foot. Then the crowd disperses, and the funeral is over.

Similar to the described rites of passage, the three calendric holidays that are observed in Svinia represent scaled-down versions of customs developed by the majority society. All Saints' Day, followed by All Souls' Day, is referred to locally by the Slovak term *dušičky*, or "little souls," and it marks the commemoration of dead relatives on the first and second day of November. Throughout Slovakia, people flock to cemeteries to clean the graves of their loved ones and adorn them with wreaths, flowers, and candles. The Roma are no exception, and the way they mark this occasion doesn't deviate from the pattern observed by the majority. The only significant distinction is that Romani graves receive fewer wreaths, flowers, and candles than Slovak ones.

The Christmas season begins with St. Nicholas Day on December 6, which is a thoroughly secular affair celebrated at school with sweets and trinkets distributed during a talent show held separately for Romani and ethnic Slovak children. Soon thereafter, some households set up Christmas trees hauled from the nearby forest. Poor people have small trees adorned rather frugally with a few sweets wrapped up in colourful foil, while rich families display more ostentatious trees covered with commercial Christmas sweets and blinking electric lights. Most children receive some presents—ranging from cheap chocolate bars to expensive electronic toys—depending on their parents' affluence and engagement. Christmas Eve and Christmas Day may be marked by a festive meal consisting of potato salad, pork cutlets, and cake. Although a few devout individuals receive a pastoral visit from the priest, the vast majority pass the season without indulging in any religious activities.

Between Christmas and New Year's Eve, small groups of children visit friendly Slovak households in the village—the priest's, the shopkeepers', the teachers'—in order to wish them a happy New Year. This thoroughly Slovak custom involves the singing of three or four traditional carols in exchange for sweets, fruits, and perhaps a few coins. The same goes on within the settlement, but here it is enacted by adult well-wishers in front of their rich patrons, who reward them with food and cash. The Christmas season ends on New Year's Eve with a large bash that leaves most residents severely hung over on the first day of the new year. Herein too the Romani ways differ little from those of their neighbours.

The third and last calendric festivity observed in the settlement is Easter. My first lesson about its importance was delivered by a young woman who arrived every morning to help out with chores around the house. On Good Friday she came to remind us not to split wood, cut bread or meat, or use any other sharp objects, in commemoration of Christ's suffering on the cross. Receiving our helper's assurance that these strictures were observed throughout the settlement, I rushed there, only to discover the usual deviations from the norm. In fact, there were some devout followers of the ritual prohibition, but there were many more who kept splitting wood and cutting bread without the least attention to these religious taboos.

Easter Saturday and Easter Sunday pass largely unnoticed except for bunches of pussy willows displayed in some households. Things change, however, on Easter Monday. In all of Slovakia, this day is celebrated with the traditional *poliévačka* or "dousing." This sexist custom pitches men against women in the performance of some pagan ritual with misogynist overtones. Men and boys, equipped with buckets of cold water, lie in wait for a passing girl or woman who is then drenched unless she buys herself free with chocolate eggs or money. The Roma engage in this immensely popular pastime with great relish. But unlike the gender-specific perform- ance practised by the Slovaks, local Roma have constructed a more egalitar- ian imitation that places buckets and pots filled with water in everybody's hands, in the expectation that anybody brave enough to venture outside gets soaked in an orgy of universal dousing.

Relations with the Outside World

Although the settlement constitutes an encapsulated community with its own history and culture, it is connected through multiple links to the outside world. Television, radio, shopping trips to Prešov, contact with relatives, prison terms, and conversations with white neighbours and officials all contribute to a certain degree of knowledge about the world beyond Svinia. But this knowledge is haphazard and distorted. Since nobody in the settlement reads newspapers and only a few watch television newscasts, local notions of current affairs and world events, but also regional and national history, geography, and politics are sketchy. I gained early appreciation of my informants' cognitive isolation when I attempted to explain the location of Canada. My pocket atlas of the world proved of little assistance, since map-reading skills are entirely absent. The news that Canada and Slovakia are separated by thousands of kilometres didn't help much either in a setting where distances are conveyed in the amount of time necessary to bridge them either on foot or on the bus. My assertion that a flight from Prague to Toronto lasts about ten hours led to some confusion, because this equalled the much shorter train ride from Prešov to Prague. Canada, on account of its great distance from Slovakia, was expected to be days and weeks away. On the other hand, during a hike to a nearby castle ruin, a teenaged boy questioned me sincerely whether Canada would be visible from the top of the hill.

Figure 2.15. Romani communities in the vicinity of Svinia

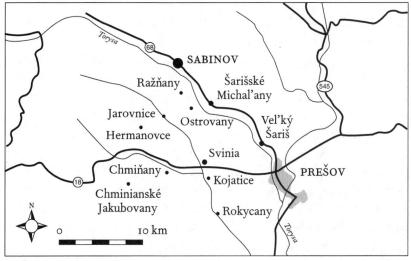

Ross Nelson & Alexander Mušinka

The compass used in Svinia for the exploration of the universe is calibrated in accordance with local needs, and the map drawn up with its help bears little resemblance to the map used by the *gadji*. For example, the Czech Republic is better known than Slovakia, because it absorbed thousands of Roma from the east during the socialist era. So it happens that major Czech towns and cities are more likely to be recognized and correctly classified than their Slovak equivalents. This means that while no local resident has ever visited the Slovak capital Bratislava, quite a few have been to Prague and possess a reasonable impression of its major landmarks. Some older men who used to work on Czech construction sites even speak passable Czech. The Czech connection endures through sporadic contact with relatives in several Czech and Moravian towns. Their (at times undoubtedly idealized) experiences, personal memories of the Czechoslovak era, and snippets of information indicating that post-communist relations with the Roma are better in the Czech Republic than in Slovakia have coalesced into widespread Czechophilism.

Within Slovakia, a reasonable grasp of the size and locations of towns and villages is confined to personally familiar communities within the Prešov region. Košice, the country's second largest city situated some 50 kilometres south-east of Svinia, remains widely unknown. Even within the relatively small Prešov region, most people are acquainted with only a handful of towns and villages that stand out for some personal reasons. Of the roughly 250 Romani settlements located in this territory, regular contact is maintained with perhaps a dozen belonging to Svinia's kinship universe. Within this pool, five communities stand out: Prešov, Jarovnice, Chminianské Jakubovany, Hermanovce, and Kojatice. None of these locations is farther than ten kilometres from Svinia, they can all be relatively easily reached by bus (an important factor in a setting where automobiles are owned by only three or four families), and they are linked to Svinia through a dense web of kinship. The high frequency of contact between these communities has resulted in various types of informal partnerships. For example, a dog owner in Svinia looking for a buyer of his pet knows whom to approach in Chminianské Jakubovany. A needy resident of Kojatice knows how to find a loan-shark in Svinia. The loan-shark, in turn, buys bootleg liquor from a partner in Jarovnice. And Svinia's lone violin maker ventures to Hermanovce in search of horse hair needed for the bows.

The contacts that prevail between Svinia and these five communities are in stark contrast to the almost complete absence of social intercourse with other, equally near and accessible settlements. Vel'ký Šariš, Ostrovany, Ražňany, Šarišské Michal'any, Chmiňany, and Rokycany are all sizeable villages with a substantial Romani presence and located within the same ten-kilometre radius, yet for the people of Svinia they constitute a foreign zone that is rarely visited. But even the "near abroad" of the five kindred communities is conceptualized as an alien territory inhabited by people that cannot be fully trusted. Jarovnice, with some 3,000 Roma the country's largest settlement, is considered a dangerous place to which few visitors go without the protection of a local relative. This rural metropolis is infamous for its dances that attract young Roma from far and wide. Several adolescent girls from Svinia who claim to have been raped suffered this misfortune while attending these night-long events. Similarly, Chminianské Jakubovany is regarded as a threatening community on account of the *degeše* status of its inhabitants. The local dog-eaters have a reputation for wild and unpredictable behaviour—some of my informants even maintained that they kill children born with hare-lip—and people from Svinia who come for a visit do so with apprehension. The social distance between the two settlements can be seen even among the closely related garbage pickers who camp on the edge of the Prešov garbage dump. The Svinia cluster pitches its primitive shelters a few dozen metres away from their *degeše* colleagues, and visitors are warned not to socialize with them.

The boundaries erected between Svinia and neighbouring settlements are maintained at both ends. While the locals badmouth the women of Jarovnice for drinking too much and for cooking *haluški* that are too big, they themselves are typecast as country bumpkins ignorant of what goes on beyond their mud huts. A less benign view of Svinia is held by the Roma of Kojatice. With barely 100 residents, this settlement is the smallest and least modernized community in the vicinity, untouched by any outside intervention. Although their needs are no less acute, local Roma live in the shadow of their more numerous and vocal neighbours. For some families that shadow is very dark and oppressive. Lacking a money-lender in their midst, they have become dependent on the services of one of Svinia's. This relationship is claimed to have led to assaults and raids carried out by the loan shark and his helpers. Yet in spite of the ensuing tension between the two settlements, all of Svinia congregates to pay last respects to Kojatice's dead, and Svinia's musicians volunteer to lead the funeral procession.

The patchwork of xenophobia, prejudice, stereotypes, and fears upholding the boundaries between neighbouring settlements rests on a bedrock of genuine idiosyncrasies that lend each community its individual flavour and identity. Remarkable as it may seem given the proximity between Svinia and the surrounding settlements, local people swear that these peculiarities extend all the way to language and physiognomy. For example, the Roma of Rokycany—separated from Svinia by perhaps five kilometres or so—are said to be recognizable by a distinctive pronunciation of certain words. The residents of Chminianské Jakubovany, on the other hand, are claimed to resemble the dogs they eat in the prominence of their incisors. While some parts of the local folk classification may be far-fetched, there *are* many observable differences. Some, such as the unique physiognomy of the people of Chminianské Jakubovany—which I myself came to recognize after a while—are clearly a vestige of endogamic tendencies perpetuated over several generations. Others are the result of a remarkable degree of cultural isolation. An interesting illustration of the latter came to my attention when an outside agency experimented with the production of handicrafts in Svinia and Hermanovce. The Czech instructor taught a number of women from the two settlements how to knit woollen hats that were then supposed to be marketed. Surprisingly, although all the students were novices exposed to the same techniques, material, and teacher, the

Table 2.1. Demographic variation between neighbouring Romani settlements

Community	Population of Roma	0–20 yrs. (in %)	above 50 yrs. (in %)
Svinia	619	69	2
Chmin. Jakubovany	869	66	2
Ostrovany	835	57	4
Vel'ký Šariš	361	56	9
Šarišské Michal'any	194	51	7

products they manufactured differed markedly from one community to the other. The hats made by the women of Hermanovce were multi-coloured and brilliantly hued, whereas Svinia's knitters adopted subdued colours and uniform patterns. Furthermore, in spite of its smaller size, the Hermanovce settlement was blessed by a higher proportion of people with advanced manual skills than Svinia. In fact, Svinia's best knitters proved to be two sisters born and raised in Hermanovce.

Perhaps the most interesting piece of hard evidence demonstrating the extent of micro-regional variation concerns the demographic composition of neighbouring settlements. Using data collected in May 1999, I compared the population distribution of Roma living in four communities located in close proximity to Svinia. The result, captured in Table 2.1, shows significant differences in the proportion of young and elderly people residing in each settlement.

In spite of the real and imagined uniqueness of each settlement, the Roma who inhabit the cluster of communities familiar to the residents of Svinia are all conceptualized as one people who share a similar language, history, and habits. As such they are set apart from linguistically and culturally more distantly related Roma, such as the formerly itinerant *Olaši* who inhabit several villages situated between Prešov and Košice as well as certain neighbourhoods of Prešov itself. To the best of my knowledge, the people of Svinia have no history of relations with the *Olaši*, and their familiarity with this branch of Roma is very limited. The greatest taxonomic distance, though, is reserved for the whites or, *gadji*. The term *gadjo/gadji* translates roughly as "non-Rom/a," and this linguistic opposition is further cemented by the notion held by some that the behavioural differences separating Roma and *gadji* are rooted in biology. Thus, according to the *vajda*, Romani blood is fiery and explosive whereas *gadje* blood is cool and thin, and this demarcates profound consequences for daily life: "... if I gave a pick to a white [man], he will throw it away. I give it to the Gypsy, and he will vent his passions with it. That's the explosiveness. And the white is more phlegmatic." The contrast may be elaborated *ad absurdum*, such as in this justification for Romani children's nakedness: "You can see some kids naked, because clothes don't agree with him. If he had the shirt on, for example, he would get dizzy in the head and could faint. This way, the breeze bathes his bare body, and that is excellent.... the blood seems to need it, because the blood is hot.... Our blood is hot."

While not everyone will agree with the *vajda*'s biological determinism, there is virtually universal endorsement of the notion that *gadji* constitute a separate category of people with a vastly different set of values, beliefs, and norms. I was reminded of this polarizing tendency every time I approached someone's hut or apartment and heard the exclamations of *gadjo! gadjo!* within and without. Although everybody knew my name, the ethnonymic designation clearly better fulfills the need for a quick and concise orientation about the nature of a visitor.

The opinions one formulates about *gadji* and their characteristics depend to a large extent on one's status. Generally speaking, the older members of the elite families—individuals born in the 1940s and 1950s who grew up during the socialist era—hold up the whites as a reference group whose accomplishments and lifestyle they seek to emulate. They often refer to ethnic Slovak *pánové*—an honorific similar to "masters" or "gentlemen"—with whom they may have crossed paths, and they emphasize their acquaintance with Slovak ways and habits. Some mention with pride an ancestor who looked and behaved so "white" that unwitting *gadji* addressed her with the term *cetka*, "aunt," which is never extended to Roma. Although this all smacks of a local version of "Uncle Tomism," it is important to bear in mind that the manifest admiration of the dominant culture doesn't preclude contempt for and occasional denigration of some of its carriers. I was told that members of the two richest Romani families in Hermanovce—high-status loan sharks who have managed to move up into the Slovak part of the village—routinely cut down their white neighbours by treating them to food served on dishes normally reserved for their dogs. Whether this really happens or not, the very existence of this belief expresses the ambiguity that seems to mark the relationship between some upwardly mobile Roma and the people they imitate.

Younger Roma, rich and poor alike, tend to be more openly critical of their ethnic Slovak neighbours. Having experienced the segregated schooling of the 1980s and 1990s, and lacking any memory of the integrative employment practices of the socialist era, people who are in their 20s and 30s have had few occasions to experience the Slovak lifestyle and even fewer to form a laudatory image of local villagers. Their stereotype of white society has been shaped by the rising inter-ethnic tensions of the waning socialist era and by the violence and racism of the 1990s. This generation's picture of ethnic Slovaks tends to be a caricature framed by personal or mitigated experiences with police brutality, skinhead violence, and the stinginess and ill will of their neighbours.

In spite of generational differences, young and old Roma alike agree on certain attributes being characteristic of the *gadji* with whom they have had meaningful contact. Foremost among them are haughtiness (a trait universally disliked by local Roma), hostility, aggressiveness mixed with cruelty, stinginess, and shrewdness. On account of these postulated traits, the world beyond the settlement tends to be feared, and forays into it evoke a certain degree of discomfort. Because these sentiments are shared across generational and socio-economic cleavages, they tend to counteract the centrifugal tendencies caused by conflict within the settlement, generating a measure of "ethnic solidarity." The single most conspicuous consequence of this solidarity is the expectation that outside agencies should be notified of local breaches of law and order only in extreme circumstances. The censure of snitching—designated by the Slovak term *bonzáctvo* which is borrowed from the subculture of prisons—prevents a man bitten by a loose dog, a girl raped by her father, or the victim of an assault from seeking the assistance of the police or some other appropriate institution. While such subordination of individual to collective interests may provide a token proof of local autonomy, in the absence of effective internal mechanisms of conflict resolution it tends to marginalize the weak and vulnerable.[7]

Notes

1. According to the 1893 Hungarian census of Roma, the entire Šariš county of eastern Slovakia was inhabited by slightly more than 3,000 Roma. The rural district surrounding Svinia and adjacent villages is shown as the home of 511 Roma (*Ergebnisse* 1895). Even with adjustments for

under-reporting it is clear that none of the communities mentioned here would have been inhabited by more than very small clusters of Roma.

2. The 1924 census was part of Czechoslovakia's—a new country that had been born only six years earlier out of the ashes of World War I—effort at limiting the mobility of Roma and thus curbing their postulated criminal tendencies (Šípek 1990). Based on the premise that enumerated Roma would enjoy legal domicile (*domovské právo*) in the community where they dwelled on the day of the enumeration, the census became an important control mechanism not only for state-level authorities but also for municipalities. Fearful that once local Roma had been registered they would be protected from future eviction by their *de facto* permanent resident status, local officials were not always keen on writing down the names of all Roma who happened to live in their village on the day of the census. So it may have happened that not all of Svinia's Roma managed to get in. But, be that as it may, we can agree with some certainty that the registration of Juraj and Hania's household reflects a willingness on the part of their white neighbours to accept them as a permanent fixture of their community. By 1924, the ancestral pair had become "*our* gypsies" and could as such find its way into local oral history.

3. Marriage and sexual relations between closely related relatives are reported from Slovak (Tokár 2001) and Hungarian (Stewart 1997) *Vlach* Roma communities, but the topic hasn't received adequate attention to allow comparison with the situation in Svinia.

4. Anthropologists have documented a rich body of rules related to the maintenance of purity among European Roma, and some scholars have sought to link them to the preservation of social boundaries between Roma and the majority society (Okely 1983; Stewart 1997). The Roma of Svinia, too, possess a corpus of rules and practices exceeding the handful of examples mentioned here. Like so much else, though, these customs are interpreted and carried on rather pragmatically and opportunistically, and daily life supplies countless instances of infractions against stated "laws" of propriety.

5. In spite of its large number of adolescents, the settlement supplied only one single recruit to the Slovak army between 1993 and 2003. Dozens of young men have been examined and deemed mentally or physically unfit for the compulsory service. In the nearby community of Chminianské Jakubovany, 25 Romani recruits were discharged due to low IQ scores in 1999 alone. However, young men don't relish the prospect of joining the

army, and I witnessed a number of occasions where recruits were being coached by more experienced friends and relatives about how to feign stupidity and infirmity.

6. A music CD that I helped produce through a professional recording studio allowed a group of talented musicians from Svinia to reach an audience far beyond eastern Slovakia. Despite its outstanding quality, the recording didn't strike a chord with North American radio stations on account of the sombre, lament-like character of most compositions. I had experienced a similar reaction from Canadian publishers of children's books asked to consider a wonderful collection of traditional stories assembled by the Romani writer Elena Lacková. The tone of the collection, furnished with haunting illustrations, was considered too sad for the tastes of North American children.

7. Few residents are likely to press charges against other Roma without first trying to compel the culprit into paying some kind of compensation to the victim. This strategy is usually fruitful and satisfies both parties. Because of this convention, police records present a distorted picture of criminal activities within the settlement.

three

ROMANI MARGINALITY IN HISTORICAL PERSPECTIVE

The essential features of the settlement of Svinia, as described in the previous two parts, provide ample illustrations of the marginality of its inhabitants. Local Roma lack access to adequate land and its resources; they live in a dirty, crowded, and unsafe environment; their housing is well below the standard of the surrounding society; they are uneducated and unemployed; they suffer disproportionately from ill health and early death; and they are exposed to widespread prejudice and discrimination that hamper their participation in local community affairs and political life. What are the root causes of Svinia's "Gypsy problem"? As I show in the following pages, the malaise suffered by local Roma is not confined to Svinia. Ever since public officials and scholars began to pay systematic attention to the position of Roma within wider society more than two centuries ago, Slovakia's "Gypsy problem" has been seen to consist of many of the same elements as those associated with the marginality of Roma in present-day Svinia. The historical excursion undertaken here serves to establish the contours of Romani marginality in Slovakia and to examine in considerable detail the course it took in post-war Svinia.

The Traditional Pattern

According to the Slovak Romologist Emília Horváthová, the more economically backward societies of the Balkans and eastern Europe made it easier for Romani immigrants to settle down and integrate into the rural economy than did the more advanced western European societies, which saw little value in the unrefined skills and products offered by Roma and therefore compelled them to remain itinerant (Horváthová 1964:28). This pattern seems to hold for the eastern Slovak region of Spiš, where Romani presence was first documented in the fourteenth century. Local nobility extended protection to a growing stream of Romani newcomers from the Balkans who settled down on feudal estates and made themselves useful in a variety of ways, including providing firewood, hauling supplies, feeding domestic animals, gathering mushrooms and wild berries, and support-ing hunting parties (Horváthová 1964:97). By the sixteenth century, the number of Roma on Slovak territory had reached several thousands, their area of settlement had expanded throughout the country, and the range of documented occupations encompassed military service, entertainment (especially through music), and metalworking (Horváthová 1964:98–101; Guy 1975; Crowe 1994). Increasingly, towns and villages also normalized relations with groups of Roma and allowed them permanent residence in exchange for useful services, such as the manufacture of metal tools and weapons. In the course of the seventeenth century, the "domestication" and settlement of these Roma was formalized by the institution of the *vajda* system, which entailed the appointment of a Romani overseer who acted as a mediator between a band of Roma and local authorities. The *vajda* came to be regarded as a judge and elder, and he was held responsible for the conduct of all "his people" (Horváthová 1964:109–112).

The fact that new groups of Roma kept arriving on Slovak territory shaped the relationship between the immigrants and the host society. By the eighteenth century there were three categories of Roma here: sed-entary groups settled on feudal estates and the margins of towns and villages; itinerants who followed a seasonal pattern of migrations within a circumscribed territory allocated by local authorities; and "illegal" Roma who continued to evade "domestication" by moving from place to place, and who made a living from criminal or semi-criminal activities. Several administrative measures enacted in the course of the eighteenth century prescribed Draconian punishment for those Roma who sought to escape registration and submission to the authorities. They culminated in the reforms of Empress Maria Theresia and her son Joseph II, which pursued a policy of complete sedentism and assimilation (Horváthová 1964; Guy 1975; Crowe 1994).

The social and cultural environment in which these reforms were drafted and enacted is illuminated by a unique document written by the scholar and Spiš resident Samuel Augustini ab Hortis (1729–1792), a man who may have been the first credible ethnographer of Roma (Urbancová 1995). Augustini's investigations took place at a time when public figures began to express concern about the rising numbers of Roma living in what was then the Kingdom of Hungary.[1] Most of the approximately 20,000 Roma believed to have resided in the Slovak part of the country had already been settled, but they continued to display wide-ranging differences from the autochtonous population. Foremost among these was their disinterest in farming, husbandry, and other pursuits of Slovak peasants, such as weaving and sewing (Augustini 1995:126–130). Furthermore, the Roma are said to have had a preference for the consumption of carcasses, tobacco smoking among both men and women, large numbers of children, and clothing designed to create the impression of elevated status. Augustini links the latter trait to "exaggerated pride," which in turn led to frequent conflicts accompanied by screams and public accusations. He singles out the proclivity to dramatic outbursts and theatricality as perhaps the most striking feature of the Romani "national character" (141).

Augustini identifies four occupations that were widespread among Slovak Roma. Metalworking assumed the highest priority, and Augustini describes how Romani blacksmiths manufactured rough tools and implements from scraps of scavenged iron. Although he allows for considerable talent, he also makes a note of a preference for rough work, which he attributes to laziness and a lack of interest in planning (131). He singles out the horse trade as another popular occupation and one associated with a postulated talent for conceit (132). He identifies entertaining as the third most prevalent source of income, with gifted musicians earning a decent livelihood through performances at village fairs, weddings, and dances. He reports that many talented musicians were known to have been fully integrated into respectable society, discarding all resemblance with their kin (1995:133). The fourth and last frequently observed occupation is said to have been the disposal of carcasses found in or near villages and towns. Dead farm animals were reportedly skinned and butchered by Roma, who kept the meat and returned the skin to the owner (133).

In spite of the many differences separating the Roma from their neighbours, Augustini was convinced that a suitable social environment would propel their assimilation. Consequently, he staunchly supported Maria Theresia's radical measures ordained between 1768 and 1773 which banned itinerancy, the horse trade, the consumption of carrion, the use of the vernacular, and numerous other "backward customs" (Augustini 1995:173).

In true Enlightenment fashion, this early Romologist concluded his trea-
tise with the prediction of a complete makeover of his subject of interest.
"Everything shall change in him," he prophesized, "not only his habits,
but even his posture and gestures will become less and less similar to those
of his parents and forebears" (174; my translation).

The acculturative effort of the latter part of the eighteenth century
failed to bring about the expected results. One important reason for its
lack of success was resistance from local authorities that were expected to
shoulder the brunt of the expenses required by the reform. For example,
the envisioned transformation of Roma into farmers presupposed the provision of plots, tools, seeds and livestock, all of which was to come from
the nobles on whose estates the objects of the reform resided (Horváthová
1964:120; Guy 1975:210). On the other hand, there are also indications
that the Roma themselves resisted the regulatory policies. For example,
in 1775 the town of Galanta built new houses for Roma after demolishing
their primitive dwellings on the outskirts. But it seems that the beneficiaries
abandoned the new homes shortly after and moved back into their ruined
huts (Horváthová 1964:124).

Attempts at assimilating Roma continued into the nineteenth century,
although they were pursued less vigorously and comprehensively. Toward
the end of that century the Hungarian government decided to initiate
another large-scale campaign against Gypsy itinerancy and backwardness,
and to this end it carried out a survey that mapped the state of the Roma
throughout the country. The results of the 1893 *Zigeuner-Conscription*—as
the German version of the census was called—are unprecedented in their
scope and reliability. For the first time in history, a government sought
and gained a thorough overview of the distribution and the economic and
social conditions of its Romani subjects in every village, town, and region.

The introduction to this seminal work, written in Hungarian and
German, explains that the survey grew out of the need to paint a reliable
picture of the country's Roma in order to formulate appropriate methods
for the solution of "one of the most difficult and interesting problems,"
namely the "regulation" of Gypsydom (*Zigeunerwesen*). If successful, it
was hoped that such an effort would result in the Roma becoming "worthy,
civilized, happy members of society, useful citizens of the state, loyal sons
of the nation and the homeland" (*Ergebnisse* 1895:4). In this respect the
census-takers were glad to discover that almost 90 per cent of Hungary's
Roma could be regarded as permanently settled (19). Since sedentism

served as the key indicator of integration and assimilation, the outcome supplied empirical evidence that the civilizing process was progressing well.

The survey established a population of 274,940 Roma for all of Hungary, which at that time included also present-day Slovakia and segments of Romania, Ukraine, and Croatia, and it revealed some very important regional distinctions, some of which continue into the present. Among the characteristics shared by the majority of Roma was their limited participation in agricultural activities. While Roma constituted almost two per cent of Hungary's population, they used—whether through ownership or leases—a mere 0.011 per cent of the country's fertile land, and fewer than four per cent engaged in some type of agriculture, be it farming, gardening or husbandry (1895:28). Although historical and economic reasons were taken into account, the authors concluded that cultural factors were at play here: "The Gypsy is not suited for agriculture," they asserted, because he lacked the necessary self-discipline, future-orientation and proclivity toward accumulation of wealth. "He lives exclusively and alone in and for the present, like the child, like the most primitive peoples of the tropical zone," they proclaimed (76–77; my translation).

The economic strategies pursued by most Roma confined them—with the notable exception of musical entertainment (1895:64–65)—overwhelmingly to marginal occupations that minimized competition with members of the majority society. The single largest occupational category was that of seasonal and occasional agricultural labourer dependent on the need and benevolence of local farmers (97). Another large segment of Roma worked as rural craftsmen, and they made a modest living as blacksmiths, brick-makers, carvers of wooden tools, basket weavers, rope and twine spinners, and so on (82). But despite their undisputed talents, these men and women rarely managed to sell their products for prices expected by their autochthonous counterparts. For example, Romani blacksmiths—who accounted for almost a quarter of the country's blacksmiths—relied on unsophisticated tools and second-rate raw materials, which produced results that couldn't compete with those of their "white" colleagues (81–83). A similar situation prevailed in the trades. Although Romani horse-dealers could make a good living, they constituted a small niche within a category dominated by pedlars, usually women, who traded in second-hand textiles, small kitchen equipment, and household implements (96). These more typical Romani "merchants" survived on the margins of the national economy and, similar to craftsmen, symbolized inferior and cheap products. Interestingly enough, only 52 Roma made a living as skilled factory workers (94), and a mere ten individuals held positions requiring higher education (74).[2]

The commentary acknowledges prejudice of the majority population as one of the causes of Romani economic marginality. But it also points out that Roma were, generally speaking, undisciplined workers who had not yet acquired marketable work habits or the ability to use their talents more rationally (73–74). Above all, they are blamed for their lack of recognition of the value of formal education. According to the figures presented, only eight per cent of all adult Roma could read and write—as opposed to 58 per cent of the general population—and the commentary attributes this sorry state of affairs to poor school attendance and parental disinterest (30–32). Completing the overview of the economic situation, the authors come to this conclusion:

> The Gypsies in their contemporary condition, then, represent a considerable economic deficit, and namely in two ways: they consume [*verzehren*] more than what they produce; they use up more than what they generate [*erwerben*], and they allow many skills suitable for production to remain undeveloped, using their strengths not for the welfare of society and themselves, but they waste these in struggling against society. (73; my translation)

While Roma throughout Hungary displayed similar characteristics, the survey demonstrates considerable regional variation. For our purposes the place of eastern Slovakia within this variation is of particular interest. Of the roughly 42,000 Roma found to have been living on the territory of contemporary Slovakia, fewer than ten per cent were fully or partially migratory, and the population was evenly split between eastern and western parts of the country. Significantly, eastern Slovakia compared unfavourably with the rest of Hungary on most important indicators of economic and social welfare. Here we find the highest percentage of segregated settlements, the smallest number of land-owning Roma, the most crowded and least durable dwellings, the lowest rates of school attendance, and the highest frequency of conflict with the majority society. Compared with the Hungarian average, Roma from eastern Slovakia were more likely to be unemployed and

Table 3.1. Social conditions of Hungarian Roma according to region in 1893

	Number of settled Roma	Average settlement size	Children below 15 years (%)	Owners of land (%)	Segregated settlements (%)	Decent homes (%)	Average number per dwelling	Villages with Roma in school (%)	Villages with complaints about Roma (%)
Hungary	243,432	34	15	3	52	60	5.3	33	32
East Slovakia	19,442	19	20	1	82	43	5.8	22	39
Šariš	3,026	14	19	0	78	47	6.8	14	45

less likely to be retained by their neighbours as farm labourers. A higher proportion depended on begging, and very few earned a living with the lucrative horse trade. While the proportion of craftsmen was similar to the situation in Hungary at large, the number of specializations was significantly lower. At the very bottom we find the county of Šariš, which encompasses much of the region surrounding Prešov, including Svinia. Here, Roma were overwhelmingly illiterate, unemployment was a more serious problem than anywhere else, trade was underdeveloped, and manufacturing was largely limited to metalworking practised by village blacksmiths. Musicians constituted the only fairly prestigious and potentially lucrative occupational group and were particularly well represented in the urban setting of Prešov. Tables 3.1 and 3.2, furnished with data extracted from the census, illustrate the precarious position of local Roma.

The First Czechoslovak Republic (1918–1938) and World War II

The new state of Czechoslovakia which rose out of the ashes of the Austro-Hungarian Empire inherited a large number of Roma, and it quickly introduced new measures designed to contain the "Gypsy problem." Motivated by the old civilizatory desire to settle down nomads as well as by a growing

Table 3.2. Occupations of Hungarian Roma according to region in 1893 (%)

	Without work (incl. children)	Beggars	Day labour	Blacksmiths	Construction (brick-making)	Other crafts	Music	Horse trade	Other trade
Hungary	41	2	25	5	6	7	6	0.5	1
East Slovakia	48	5	14	8	6	6	7	0	1
Šariš	54	12	13	11	1	1.5	6	0	1

list of complaints about criminal tendencies of wandering Roma, in 1927 the government passed a "Law concerning itinerant gypsies." This edict required all "wandering gypsies" to register and seek a special permit, which regulated the size of their groups, the length of time they could spend in a single community, the regions they could visit, and the commercial activities to be carried on (Senát Národního shromáždění 1927; Šípek 1989, 1990). Some municipalities particularly opposed to travelling Roma used this law to restrict or completely ban itinerants from their territories. For example, resorts in the High Tatra region of Slovakia did so as early as 1928 (Kollárová 1992:66). Prague and several popular Czech spa towns followed suit in the early 1930s (Šípek 1991).

The regulatory attention resulting from the 1927 law led to the compilation of fairly reliable data about the Roma living in the country. Akin to the Hungarian census of 1893, the enforcement of the Czechoslovak legislation required an overview of the distribution and socio-economic condition of travelling as well as settled Roma. The country-wide survey carried out for this purpose in 1924 enumerated approximately 60,000 settled and 2,000 itinerant Roma in all of Slovakia (Horváthová 1964:160). The highest concentration—18,263 people—was found in the eastern Košice district, which at that time comprised the counties of Zemplín, Spiš, and Šariš (Horváthová 1964:156; Nečas 1986). The vast majority of the eastern Slovak Roma lived dispersed in more than 570 rural settlements designated then as "camps" (tábor) and situated near or on the margins of villages (Nečas 1986). More than half of these, including Svinia, had fewer than 50 residents. Perhaps 2,000 Roma lived in towns and cities, but here the concentrations were very small as well. Prešov had fewer than 150 resident Roma; Košice boasted the biggest Romani population with almost

Table 3.3. Occupations of Roma in eastern Slovakia in 1924

Size	Children 0–14 yrs.	Without work	Working adults	Servants and labourers	Musicians	Blacksmiths	Craftsmen	Traders	Others
18,263	41%	14%	6,791	5,681	552	257	187	63	51

800 people concentrated in a number of neighbourhoods; and the towns of Trebišov and Humenné followed with just under 300 and just above 200 residents respectively. Table 3.3 captures the occupational distribution of this population (after Nečas 1986).

The data presented here are undoubtedly somewhat distorted. The Romani population in individual communities tended to fluctuate, the determination of age was subject to error, and many people had multiple occupations. But even so, some conclusions can justifiably be drawn, especially in comparison with the material obtained from the previous census held in 1893. The sharp increase in the number of children and adolescents—from 20 per cent to over 40 per cent—indicates a rapidly growing population, a trend reflected in the expansion of the overall number of Slovak Roma from roughly 42,000 in 1893 to some 62,000 thirty years later. Although most Roma continued to reside in small and dispersed communities, their average population size had risen by more than 50 per cent—from 19 in 1893 to 31 in 1924. The occupational structure shows that unskilled labour continued to prevail as by far the most frequent type of work performed by Roma. The relatively high percentage of people making a living with music—a prestigious and reasonably well-paid occupation—predominated in urban settings. For example, all the 93 adult male Roma registered as living in the town of Michalovce made a living in this way; in Košice, 131 Roma earned their keep as musicians (Nečas 1986). Now as before, farming—the modal occupation of the majority population—was almost entirely absent. Only five persons could be unambiguously classified in this category (Nečas 1986:219).

The lifestyle pursued by most Slovak Roma during the inter-war period differed little from the pattern developed earlier. According to the "primordialist" hypothesis of the Slovak ethnologist Emília Horváthová, the prevailing relationship between Roma and their neighbours enshrined principles of caste-like distinctions brought from India. In this model, the Roma performed tasks and services considered inferior by the majority society in exchange for food, clothing, and protection extended by their "higher-caste" patrons (Horváthová 1964:177). Hence Slovak farmers owned all local resources—land, forests, livestock, raw materials—while the Roma were entitled merely to rejected or surplus resources, and even then only in exchange for their labour. A certain proto-symbiotic relationship did emerge here whereby both sides benefitted from their respective specializations. But the nature and the extent of the relationship were determined unilaterally by the villagers and designed to magnify their advantage. For example, villagers bartered *válki*—the traditional unfired bricks—from Roma, but the manufacturers couldn't expect a fair price simply because there was an abundance of brick-makers and *válki* (Horváthová 1964). Even in the more refined field of metalworking, Romani blacksmiths usually drew the shorter end. Although farmers normally equipped their horses with horseshoes made by Romani blacksmiths, they usually left the shoeing itself to a Slovak "specialist" who purchased the necessary products from a Romani "generalist" (Mann 1992:110). Thus, although the blacksmith, or *kováč*, occupied a prominent place among rural Roma, the earnings from his trade often had to be supplemented by other activities (Nečas 1986; Kollárová 1992:64). In the rare cases where a blacksmith managed to challenge the traditional division of labour, he began to associate more with members of the majority society, which often led to complete assimilation (Mann 1992:111).

Such was also often the case in the lucrative and prestigious music profession. As in previous decades and centuries, the majority society retained its willingness to exempt successful musicians from the general contempt in which Roma were held. Throughout the 1920s and 1930s, Romani performers entertained the clients of urban cafés, restaurants, and dance halls in most Slovak towns and cities. This "Gypsy nobility" became a caste-like group with its own code of conduct and appearance, and, occasionally, professional organizations. For example, the Romani musicians of Košice had their own "Association of gypsy musicians," *Lavutaris*, and they were well integrated into the city's institutions (Davidová 1995:58). They lived in respectable houses, and their children attended regular schools (Horváthová 1964:168).

Another position that conferred relatively high status was that of the *vajda*. Traditionally associated with the need of local authorities to maintain "law and order" in settlements, the position was formalized in the early

1940s when the *vajda* was placed under the authority of village mayors. In exchange for his collaboration with the state, the *vajda* received a small salary and a share of useful resources, such as firewood (Kollárová 1992:64).

As Table 3.3 demonstrates, only an exceedingly small number of rural Roma enjoyed such privileged positions. Most lived in abject poverty, and the growing population, combined with the inability to keep pace with changes in the economy, exacerbated their marginality. The inter-war period saw the introduction of new manufacturing techniques into the Slovak countryside, and these innovations made the services and products offered by Romani craftsmen and traders increasingly obsolete. As one scholar put it, their "selling" degenerated into "begging" supplemented by occasional stealing (Horváthová 1964:167). The proto-symbiosis that had developed with the majority society began to crumble, and growing numbers of rural Roma came to depend on charity (Horváthová 1964; Kollárová 1992).

Although Czechoslovak Roma officially enjoyed the same legal status as any other citizen, contemporary accounts reveal deep-seated prejudice in all walks of life. The tone of public discourse in which Roma were discussed can be surmised from newspaper accounts of a highly publicized show trial that took place in Košice between 1927 and 1929. It concerned several dozen members of a Romani criminal gang who stood accused of killing and eating a number of Slovaks. The proceedings attracted extraordinary attention from domestic and foreign journalists who surpassed one another in animalistic depictions of the Roma. According to one excerpt from the local press, "None of the accused ... has a head that could be considered human.... [It is] as if monkeys taught to speak had been gathered here" (quoted in Šalamon 1988:148; my translation). Another domestic account postulated, "Gypsies are a different breed from the rest of the population. Even though they have lived for centuries beside us, we are still as foreign to them as when they arrived" (149).

There is evidence of growing inter-ethnic tensions and occasional violence occurring in some rural locations during the inter-war era. For example, several pogroms took place in the east Slovak county of Spiš whereby groups of villagers damaged and even demolished neighbouring Romani settlements. In one such case, which happened in 1933 in Spišská Bystrá, the Roma were punished for refusing to play music at the firemen's ball (Kollárová 1992:64). The most tragic of these altercations transpired in 1928 in the southwestern part of Slovakia, in the village of Pobědim. Driven by the desire to extract revenge for some perceived injury, 40 armed men invaded the local settlement, ravaged it, and left six of its residents dead and 18 wounded (Horváthová 1964:163–165). There were other, less violent, conflicts that led to segregationist measures among the Slovaks. Often these were precipitated by outbreaks of infectious diseases in the settlements, such as a flare-up of stomach typhus in 1918 which killed twelve Roma in the Spiš community of Letanovce and prompted local villagers to move the settlement farther away (Kollárová 1988:138).

The state responded to the escalating "gypsy problem" in three ways. As mentioned, it drafted and enforced legislation to control the most unruly segment of the Roma—the itinerants. Second, among settled Roma, public authorities began to pay more than passing attention to the provision of elementary education. Starting in 1926, it began setting up special "gypsy schools" in several eastern cities, towns, and even villages. The first such institution emerged in the Sub-Carpathian metropolis of Užhorod—where it still exists today—followed by Košice and Levoča (Horváthová 1964; Kollárová 1988, 1992). Here Romani children followed a basic and practical curriculum designed to provide a rudimentary level of literacy and "life skills." Where numbers didn't warrant a separate building, segregated "gypsy classes" were set up within existing schools. The perception of the children constituting a health risk on account of their unhygienic living environment supplied the most frequent rationale for keeping them segregated (Kollárová 1988:139–144).

The third important type of state intervention was the provision of welfare. In view of the growing gap between the size of the Romani population and the resources available to it, public welfare became a necessity in some locations during this period. Assistance took the form of an ongoing distribution of food in particularly destitute families, as well as occasional donations of food and clothing in times of crisis (Kollárová 1992). That the Roma were exceptionally needy is disclosed by a Slovak-wide registry of welfare recipients set up in 1940. Out of the 32,575 persons receiving assistance at that time—12 per cent of the general population—more than 25 per cent, or 8,939, were Roma. A related registry capturing the number of "professional" beggars, lists 10,763 individuals country-wide. Roma accounted for more than two thirds—7,599. Within the county of Spiš, Roma represented more than 30 per cent of all welfare recipients—962 out of 2,997—and the overwhelming majority of "persons subsisting on begging"—1,477 out of 1,564 (Kollárová 1992:66–67).

The poverty experienced by most Roma during the early part of the twentieth century deepened during World War II. In 1939 Czechoslovakia disintegrated into the German-controlled Protectorate of Bohemia and Moravia and the nominally independent Slovak State that collaborated with Hitler's Nazi régime. From the approximately 12,000 Roma who resided in the Czech lands at the beginning of the occupation, some 5,000 left for Slovakia right away in order to escape repressive measures (Šípek 1991). These included a total ban on travelling, which at that time was still practised by the majority of Czech Roma, followed in short order by the deportation of most Roma to forced labour camps from which few returned (Nečas 1981; Šípek 1991).

The much larger number and greater differentiation of Slovak Roma, as well as the country's nominal independence, made the execution of Nazi racial policies less consequential. Most did survive the war era, albeit ravaged and intimidated. One of the first laws issued by independent Slovakia stripped Jews, "half-Jews," and "unregulated" travelling Roma of citizenship (Nečas 1988:127). All remaining Roma were banned from popular tourist areas, and in some locations curfews were imposed (Nečas 1988:131; Kollárová 1992:67). In 1941 the itinerancy permits issued after 1927 were rescinded, and all forms of travelling were outlawed. Simultaneously, many settled Roma were ordered to move their dwellings to designated areas located at a prescribed distance from neighbouring villages (Horváthová 1964; Nečas 1988; Lacková 1999). By 1942, "gypsy asocials" began to be shipped to labour camps set up in several districts. Their inmates repaired roads, built a new railway line, and maintained military fortifications (Davidová 1965:29–30; Kollárová 1992; Fedič 2001). Following the 1944 Slovak National Uprising, Roma were increasingly subjected to pogroms and mass executions, usually carried out by German soldiers (Horváthová 1964:171; Davidová 1965:29–30; Nečas 1988:131–132; Kollárová 1992:68; Fedič 2001).

The Socialist Era (1948–1989)

The postwar period found the Roma reduced to a few hundred survivors in the Czech lands and their Slovak kin still numerically robust but socially and economically more isolated from the surrounding society than ever before. The first significant response to the devastation inflicted by the war was a massive emigration of thousands of Slovak Roma to Czech territories in need of an industrial labour force. The strength of this wave can be gathered from the first postwar census of Czechoslovak Roma held in 1947. From the total figure of 101,190, Czech territories accounted for 16,752, but since local Roma had been almost completely exterminated, it is evident that most of the "Czech" Roma hailed from Slovakia (Jurová 1993:24). The roughly 85,000 Roma who remained in Slovakia continued to live mostly in rural settlements, with the highest concentration seen in the eastern counties (Horváthová 1964:285–286).

After the communist takeover in 1948, the so-called gypsy question assumed considerable ideological importance. Having adopted the egalitarian principles of a people's democracy, Czechoslovakia's new socialist government displayed a sincere effort to reduce the social and economic marginality of the poverty-stricken Roma. The first step in that direction occurred in the early 1950s with a thorough investigation of their living conditions (Jurová 1993:38–39). The problems identified in the course of this preliminary analysis seemed overwhelming. Unemployment was rampant, especially in eastern Slovakia where only some 30 per cent of all employable Romani men held permanent jobs of any kind. More than 80 per cent of Roma living in this region were illiterate, and the majority of local children didn't attend school (Jurová 1993:40). In the summer of 1955, public health officials conducted a survey of living conditions in dozens of rural settlements. They described the situation as "catastrophic" (Jurová 1993:43). In one half of the inspected dwellings the floor consisted of stamped earth; eighty per cent were in a state of serious disrepair; most settlements lacked a single outhouse or sewage disposal of any kind; drinking water was hauled from polluted creeks; dwellings were crowded, and the average number of six occupants per room placed the settlements well below the national standard (Jurová 1993:43; Horváthová 1964:361). All these factors were believed to play a part in the prevalence of serious and contagious diseases, such as tuberculosis, typhus, trachoma, and syphilis, which occurred here far more frequently than in villages inhabited by ethnic Slovaks (Jurová 1993:43–45). Another, smaller, study conducted in late 1955 and concerned with social and economic conditions in a number of eastern Slovak settlements disclosed an adult illiteracy rate of 80 per cent, widespread incestuous relations among close relatives, cases of *de facto* polygyny, and rising rates of criminality embedded within rapidly worsening relations with the majority population. Only 13 per cent of employed Roma carried out work requiring some degree of specialized education or training, such as bricklaying, blacksmithing, or shoemaking. This wasn't expected to change any time soon because of the exceedingly low participation rate of young Roma in formal education. Significantly, only four per cent of working Roma engaged in some form of agriculture (Osvetové ústredie 1956).

Despite the continuous emigration of Roma to the industrial districts of Bohemia and Moravia, their number in Slovakia continued to rise, and by the middle of the 1950s it hovered around 115,000 (Jurová 1993:47). Although natural increase accounted for much of this, a not insignificant part seems to have been played by the arrival of at least a few thousand itinerant Roma from Hungary soon after the end of the war (Jurová 1993:20, 22, 45). A government census taken in 1958 claimed 46,000 "itinerant persons" for all of Czechoslovakia (Zeman 1959:8), and while the figure is probably inflated due to a variety of factors (Lindnerová 1993:196), the number of travelling Roma had undoubtedly increased. This is reflected in reports filed by local authorities in several Slovak districts as early as 1945, raising concerns about itinerants and attributing to them various crimes and social problems (Jurová 1993:20–24, 45). The perceived need for "law and order" increased with the communist takeover, bringing to power a political party that had very little tolerance for marginal members of society who shunned regular employment and daily supervision.

Thus the "gypsy question" as it (re)emerged during the first few years of the communist era required a two-pronged attack. On the one hand, the Roma settled in their primitive rural communities had to be helped with the attainment of a living standard befitting socialist villagers. As one politically aware ethnologist defined it, the "gypsy question" represented "an accumulation of problems deriving from distinctions caused by the Gypsies' backward forms of lifestyle and culture, which it is necessary to eliminate in accordance with changes wrought in their economic position by socialism" (Davidová 1965:35; my translation). On the other hand, the perceived presence of a large segment of Roma "roaming" the countryside without a fixed abode or suitable employment challenged the party and state apparatus in its determination to control and determine the destiny of all citizens. It was the dual need for socio-economic improvement *and* administrative control that shaped the communist-era policies towards Roma.

Although the goals of the socialist modernization campaign were determined early on in the 1950s, the means by which these were to be attained weren't agreed on until the late 1950s (Grulich and Haišman 1986; Jurová 1996). A largely internal debate went on for almost ten years concerning the most effective methods to be pursued. The liberal-progressive participants in this debate—mostly enlightened bureaucrats and academics—favoured an emancipatory approach that called for the recognition of Roma as a separate ethnic minority, possibly a degree of territorial autonomy in some parts of Slovakia, and a pattern of integration determined by the Roma themselves (Jurová 1993:34–37). This approach took into account the emergence in 1948 of the Association of Slovak Roma, which represented a growing number of Romani intellectuals, artists, and community leaders interested in playing an active part in the integration of their compatriots into mainstream society (Jurová 1993:25–26). At the other end of the bureaucratic spectrum, conservative apparatchiks demanded a paternalistic, Party-controlled approach that would be heavily assimilationist in its outcome (Davidová 1965; Grulich and Haišman 1986; Jurová 1993).[3]

The two alternative strategies were discussed in 1958 by the Central Committee of the Communist Party—Czechoslovakia's highest organ of power—in order to issue appropriate and final guidelines. The Committee members deliberated and then concluded that, from the perspective of Marxism-Leninism, the Roma lacked basic prerequisites of a separate nationality, such as a common territory and a single shared language (Zeman 1959:22). Hence they warned that the recognition of ethnic uniqueness would "slow down the resocialization of gypsies, strengthen [their] undesirable isolation from other workers, [and] aid in the conservation of the old primitive gypsy lifestyle" (Zeman 1959:22; my translation).

The timing of these deliberations is of some interest. They coincided with feverish preparations for Czechoslovakia's appropriation in 1960 of the attribute "*socialist* republic." Since the "gypsy question" was seen as constituting a major obstacle to the factual realization of socialism, a concerted effort had to be made to solve it as quickly as possible (Guy 1975). The centre-piece of this endeavour became the Central Committee's order that itinerancy was to be eradicated by the end of 1959, leading in turn to the promulgation of the communist era's most important regulation concerning Roma: "law no. 74 about the permanent settling down of itinerants" in October 1958.[4] While the manifest target of this law was itinerants, the seven pages of elaborations that accompanied it provided a comprehensive set of measures to be used by local authorities in their dealings with all Roma. Their ultimate goal was assimilation into mainstream society in order to complete the socialist revolution for all segments of the population.

The Party apparatchiks responsible for promulgating and overseeing this policy were no naive ideologues detached from social reality. They knew very well that much of the success of the assimilationist effort depended on the goodwill of the majority population. As one Party official explained, "While capitalist states solved and solve the gypsy question by means of the sharpest racial discrimination and isolation—Nazism even with geno-cide—in the countries of the socialist camp we approach the solution ... on the basis of socialist humanism" (Zeman 1959:6; my translation). This was not meant to be a hollow promise. The Party did indeed expect that communism would make a difference in the treatment of Roma by officials and ordinary citizens alike. In the words of the deputy minister of the interior,

> the basic and key precondition for the solution of the gypsy question will be the emergence of a correct, new attitude of all citizens to the gypsies. It is about not driving these people into isolation but rather to enable them to attain the cultural niveau of other citizens. To accomplish this it is necessary that other citizens make this possible. (Kotal 1959:59; my translation)

Law no. 74 and accompanying directives triggered a modernization campaign of unprecedented magnitude. It aimed at eliminating Romani "backwardness" (*zaostalost*) in all realms of life and at integrating Roma physically and socially into mainstream society. Although by virtue of their most striking "otherness" the itinerants were presented as the primary objects of the legislation, once they had been settled in appointed munici-palities, the social engineers responsible for the "gypsy question" turned their attention to the more general problem of the far-reaching marginality faced by most Roma in all walks of life. The vehicle for simultaneously overcoming backwardness and attaining integration was to be an ambitious program designed to liquidate the most primitive and isolated settlements and to move their residents to new dwellings situated in integrated neigh-bourhoods of nearby villages and towns (Zeman 1959:12, 14). This was no small task. Figures released in 1956 disclosed 1,305 settlements dispersed throughout Slovakia and inhabited by some 95,000 Roma in 14,935 dwell-ings (Jurová 1996:404).[5] While the initial phase of the colossal project was to see the elimination of 286 settlements with 3,158 dwellings (Jurová

1996:620), top officials realized that the entire process would require at least 20 years (Jurová 1996:404). The complexity of the resettlement scheme may be illustrated with a sketch of events that accompanied the liquidation of a medium-sized community in the district of Poprad in 1961. Its 110 residents were dispersed into newly constructed apartments in eight different municipalities. Here is how a sympathetic observer describes the various steps involved:

> First, all these Gypsies were de-loused and bathed in the nearby spa ..., and then subjected to a thorough medical examination. Children were inoculated as well. After receiving clothing and refreshments, they were transported by buses to specific municipalities of the Kežmarok district with their new homes. In each village representatives of the local administration and population awaited these families in readied and basically furnished apartments to welcome them and here and there also to help overcome the first difficulties.... Beside the fundamental conditions—accommodation and employment—these families also needed new clothing, household equipment, and food for the first few days.... Right after the departure of its residents the old gypsy settlement was burned down and levelled with the ground to prevent the return of any inhabitants. (Even so, one of them—old Pompa—came back in the evening and slept the whole night on the spot of his former abode. It pulled him to the old place, but then he understood.) And in a short while this whole location...grew over with grass and its former inhabitants began to get accustomed to a different lifestyle in their new homes. (Davidová 1965:104; my translation)

While the "liquidation and dispersal" campaign was undoubtedly the most challenging component of the socialist modernization project, there were many other tasks. Tens of thousands of children and adults had to be x-rayed, immunized, and periodically examined in an effort to stem the spread of communicable diseases that had already been brought under control in the majority population (Ministerstvo zdravotnictví 1959:77–78). In accordance with new socialist legislation guaranteeing employment for all able-bodied citizens, jobs had to be found for thousands of often under-skilled Roma. State and party officials realized that the goal of universal and meaningful employment couldn't be attained without a dramatic improvement in educational standards, and to this end a complex set of innovations was to be introduced. The ministry of education promised the provision of universal and subsidized daycare to all Romani parents in an effort to prepare their children for school—and to minimize the exposure of impressionable children to "harmful customs" (Ministerstvo zdravotnictví 1959:73–74). The same provision was made for lunch and after-school programs of elementary students. Cognizant of some of the causes of prejudice against ethnically mixed classes, ministry officials ordained that all Romani children attending school be de-loused with DDT in order to forego the de-humanizing removal of hair. The ministry also promised an adequate supply of specially trained and motivated teachers who were to provide the highly individual attention required by most Romani students. Where this proved insufficient, special classes and even schools could be created for "youth requiring special care." Aware of the potential of such segregationist measures to slow down the integration process, the ministry emphasized that these would be employed only in exceptional circumstances as a provisional instrument allowing disadvantaged children to catch up and be transferred, as promptly as possible, to regular classes and schools (Ministerstvo zdravotnictvi 1959:72–74). Great pains were taken to distinguish such temporary institutions from regular special schools for mentally retarded children. As one education expert put it, "Gypsy children are, with some exceptions, entirely normal and intelligent; they are only neglected. Therefore, [...] gypsy children don't belong to special schools" (Bacíková 1959:40).

The first phase of the modernization campaign ended with mixed results. By 1965, only 45 settlements had been liquidated, resulting in the relocation of some 3,000 people, but explosive population growth increased the number of settlement-based residents by another 5,000 (Davidová 1965:201; Jurová 1993:75). Worse, the overcrowding problem of individual dwellings became further exacerbated as the average number of occupants climbed from 6.1 to 7.4. Even many former itinerants, who were at the centre of government attention, ended up in provisional quarters that were neither integrated into ordinary villages nor equipped with services prescribed by public health authorities. In the end, the engineers of the resettlement scheme authorized exemptions that saw former itinerants continue to live in their wagons, albeit only after having the wheels removed and their horses confiscated (Ministerstvo vnitra 1959:66; Zeman 1959:11–13).

Initiatives in the crucial realm of education were also plagued with problems. Contrary to the exaggerated expectation that illiteracy would be eradicated within a couple of years (Zeman 1959:19), it persisted as a formidable problem for decades to come. By the early 1960s, only a very small minority of Romani children had been enrolled in daycare and kindergarten, and of the more than 32,000 children of school-going age merely 11,000 attended school regularly (Jurová 1993:68). In spite of the warning that "the massive immersion of gypsy children into special schools is in direct contradiction to the conclusions of the Central Committee of the Communist Party and must therefore end" (Bacíková 1959:40), this temporary measure was soon to become a permanent feature. The number of students seeking post-elementary education of any kind was abysmally low, and most of the employment opportunities created for Roma consisted of unskilled, manual labour, much of it seasonal; this was a particularly persistent problem in eastern Slovakia (Jurová 1993:67–70).

There is considerable evidence suggesting that while technical problems—such as the availability of finances and material for the construction of new houses or the shortage of experts required in many areas (Davidová 1965:105)—and exaggerated goals are partly to blame for the slow and incomplete progress of the modernization program of the 1950s and early 1960s, the "human factor" of prejudice, resistance to change, and outright sabotage played an equally important role. As we have seen, Communist Party officials were aware that the ideals of "socialist humanism" hadn't been universally accepted and that centuries-old patterns of prejudice against Roma couldn't be expected to vanish overnight. Special citizens' committees were to be set up in each ethnically mixed community in order to assist with the local implementation of the resettlement project. There were hundreds of standardized lectures called "improving our relations with Gypsies" (Jurová 1993:68). And there were appeals to local chapters of various "mass organizations"—such as the Young Pioneers and the Socialist Youth Union—to extend assistance to newly integrated Roma. Students were expected to strike up partnerships with Romani children who needed help at school (Zeman 1959:19). Adults were encouraged to take an interest in the affairs of Romani colleagues and neighbours. In the words of one senior Party official, "we always find devoted comrades who occasionally drop in for a neighbourly visit in a gypsy family, help overcome initial difficulties, and teach them [...] the cultured way of living and housekeeping" (Zeman 1959:13; my translation).[6]

The way in which the attempted integration of Roma unfolded at the level of individual communities differed strikingly from the "socialist humanism" model envisioned by armchair social engineers in Prague and Bratislava. Official reports documenting the modernization campaign of the late 1950s are replete with observations of passive and active resistance rendered by ordinary citizens as well as local officials. Most of it extended to the dispersal of resettled Roma into neighbourhoods inhabited by the majority population. Land owners refused to sell parcels of land earmarked as building lots for needy Roma. Officials slowed down or outright sabotaged procedures required for the issuance of building permits and the purchase of building material (Davidová 1965:101, 105–106; Jurová 1996:368, 370, 374, 376–377, 400, 621; Haišman 1999:169). In some municipalities local authorities permitted the construction of new homes within settlements targeted for liquidation (Davidová 1965:107). Elsewhere, mobs of villagers attacked and destroyed new houses situated "outside the pale," convincing the builders to retreat into their traditional territory (Přívora 1959:48). Research carried out in ethnically mixed communities revealed extremist views held by many members of the majority, advocating castration, expulsion to an uninhabited island, and the burning down of settlements as the preferred solution to the "gypsy problem" (Osvetové ústredie 1956:44).

But it wasn't just the "whites" who failed to meet the Party's expectations. There were complaints about some beneficiaries' disinterest in contributing to the modernization effort (Jurová 1996:400), and in a few locations the attention and generosity displayed toward the Roma are reported to have made them disrespectful and rowdy (375). The worst complaints, however, came from municipal and police authorities in the Czech towns and cities where many of the Slovak Roma had been resettled. For instance, the northern Bohemian town of Most and the surrounding district attracted some 5,000 Slovak Roma who had arrived in the late 1950s in search of employment in local industries. According to a police report addressed to the Central Committee of the Communist Party, most of the housing assigned to the newcomers in the town itself was destroyed within a short period of time by people unaccustomed to urban amenities. Hardwood floors were ripped up and burned, beams were sawed off and used as makeshift furniture, and copper wiring and water pipes were removed and sold off; as a consequence of these alterations, around one hundred houses

Table 3.4. Romani population trends, 1947–1967. Based on government figures
(Jurová 1996:1020–1023)

	Czechoslovakia		Slovakia		East Slovakia	
	No. of Roma	0–14 yrs.	No. of Roma	0–14 yrs.	No. of Roma	0–14 yrs.
1947	101,190	38.8%	84,438	39.3%	42,354	40.4%
1967	223,993	46.0%	164,526	45.2%	89,697	47.5%

in the historic part of Most had to be demolished as hazardous dwellings
(Ministerstvo vnitra 1962). The town council attempted to stem the influx
of new migrants, and some parties were simply loaded up onto trucks and
tractors and deported to surrounding villages. In one instance described by
the police report, "local citizens hindered with pitchforks, axes, and other
implements the unloading of the Gypsies and forced them to return to
Most where they were left behind on the town square" (Ministerstvo vnitra
1962). From here they surreptitiously moved into empty apartments and
proceeded to occupy them illegally.

In 1965 the Central Committee of the Communist Party reviewed the
progress of the "liquidation and dispersal" program and expressed dissatisfaction with the results. Not only was the measurable outcome relatively
modest; it also was unevenly distributed in favour of central and western
Slovakia. The vast majority of liquidated settlements was found in the
highly visible tourist areas of north-central Slovakia, whereas the most
underdeveloped communities in the east had received insufficient attention
(Jurová 1993:72).[7] A similar asymmetry prevailed in improvements made
in the fight against illiteracy and absenteeism (73). The only area where
really significant strides had been made was health care. A growing number of births was taking place in hospitals, resulting in a marked decline in
infant mortality. This, combined with improved post-natal care by means
of frequent check-ups and the introduction of compulsory immunization
resulted in a rapid increase in the country's Romani population (Jurová
1993:71). Table 3.4 captures changes that occurred between 1947 and 1967.
It reflects the dramatic growth of the Romani segment and its high concentration in the eastern regions of the country.

The 1965 review took into consideration the population explosion that
was particularly striking in the rural districts of eastern Slovakia and the

strain this was placing on the already disastrous housing situation. A new plan hatched by government officials foresaw a dramatic intensification of efforts in both components of the "liquidation and dispersal" program. It called for the elimination of more than 100 settlements per year and for the dispersal of 63,000 rural Roma within five years. In addition, some 14,000 were to be transferred to industrial "partner districts" in Bohemia and Moravia (Jurová 1993:79; Davidová 1995:203–204).

This second phase of the modernization campaign didn't attain the set targets either, since local prejudice and resistance to externally imposed policies proved a major stumbling block again (Haišman 1999:172–173; Víšek 1999:213). However, there were some undeniable successes. Almost 24,000 rural Roma found a new home in integrated neighbourhoods and villages, 4,700 inadequate dwellings were liquidated, and thousands of people moved to Czech urban centres where they adjusted to a radically different lifestyle (Jurová 1993:93). The 1970s brought a new emphasis on gradual integration by means of improved education and life skills (93–95), but the liquidation and dispersal initiative continued, albeit in a less systematic and more gradual fashion, until the end of the socialist era (Davidová 1995:205–210). This combination proved rather successful. Between 1970 and 1980, the failure rate of Romani students attending Slovak elementary schools declined from 40 to 17 per cent (Lindnerová 1993:201). The participation rate of Romani children in daycare and kindergarten rose from 33 per cent in 1975 to 76 per cent in 1988 (Lindnerová 1993:200; Jurová 1993:101). Whereas in 1970 there were only 39 Slovak Roma with completed university education, by 1980 that number had increased to 191 (Jurová 1993:102). Even the settlement liquidation program bore significant fruits as the number of segregated communities declined to 278 in 1988, with only just under 15,000 people still living in inadequate dwellings slated for elimination (Jurová 1993:104–105; Davidová 1995:216). Many rural residents flocked to towns and cities. The number of urban Slovak Roma rose from 49,000 in 1970 to almost 80,000 in 1980. Now, as before, the eastern metropolis of Košice accommodated the largest population of urban Roma in the country. By 1980 it had climbed to more than 8,600 (Srb 1986).

Several other processes of considerable significance unfolded during the last twenty years of the socialist era. The permissive 1960s ushered in a short-lived but nevertheless important period of emancipation that saw the Roma finally being recognized as a genuine ethnic group (Davidová 1995:205–208). The politically repressive 1970s put a damper on their activism, but toward the end of that decade the quest for Romani emancipation began to play a part in the growing dissident movement rallied around Václav Havel and the Charter '77 initiative. Havel and his collaborators condemned the refusal of the Communist Party to grant the Roma at least a measure of self-determination, and they accused those behind the assimilationist policies of attempted genocide (Davidová 1995:211–214). Within ten years, criticism of state paternalism became widespread (Gruska 1988), and soon even highly placed officials began to advocate "positive ethnic emancipation" for the Roma (Víšek 1988:37). One of the final gestures of the last communist government was to encourage the formation of Romani organizations and their participation in tackling the many problems that the paternalistic approach of previous decades had failed to address satisfactorily (Lindnerová 1993:202).

The emergence of a Romani political elite in the course of the 1970s and 1980s was a logical consequence of the integrationist policies pursued by the Communist Party. Although the proportion of university-educated Roma continued to lag behind that found in the majority society, it had undeniably increased and contributed to the growth of incipient Romani nationalism. Significantly, the emancipatory movement was born in the Czech Republic, and its most influential exponents were emigrants trans-planted from rural Slovakia as part of the dispersal campaign of the 1950s and 1960s. This fact reflects the wider phenomenon of socio-economic differentiation within the Romani population and its consequences for the Roma left behind in eastern Slovakia. The social engineers respon-sible for the socialist-era modernization program recognized that the rural communities that they were seeking to change exhibited some degree of social, cultural, and economic heterogeneity. While almost everybody was wretched compared with their ethnic Slovak neighbours, wretchedness itself came in many different shades (Lacková 1999). The modernizers sought to capture the essence of the variation found among their clients by subdividing them into three categories. Category I consisted of Roma who had already left the ethnic ghetto and had dispersed among the majority population. Category II comprised "adaptable" individuals and families. And category III referred to the "most backward" (*najzaostalejší*) mem-bers of a given community (Jurová 1996:1023). This classification system was used throughout the socialist era, and it allowed for the tabulation of quantifiable and comparable changes. Predictably, perhaps, category III Roma rarely registered for the long-distance move to Czech territories,

Table 3.5. Socio-economic differentiation of Czechoslovakia's Roma in 1967

	Czech territories	Slovakia	East Slovakia
No. of Roma	59,467	164,526	89,697
Category I	40.1%	27.7%	17.7%
Category II	41.4%	34.9%	35.7%
Category III	18.0%	37.4%	46.6%
Employed adults	66.0%	50.5%	40.9%

nor were they welcomed by Czech officials who had their eyes on the best possible immigrants, drafted from category I and the upper end of category II (Haišman 1999:181). The direction and consequences of this brain drain can be assessed from Table 3.5. It captures the unequal distribution of the three categories of Roma as identified by census-takers in 1967 (Jurová 1996:1023).

Considering that the majority of the Czech Roma represented in this tabulation originally hailed from eastern Slovakia, the degree of polarization between "eastern" and "western" Roma that transpired within 10–15 years is remarkable. It must be taken into consideration in the evaluation of the impact the modernization campaign had on the lives of average people. Generally speaking, the further east we look, the lower the standard of living and the higher the degree of separation from the majority society. As revealed by Table 3.5, this expectation holds not only for Czechoslovakia at large but also for the smaller spectrum of Slovakia. Additional evidence confirms eastern Slovakia as something of a cesspool that continued to shelter the country's most marginal communities of Roma. For example, of the 278 segregated settlements left in the country by 1988, only 48 were located outside the eastern zone of deprivation. Similarly, 85 per cent of the substandard huts that continued to withstand the liquidation program stood in the eastern counties (Jurová 1993:105).

The east-west divide didn't escape the scrutiny of government officials, especially since it seemed to coincide with demographic distinctions that appeared to accelerate the reproduction of Roma belonging to the most backward category. The results of the 1980 census led to alarm in some quarters because they revealed a spectacular and growing gap between the demographic profiles of Roma and the majority society, as captured in Table 3.6 (Bačová 1988:25; Jurová 1996:1016).

Table 3.6. The demographic divide in eastern Slovakia (*Východoslovenský kraj*). Based on 1980 census

	Size	0—14 yrs.	Average age (m)	Average age (f)
Entire population	1,401,759	28%	30.2	32.3
Roma	108,356	46%	20.1	20.9

Table 3.7. Slovakia's Romani population based on census figures (Jurová 1993:98–99; Davidová 1995:215)

	Slovakia	central and western regions	eastern region
1970	159,275	75,596	83,579
1980	199,853	91,497	108,356
1989	253,943	113,702	140,241

By this time, Party and government officials had come to express the view that since the socialist order provided full opportunity for integration, the apparent failure of some Roma to attain a position of socialist respectability resulted from their own choice to adhere to a pathological culture and to embrace a deviant lifestyle (Víšek 1988:37; Jurová 1992:98). Worried by the explosive growth among what the officials called "non-integrated gypsy citizens," the government began to encourage voluntary sterilization for particularly fecund Romani women in 1972 (Mann 1995:61). In 1974 the Slovak ministry of health set up a family-planning program directed at Roma, renewed in 1983, in an effort to reduce "the high proportion of the unhealthy population" (61). Its core ingredients were abortion on demand and sterilization rewarded with handsome cash incentives. The steep rise in the value of the benefit—it went up from 2,000 crowns in 1986 to 25,000 in 1988 (Mann 1995:61–62)—mirrors the growing unease with which the government viewed the rapid reproduction of Roma (Víšek 1988:35–37). Table 3.7 depicts the population trend as it prevailed in Slovakia between 1970 and 1989. The latter year is the last date for which reasonably accurate figures are available.[8]

Post-war Modernization in Svinia

Although there are few dependable sources from which to reconstruct the history of Svinia's Roma during the war and the early socialist era, a handful of oral accounts suggests that the war years caused less upheaval here than in some neighbouring communities. Unlike nearby Jarovnice or Velký Šariš where Roma were systematically terrorized and dislocated (Lacková 1999), the smaller community in Svinia escaped major harm. Two men were confined to a labour camp in the vicinity of Prešov, and a handful of men were drafted into the Slovak army where they seem to have performed auxiliary tasks, such as the digging of graves. The women who stayed behind were subjected to occasional harassment from soldiers and Hlinka Guard members looking for sexual gratification, but popular defensive strategies—such as the feigning of typhus and other contagious diseases (see Lacková 1999)—seem to have kept major harm at bay. Romani informants in Svinia tend to associate war-time brutality almost exclusively with guardists from other communities and with German soldiers of the Wehrmacht—who appeared in Slovakia only in 1944. Local whites are praised for occasionally intervening in defence of "their" Gypsies. Toward the end of the war, several villagers and Roma seem to have banded together and joined the partisans operating in the area.

The seemingly harmonious inter-ethnic relationship endured into the post-war and early socialist era. Both Romani and white informants confirm godparenthood as an important expression of the villagers' goodwill toward the Roma, which survived into the 1960s. Another most significant sign of inter-ethnic tolerance was the willingness of the villagers to accept the dispersal of some Roma beyond their traditional boundaries. I have already sketched the "exodus" of the two siblings Józef and Alžbeta, accompanied by their spouses and offspring, from their ancestral home by the creek, but we must return to it because of the extraordinary significance it played in the local version of the socialist modernization program.

Although the precise timing and the exact circumstances of the two siblings' abandonment of the old settlement cannot be recalled in detail by surviving witnesses, there is agreement on a number of factors. The move happened shortly after the end of the war, and it was preceded by the death of Juraj Kaleja, the founding patriarch of the community. It seems that Juraj's death created a leadership vacuum and precipitated a process of segmentation among his numerous offspring. Two of them, Józef and

Alžbeta, with their relatively acculturated spouses from elsewhere, had by then clearly gained a reputation for diligence, astuteness, and good relations with the villagers. Thus when they approached the village administration and sought permission to leave the strife-ridden settlement, there was little resistance to their moving to the north-eastern edge of the village, to a location called Dudkov (see Figure 1.2). The chosen site had been part of the holdings owned by the Hungarian noble Sinai, who had been expelled and expropriated by the reconstituted Czechoslovak regime. Both Romani and white informants agree that the move had been approved by the *výbor*, the post-war equivalent of a municipal council, which gave it an official imprimatur that the descendants of Józef and Alžbeta interpret as an invitation extended to their parents to join the village community. Villagers, on the other hand, underline the precarious legal status of the site, which had made it something of a no man's land.

Significant as it was, the relocation to Dudkov didn't dramatically alter the status of the two families. They remained landless squatters dependent on the benevolence of their white patrons. The move had indeed lessened their social and physical distance from the village proper, but Dudkov was still very much on the geographical margins of Svinia. Several years later, in the early 1950s, after the new settlement had expanded to seven huts, its residents left it for another site of uncertain legal status, a meadow called *farská lúka* adjacent to the main road connecting Prešov with central and western Slovakia. The land on which the relocated colony was built had also been expropriated from its former owner—this time the Roman Catholic Church. Villagers who recall the details of the situation assert that the "colonists" had been invited by communist officials eager to demonstrate the progressive consequences of the repressive measures to which the church had been subjected.

But the sojourn on the south-western margin of the village was also short. Increased road traffic exposed the unkempt settlement to the eyes of a growing number of passersby, and the white establishment began to look for a less conspicuous location. In the words of one of the sons of Józef Kaleja, "We were close to the road. We had wooden huts, and it was visible. High officials [*pánové*] from abroad travelled there, and all of that was visible...."[9] So the upwardly mobile families of Józef and Alžbeta were compelled to move once more, this time to Svinia's north-eastern edge where the upper settlement was to become their home for the next 30 years. I will return shortly to the circumstances leading to this move, and its consequences for local inter-ethnic relations.

The entrenchment of socialism during the 1950s

The 1950s were a decade of profound social, political, and economic transformations in Svinia as well as other rural communities. It was very much a liminal period during which people who had just gone through the traumatic experience of the war were now subjected to the numerous changes imposed by the communist régime while simultaneously still clinging to traditional values and norms generated during, and for, a different era. Accustomed to a life whose contours had been delineated by personal talents and concerns, the villagers were challenged by post-war developments to surrender a great deal of their autonomy to an intrusive new political order, and to redefine their notions of progress. The biggest and hardest change introduced during this unsettling decade was the collectivization of agriculture. It was initiated by a preparatory committee of eleven landowners in 1951, but it took until 1959 before the agricultural cooperative could be officially established with 91 members (*Pamätná kniha*, vol. I, p. 72). The almost decade-long process wouldn't have been completed without considerable economic and social pressure, including escalating taxes and levies imposed on recalcitrants. As the traditional agricultural economy began to crumble, new forms of employment opened up in industrializing towns and cities nearby. By 1951, 31 of Svinia's residents commuted daily to Prešov where they had found work in new plants and enterprises (*Rada MNV*, 13.2.1951; 236/1).[10] The narrowing of the gap between town and village—one of the major goals of state socialism—was encouraged by new forms of patronage (*patronát*), such as the linking of the agricultural cooperative with selected enterprises in Prešov that offered technical assistance and managerial advice to their inexperienced rural colleagues. Such linkages and direct recruitment campaigns (*nábor*) increased the interest of villagers in abandoning agriculture in favour of industrial work—a trend desperately needed by new enterprises that suffered from chronic labour shortages (*Rada MNV*, 13.2.1951 & 12.6.1951; 236/1).

The building of socialism brought many other far-reaching consequences. Development plans drawn up locally during the 1950s included numerous public works, such as improvements to the municipal infrastructure and a sprawling complex of buildings required by the agricultural cooperative. Other innovations included the gradual electrification of the entire village, improved bus connection with Prešov, asphalt roads, a post office, a daycare, and numerous cultural initiatives, such as film screenings, a public reading room, and a dance and theatre ensemble (*Plénum MNV*, 21.1.1953 & 10.5.1956; *Rada MNV*, 10.11.1960; 236/1). In line with the socialist promotion of collectivism, local residents were expected to make a contribution to the attainment of these improvements in the form of *brigády*, a uniquely period-specific concept that may be loosely translated as "volunteer labour." Those who failed to put in a sufficient number of hours could, under extreme circumstances, face criminal charges (*Plénum MNV*, 1.2.1956; 236/1).

The socialist transformation also required participation in a large number of political organizations and initiatives designed to promote and entrench the new political order. Svinia saw the establishment of Young Pioneers at the local elementary school, a commission for world peace, people's courses in Russian, and a chapter of the Czechoslovak-Soviet Friendship Society; and there were numerous public displays of political correctness, such as the annual commemorations of various revolutions, liberations, and other important events in the calendar of socialism. An impression of the size and significance of some of these may be gained from the fact that the 1952 May Day celebration in Prešov was expected to draw 150 participants from Svinia, equipped with appropriate pictures and banners supplied by the municipal administration (*Rada MNV*, 29.4.1951; 236/1).

But the implementation of these far-reaching changes didn't pass unchallenged. Svinia in the 1950s was still in many respects a traditional rural community whose members looked askance at the profound transformations of the post-war era. In spite of rapid modernization, few villagers listened to the radio or read newspapers, and their main medium for the dissemination of information remained the customary village drummer who made his daily rounds through the community and announced public news at designated locations (*Plénum MNV*, 6.6.1954; 236/1). Elements of local custom also continued to leave an imprint on the composition and work methods of the municipal administration. Although officially "modernized" by its incorporation into a regional apparatus that was closely supervised by the communist party, Svinia's local government continued to be staffed by amateur administrators who had difficulty with written Slovak and refused to address their fellow villagers by the imposed title of "comrade." The lack of socialist-style professionalism displayed by the officials of this transitional era can be seen in the honesty, and often sympathy, with which they entered the complaints of their constituents in the reports compiled at every public meeting. These reports testify to the overwhelming opposition of the vast majority of Svinia's farmers to the principles of collectivized agriculture and the imposition of discriminatory quotas on "independents." These two related topics dominated public discourse throughout the 1950s (*Plénum MNV*, 6.1.1955 & 9.11.1956; 236/1). On a number of occasions, public officials not only sympathized but clearly collaborated with their constituents against the implementation of orders issued from "above." For example, the request for a list of "village magnates" (*dedinský boháči*—the Slovak equivalent of Russian *kulaks*) was answered with the firm assurance that no such people existed in Svinia (*Rada MNV*, 4.3.1953; 236/1). A directive demanding the redistribution of excessive residential space in favour of local paupers triggered a similar reply, which suggested that Svinia had neither excessively rich nor excessively poor inhabitants (*Rada MNV*, 10.4.1958; 236/1). This and other instances of insufficient local attention to goals formulated at higher levels led to rebukes from regional cadres (*Plénum MNV*, 25.2.1956 & 20.6.1960; 236/1).

In view of widespread opposition to the collectivization of agriculture which, as the backbone of the local economy and society, affected everyone rather profoundly, one must ask what convinced the people of Svinia to eventually join the "forces of progress"—as they manifestly did between the late 1950s and early 1960s. I think that the promise of material advancement made by the communist régime had much to do with that. Although not stricken by poverty, pre-war Svinia was not a village of excessive wealth either, and its location in the most backward region of Czechoslovakia placed very real limits on economic development. The introduction of socialism changed that very quickly. Aided by massive state subsidies and the communist inclination toward megalomania, eastern Slovakia was soon dotted with huge steel mills, cement manufacturing plants, chemical factories, and other industrial complexes. The impact of the post-war industrialization and large-scale modernization on rural communities was swift and comprehensive. Agricultural cooperatives not only encouraged more technologically advanced forms of production—by means of tractors, combines, threshing machines, and so on—but also acted as a channel for the electrification and mechanization of the countryside. An improved transportation network, essential for the region's industrialization, increased the mobility of villagers and enabled them to take advantage of employment outside the home territory. Innovations in the construction industry encouraged the building of larger and more durable homes equipped with running water, bathrooms, and indoor plumbing.[11]

It was this material progress that eventually convinced Svinia's residents of the blessings of socialism. They continued to bemoan the loss of independence brought about by collectivization, but they recognized and took advantage of the perks presented by the rapid modernization of their village and region. Here and there a particularly free-wheeling innovator indulged in the acquisition of genuine luxuries—by 1959 Svinia boasted its first television set and its first private automobile (*Pamätná kniha*, vol. I, p. 83)—but for the majority the most desirable and coveted by-product of socialism was without doubt the opportunity to obtain a new house. Svinia's municipal annals overflow with records related to the desire of the villagers to take advantage of a comprehensive strategy encouraging rural residents to participate in "individual home construction" or, as it came to be abbreviated, IBV (*individuálná bytová vystavba*). This scheme provided access to interest-free loans, modern and affordable building material, and, where necessary, cheap lots. The first phase of IBV between 1952 and 1958 saw the construction of at least 19 new family residences (*Stavebné povolenie, MNV*, 1953–1960; 236/2), and many more would have been built had it not been for shortages of construction material (*Plénum MNV*, 23.7.1957; 10.5.1956; 236/1). Several families benefitted from the expropriation of the Hungarian nobleman's estate. The subdivided park around his château yielded three sizeable building lots and two respectable fields, which were then sold to needy villagers for a pittance (*Prídelová listina, MNV*, 1958; 236/2).

What role did local Roma play in the initial phase of the socialist modernization of Svinia? First of all, during the 1950s they still constituted a relatively small minority. Toward the end of that decade Svinia was inhabited by approximately 600 whites and only around 75 Roma (*Domovná kniha, MNV*, 236/1). Some 50 per cent of the Roma consisted of children under the age of 15, and there were at least 15 men of employable age, that is, between 18 and 59 years. This is an important piece of information, because the very first historical reference to Roma during this period, made at a municipal council meeting in 1951, postulates that "the village [has] many gypsies who have not been employed, and who don't want to [accept work]" (*Rada MNV*, 12.6.1951; 236/1). This remark was made in conjunction with a request from the Prešov district administration for workers willing to take up jobs in the city's new industries. Although the Svinia municipal council appealed to the district administration to coax local Roma into accepting work, the situation doesn't seem to have changed. A 1955 entry in the village chronicle claims that Roma "have difficulty entering into regular employment. Only [two] go to work, and the rest remain at home" (*Pamätná kniha*, vol. II, p. 49).

These first public complaints about the deficient work ethic of local Roma are embedded in a wider framework of general dissatisfaction with their lifestyle and conduct. In 1954, the municipal council instructed several officials to "again visit the homes of children of gypsy ancestry and convince the parents to provide them with the most necessary clothing, so that they can participate [in school] regularly" (*Rada MNV*, 30.1.1954; 236/1). The following year, the village chronicler observed,

> Very unfavourable conditions prevail among citizens of gypsy ancestry who don't want to adjust to a more cultured way of life.... They receive handsome incomes together with family allowances. They don't know how to manage money properly, they often get drunk, and so their families suffer from a lack of food and clothing. Children go to school irregularly, they have nothing to put on, and often nothing to eat. These residents are called to order by local officials, but that helps little. They know their rights very well, but they refuse to submit to civic duties. (*Pamätná kniha*, vol. II, p. 49)

In 1958, when the same source reviewed the first decade of socialism, it concluded that "the standard of living of workers in our village is higher, except for citizens of gypsy ancestry who are adjusting to progress with difficulties" (70).

When the country-wide settlement liquidation and dispersal campaign reached Svinia, officials more or less naturally targeted the "secessionists" around Józef and Alžbeta Kaleja. These people had chosen to leave the backward ancestral settlement, and there was some evidence of their adaptability. Indeed, the male leaders of the emigrants, Józef Kaleja and his brother-in-law Ján Čikala, had been explicitly exempted from the unfavourable comments about the work ethic of their kin (*Pamätná kniha*, vol. II, p. 49). In 1959, on the eve of Czechoslovakia's official attainment of socialism, it was therefore this group that was chosen for the integrative experiment. It entailed its relocation from the visible but peripheral location by the main road to a more central site slated for future development. The agricultural cooperative was about to begin construction of its headquarters here, and a new residential subdivision was taking shape right across the road. Here, the Prešov district administration set aside five building lots of 480 square metres each and assigned them to senior members of the two resettled Romani families (*Prídelová listina, MNV,* 1959; 236/2).[12] It put in electricity and a well and began construction of five small family homes made of cinder blocks (*Pamätná kniha,* vol. II, p. 87), of which only two seem to have been completed. This modest development constituted the apex of the "liquidation and integration" program in Svinia. It was one of its first applications in the Prešov district, and higher-level authorities expressed satisfaction with its results (Jurová 1996:600, 620–621).

Uneven development during the 1960s

The first decade of official socialism began, appropriately, with the election of a new chairman of the municipal council. Nominated by the communist party, this new official was not only politically reliable but also well educated—two qualities that seem to have been in short supply during the transitional 1950s. Virtually overnight, the parochial, idiosyncratic, and ungrammatical Slovak of previous council secretaries gave way to a techno-political jargon spiked with buzz words and slogans imported from Bratislava and Prague. Appropriately, the cosmopolitan "comrade" replaced more traditional terms of address during council meetings.

The reformed leadership presided over a rapidly modernizing community. Attracted by high wages and a diversity of opportunities, more and more villagers chose to work in Prešov. The number rose steeply from 31 in 1951 to more than 100 in 1961 and 150 by 1965 (*Pamätná kniha,* vol. II, pp. 97, 162). This led to an acute shortage of workers, especially younger ones, at the expanding agricultural cooperative (*Rada MNV,* 28.12.1960; 236/1). Although the latter couldn't compete with Prešov-based enterprises in the wage sector, it sought to attract young employees by offering technical upgrading for drivers of trucks, combines, and bulldozers (*Rada MNV,* 11.5.1961; 236/4), as well as modern flats in new apartment buildings (*Plénum MNV,* 5.5.1965; 236/3). Whereas the rental flats were

intended for young families without sufficient resources for the purchase
of a house, older and better endowed residents continued to take advantage
of the subsidized IBV scheme at an increasing rate. The number of private residences built during the 1960s averaged 5 to 7 annually (*Pamätná
kniha*, vol. II, p. 174). Commenting on the rising standard of living, the
community chronicler stated that "village life is improving. There are better employment opportunities, people are striving to build new homes and
to acquire attractive furnishings, home appliances, radios and televisions"
(106). By the end of the decade, the 164 households of Svinia boasted 14
motorcycles, 20 automobiles, 116 television sets, and 139 washing machines
(203). Another telling innovation was the replacement in 1965 of the village
drummer with a state-of-the-art public announcement system that reached
every section of the rapidly expanding and modernizing village (*Plénum
MNV*, 23.12.1964; 236/3).

The spectacular improvements attained by Svinia's inhabitants during
the 1960s weren't shared by the Roma. Indeed, every time the community
chronicler took note of the rising standard of living of his neighbours, he
felt compelled to add a qualifying note to the effect that "only citizens of
gypsy ancestry live very backwardly, even though they too have employment opportunities. Alas, they don't know how to take advantage of them;
they are irregular in work, and they don't know how to manage finances
effectively" (*Pamätná kniha*, vol. II, p. 106). To be sure, the first decade
of proclaimed socialism began with optimism that the "gypsy question"
would be settled satisfactorily. The first few meetings of the new, techno-
cratic municipal council assembled in 1960 carried out several measures
to that effect. A commission "for the solution of the gypsy question" was
appointed and charged with several tasks, including a monthly inspection
of the health situation among the Roma, and assistance with problems
related to hygiene and school attendance (*Plénum MNV*, 15.7.1960; *Rada
MNV*, 8.7.1960; 236/1). Another committee, called the "penal commission," was struck in order to help maintain public law and order (*Plénum
MNV*, 15.7.1960; 236/1), and elementary school teachers were instructed
to increase their attention to Romani children on account of a growing
incidence of "various forms of filthiness" and jaundice (*Plénum MNV*,
21.9.1960; 236/1).

The higher level of attention paid to Roma during this period bore some
fruits in the area of employment. By 1965 the agricultural cooperative
employed five Romani men and planned to hire three more in the near

future (*Rada MNV*, 11.5.1965; 236/4). But this achievement seems to have been triggered largely by the aforementioned shortage of workers suffered by the cooperative as well as orders from the Prešov district administration. The municipal council had to pledge "to pay attention to the gypsy question, and to see to it that all male labour force of gypsy ancestry be employed among the members of the agricultural cooperative" (*Rada MNV*, 11.5.1965; 236/4). Although significant, the new work opportunities gained by Roma did little to change their social status. One reason for this was the nature of the work carried out by Romani employees of the cooperative. Without exception, they received jobs that required no skills beyond pure strength, reasonable endurance, and some degree of manual dexterity. They ended up feeding animals, loading heavy sacks of potatoes and other agricultural produce onto trucks, and shovelling manure from stables. More technical and better-paid positions they were barred from, ostensibly on account of their deficient education.[13] The Prešov district authority attempted to do something about that by instructing the school principal to organize literacy classes for adult Roma (*Rada MNV*, 10.11.1964; 236/4), but the outcome of this initiative remains unrecorded.

The frequency with which the district government—itself an extension of regional and national communist party networks—intervened on behalf of the Roma demonstrates a widening rift between higher-order policies formulated in support of Romani integration and the willingness or ability of local cadres to implement them. Having initiated and financed the 1959 resettlement of Svinia's category II Roma, the district government now expected their transformation into fully integrated, category I, members of the community. Cognizant of the tendency of some local authorities to sabotage such efforts, the district delegated officials to attend municipal council meetings dealing with Roma-related issues, ensuring that local cadres remained faithful to the party line. The records of such meetings show a growing tendency of the local administration (and population) to adopt a punitive and segregationist approach toward the Roma, which challenged the district representative, his superiors, and the policies they sought to implement. By 1964, this conflict manifested itself in a number of "reactionary" initiatives sought by vocal segments of the villagers and at least implicitly endorsed by the municipal council. One of these was the demand for special, that is, segregated classes for Romani pupils, which was justified largely in terms of their lack of hygienic habits. The demand was first expressed publicly by the school principal—a highly regarded communist—in a written recommendation to the municipal council. He justified it by pointing out that "children of gypsy ancestry come to school very dirty, which makes it unpleasant to put them together with the children of ordinary citizens" (*Rada MNV*, 10.9.1964; 236/4). Dirtiness, clearly, wasn't the only problem. The principal went on to complain about his inability to ascertain some children's dates of birth and even correct names.

There is no record of the outcome of the discussions concerning the request for segregated classes that went on between the chairman of the municipal council and his district superiors (*Rada MNV*, 19.9.1964; 236/4). Older Roma, though, claim that a partial segregation was implemented around this time. It effectively split the body of students into three groups. Ethnic Slovaks and children from the upper, "integrated," settlement attended school in the morning, but although they seem to have shared the same classrooms, Romani students were confined to the back rows where interaction with the teacher was limited. Children from the lower settlement came to school in the afternoon after the other two groups had left. Middle-aged Romani assimilationists who grew up in the upper settlement see this arrangement as proof of their superior position compared with the backward *cigáni* from the lower settlement.

In spite of its somewhat elevated status, it was only a matter of time before the upper settlement became the object of segregationist sentiments as well. In late September 1964 a public meeting of 41 concerned citizens "demanded to solve the resettlement of citizens of gypsy ancestry." Their proximity to the agricultural cooperative was seen as causing "serious danger of fire" and as increasing the potential for theft of property held by the enterprise (*Plénum MNV*, 20.9.1964; 236/3). As we shall see shortly, it wasn't long before this still somewhat vague challenge turned into a firm determination that the candidates for integration and assimilation be returned to the ancestral settlement inhabited by their backward kin.

Criminalization and segregation in the 1970s

The era of progress and accumulation of wealth begun in the 1960s reached its zenith during the 1970s. The quality of life of the villagers continued to improve with the addition of several public buildings, includ-ing a large community hall (*kulturný dom*, literally "house of culture"), a fire hall, a school canteen, and a complex of three apartment buildings for the employees of the agricultural cooperative. A managed waste disposal site was set up and trash bins distributed to all households in an effort to promote public cleanliness (*Plénum MNV*, 12.12.1977; 236/3). The main street received a coat of asphalt, and plans were made for the upgrading of side streets as well (28.8.1979). The construction of private residences continued at a frantic pace, hampered only by a chronic shortage of building lots (27.10.1978; 21.12.1979). By 1975, the village boasted 150 radios, 142 television sets, 38 automobiles, 89 residents with completed high-school education, and 14 with university degrees. Residents employed outside Svinia numbered 273, and 117 homes had been constructed since the end of the war, of which 89 had been completed between 1961 and 1975 (*Pamätná kniha*, vol. III, pp. 4–6, 173).

The progressive gentrification of Svinia's inhabitants can also be seen in changing tastes and pastimes. *Kultúrnost'*, a concept that denotes urbanity and civilized deportment, became a much sought-after ideal. It explained the need for sidewalks, so that children didn't have to wear rubber boots to school (*Plénum MNV*, 16.3.1976; 236/3), as well as daily broadcasts of admonitions directed at those citizens who continued to disregard public ordinances about proper garbage disposal (18.7.1975). The quest for *kultúrnost'* was behind the construction of the municipal "house of culture"—with its reading room and dance floor—and the annual quiz "what do you know about Lenin?", which coincided with the role model's birthday (21.4.1978). The changing sensibilities of the urbanizing villagers—more than 200 of whom by now commuted daily to the nearby metropolis of Prešov—prompted a request to replace the traditional live music played during funerary processions with recorded classical tunes beamed from the public broadcast system (24.4.1979), and they inspired monthly dances and annual competitions organized by Svinia's gardeners' club. The 1971 event attracted 91 participants (*Pamätná kniha*, vol. II, p. 218).

The Roma continued to fail the test of *kultúrnost'*. They partook of few of the material and cultural improvements attained by the villagers, and they began to be perceived no longer as a nuisance but as a deviant element that threatened the welfare and security of the community. The growing concern with deviant and, increasingly, criminal tendencies of the Roma is mirrored in the establishment of a second municipal committee with direct responsibility for the "gypsy question," the "commission for the protection of public order." This body came to function more or less explicitly as the defender of the local white establishment against challenges emanating from the two settlements. The expanding racialization of local views of public order and criminality was justified by periodic reports that charged the Roma with the majority of misdemeanours and crimes (*Plénum MNV*, 26.8.1972; 263/3). For example, the commission for public order convened twelve times during 1977, and most of the four to six infractions and offences it discussed each time were attributed to Roma (*Pamätná kniha*, vol. II, p. 71). A more precise count, carried out in 1979, established an annual ratio of 30:14 against the Roma (*Plénum MNV*, 24.10.1979; 236/3).

Although most of the infractions seem to have been relatively minor—such as school absenteeism or outstanding fees for dog licences—there were also some serious problems that hadn't occurred before. One of them was the rapid growth of the Romani population and the consequences this had for its coexistence with the ethnic Slovak majority. Local officials began to pay attention to this issue in the early 1970s when they started to keep race-specific birth records. Although "white" births continued to outnumber Romani ones, two factors somewhat dampened the advantage: a growing tendency of young villagers to move permanently to Prešov and other urban centres, and the perception of a substantial immigration of Roma from other locations (*Pamätná kniha*, vol. III, p. 93). Although municipal records don't indicate an unusually large wave of newcomers, contemporaries clearly viewed the "foreigners"—who had arrived, for the most part, to marry local Roma—as a cause for concern. They were dubbed *privandrovalci* (akin to "trashy newcomers"), and vocal villagers periodically called for their expulsion (*Plénum MNV*, 22.4. & 30.6.1977; 236/3). But, with or without the immigrants, the number of local Roma kept going up, and this placed considerable pressure on their housing situation. They responded with the construction of new huts, which, having been erected without building permits, aroused further indignation among the villagers (*Plénum MNV*, 22.6.1978; *Pamätná kniha*, vol. III, p. 93).

The second serious obstacle impeding relations between the two groups was a rising incidence of public disturbances attributed to Romani "troublemakers," and of displays of "uncultured" behaviour. These ranged from drunkenness and unbecoming conduct (*Plénum MNV*, 30.6.1977 & 21.4.1978; 236/3) all the way to unhygienic and unsavoury habits allegedly indulged in by most Roma. As the community chronicler put it, the "culture [*kultúra*] of living, eating, [and] dressing is below the dignity of people living in a socialist society" (*Pamätná kniha*, vol. III, p. 73).

The explosion of complaints directed at Roma during the 1970s was accompanied by a diversification of strategies employed to solve the "gypsy problem." On the one hand, higher-order assimilationist policies continued to be felt and applied at the local level. The buzz word here was "re-educa-tion" (*prevýchova*)—occasionally even "re-birth" (*prerod*)—of the Roma as a means to improving inter-ethnic "coexistence" (*spolunažívanie*), and several initiatives were dedicated to this lofty goal. For example, the Svinia chapter of the Slovak Women's Association organized cooking and baking classes for Romani women (*Pamätná kniha*, vol. II, p. 307), and even the combative members of the public order commission seem to have conducted occasional educational meetings with Roma receptive to advice concerning "improved hygiene, school attendance and coexistence" (*Plénum MNV*, 24.10.1979; 236/3). From time to time, the municipal council invited a Romani "singers' group" to perform at some festive gathering (25.8.1978).

This "soft" approach didn't please a growing number of hard-liners who demanded strict disciplinary measures against deviants, such as a ban on the sale of liquor to Roma on days when they received salaries (*Plénum MNV*, 24.10.1979; 236/3), fines for parents whose children didn't attend school (*Plénum MNV*, 5.5.1972; *Pamätná kniha*, vol. II, p. 244), and police intervention in matters affecting public order and the presence of unreg-istered "immigrants" (*Plénum MNV*, 30.6.1977 & 21.4.1978;). Records of municipal council meetings suggest that a call for punitive action was usu-ally made by a few vocal hard-liners who convinced other assembled citi-zens and eventually council members themselves of the need to adopt firm measures against "gypsy fellow citizens" (*cigánskí spoluobčania*), as Roma came to be officially designated toward the end of the decade. At times, this led to disagreements with the council chairman who was, after all, expected to defend and propagate the official approach based on the notion of vol-untary resocialization governed by the methods of "socialist humanism." For example, the chairman objected to the council's ban on liquor sales to Roma, which was clearly a discriminatory measure that violated the law (24.10.1979). District authorities were also aware of the rising tendency to bypass official guidelines, and a review conducted in 1979 criticized the municipal council for shortcomings in its dealings with Roma, including inadequate attention to the need for resocialization (21.12.1979).

In the end, the two approaches coalesced into something of a compro-mise that defined a local strategy for coping with Roma that has prevailed until now. "Strategy" is perhaps too technical a term for this rather implicit consensus based on two seemingly contradictory goals embraced by the majority of the villagers. It was anchored in the conviction that while local

Roma should be encouraged to acquire *kultúrnost'*—by means of education, regular employment, and imitation of their Slovak neighbours—the coexistence of the two groups was so problematic that only pervasive physical and social segregation could guarantee a reasonable degree of harmony. In essence, this local preference may be dubbed "integration through segregation."

We have already seen that the local segregationist preferences came to be publicly affirmed only five years after the biggest integrative measure in Svinia's history, namely the 1959 foundation of the upper settlement. This resolve strengthened in the course of the late 1960s, and by the early 1970s this was no longer a demand for *moving* the upper settlement to some less problematic site but rather a specific plan calling for the *return* of its residents to the ancestral location by the river (*Plénum MNV*, 18.12.1971 & 9.2.1972; 236/3). This plan was endorsed by the municipal council and forwarded to district authorities for approval (9.2.1972). Although clearly segregationist, the *vox populi* expressing this demand was not indifferent to the aspirations of Roma for a higher standard of living. This was recognized as a legitimate need, and soon after passing the segregationist motion the council approved a plan for the construction of fifteen family residences earmarked for Roma (*Pamätná kniha*, vol. III, p. 51).

Probably the best illustration of the application of the "integration through segregation" approach comes from educational initiatives spearheaded during this decade. Although the number of Romani children was still relatively small (in the 1971–72 school year, only 35 out of 257 students were Roma), their failure rate was disproportionately high, and this was seen as a cause for concern (*Plénum MNV*, 23.6.1972; 236/3). Fines meted out to reduce absenteeism, the determination of the public order commission to pay special attention to Romani students (5.5.1972), and the principal's study trips to schools with high ratios of Roma (22.4.1977) all indicate a sincere effort on the part of local officials to make a contribution to the raising of *kultúrnost'* among the young generation of Roma. These initiatives were complemented by the establishment of a subsidized daycare/kindergarten program where young children were expected to acquire essential skills and habits necessary for successful participation in school. But in line with local sentiments, both institutions were segregated along ethnic lines, with separate "gypsy classes" firmly entrenched during the 1970s (22.4.1977; *Pamätná kniha*, vol. III, p. 78). With the informal system of previous decades no longer prevalent, by now the school principal employed psychological tests and medical examinations as justification for the isolation of Romani students (*Plénum MNV*, 28.8.1979; 236/3). The Romani daycare/kindergarten, at first situated in the same building as its white counterpart, was moved in 1978 into separate quarters that minimized interaction between the two groups (25.8.1978; 22.12.1978; *Pamätná kniha*, vol. III, p. 143).

This overview would remain incomplete without attempting to explain more fully the apparent failure in Svinia of Czechoslovakia's integrationist policies. Partial successes notwithstanding, such as improved school attendance and work-force participation, the main goals of residential integration, improved standard of living, and assimilation were not attained, and the socio-economic differences separating Roma from ethnic Slovaks kept growing rather than diminishing. The failure is the more puzzling in view of the initial successes experienced during the 1950s by the adaptable category II secessionists who had managed to attain partial acceptance into the white community. What prompted the villagers to give up on the seekers of integration, and to do that so quickly after the establishment of the upper settlement?

Discussions of this topic with former inhabitants of that site reveal two main themes. One revolves around the assertion that white residents of Svinia became distant and hostile to the Roma in consequence of their rising standard of living in the 1960s and 1970s. As they grew rich, the argument goes, the villagers began to demean and belittle the Roma more frequently. The second theme underlines the role of internal developments among the secessionists, in particular the coming of age of a new generation of young parents who failed to maintain adequate discipline among their children. This, it is said, led to increasing incidents of disruptive and destructive behaviour within as well as outside the upper settlement and of hostile confrontations with white neighbours. It would be foolhardy to expect to isolate a single cause of as complex a problem as the inter-ethnic conflicts of the 1960s and 1970s. But it is worthwhile to pursue and develop the two themes a little further in order not only to shed additional light on local relations, but also to understand more fully the social dynamics of the reunited Romani community.

A striking feature of the upper settlement was the remarkable differentiation that took place among the descendants of the two founding couples. Unlike the lineages engendered by the three remaining Kaleja brothers on the ancestral site, which developed into similar clusters of garbage-pickers

Figure 3.1. Residents of the upper settlement in front of one of the cinder-block houses built by district authorities

Magda Balčáková

and other low-status semi-untouchables, the two upwardly mobile lineages established by Józef Kaleja and his sister Alžbeta proliferated into groupings marked by considerable status distinctions and dissimilar proclivities. Here we need to follow only two of these strands. They both descend from Józef Kaleja and his wife Mária in the form of a son and a daughter and their respective offspring. While the daughter raised a family of successful money-lenders and assimilationists, her brother propagated aggressive fighters whose relations with the villagers have been riddled with conflict. According to the head of the money-lending assimilationists, a woman whom we have already encountered under the nickname Velryba, it was the aggressive conduct of her brother and his children that precipitated the eviction from the upper settlement. A few excerpts from the biography of this bellicose man are instructive.

Velryba's brother, whom I shall refer to as Mirga, is one of the oldest local Roma. Born in 1936, he belongs to a generation that experienced both traditional white patronage and the growing tensions of the socialist era. Like all his contemporaries, he had Slovak godparents who helped out with his upbringing according to their ability and, to some extent, self-interest. In Mirga's words,

> I used to work there [in his godparents' household] with horses. I liked horses very much, and I worked with them there, fed cows, brushed horses, took care of cows, spread manure in fields, I worked for them from childhood, and they raised me.... I went there all the time, because I wasn't really interested in school.... Even father visited school and asked the teacher why I am stuck all the way in the corner. "There are no benches" [answered the teacher]. "What do you mean, no benches, when I see empty benches ... and gypsies, all of them sit in the back corners, and all whites in the front, so the whites are learning, and the black race they are just listening, or what?"—"if you don't like it, your children need not come to school" [said the teacher], and then father said that the boy will grow up on his own.... So, I grew up there [in the godparents' household], there was lots of food, they even gave some to mother: flour, potatoes, milk, cabbage, they gave it to her and said that I earned it through my work. Yes, they were good people,... and for my work they gave mother food,... and at times they even hauled firewood with horses from the forest, so I would have enough for the winter.

The protection provided by Mirga's white patron extended beyond the household, as the following excerpt makes clear:

> When I grew up a little, I started to get into fights with *gadje* boys. I would venture onto the street, and right away these boys, big ones, began to beat me. So I told P. [the employer], "Uncle, I cannot take the horses and wagon along the street, because they throw rocks at me." And he went and complained to the chairman [of the municipal council], because old P. was a decent fellow, and also the aunt, and so he complained, "how come my servant can't take out manure, because they pelt him with rocks?" [But this didn't help] and I made myself a fine stick,... put it in the wagon,... and jumped off and chased them with the stick, and beat them on their legs and arms, and

that's how I grew up.... And they went and complained to P.,
"Uncle, he beats us."—"Leave him alone then, he won't let
you beat him up. I told him not to let you beat him. If you beat
him, he will beat you back."

By the time he was in his late teens, Mirga ended up in prison for a series of
public disturbances that included fights in the village tavern. This began a
pattern that lasted for much of his adult life. While many of the skirmishes
may have been fairly innocuous brawls, there were also some major altercations, such as this one, precipitated by a conflict between Mirga's father
and the police:

> [The police arrived to interrogate father, but he was absent]
> and I had been drinking a little and was having a nap at the
> table.... And the chairman says, "this one here is such a good-
> for-nothing, came back from work and is drunk already.... get
> him out and give him a fine one." And we had a small garden,
> and people from the cooperative, and our neighbours living
> around us, they were watching what was going to happen to
> me. They began to beat me [with a stick], but I was drunk
> and didn't feel any pain, and so one kicked my nose with a
> heavy boot, and that was like a lightning, and I look up and
> see a uniform, and K. [the chairman] is screaming, "beat him,
> he is a lout, he should be killed!" And they went on kicking
> me.... I wanted to defend myself, but they shot me in the leg.
> Even soldiers arrived, police with dogs, and then they took me
> away.... They took me to Prešov, hauled me into the basement,
> tied me onto a table, and one had a bucket with water, and
> they asked me to choose a truncheon.... And they tied me to
> the table and began beating. They went on and on, and when I
> fainted, they threw water over me and beat me again.

According to Mirga, the injuries sustained during this beating required extended hospitalization, followed by a prison term that kept being extended
until it reached seven years.

What caused Mirga's ongoing tensions with the villagers? One of his
daughters—herself a bellicose woman with a long history of prison
terms—claims that the villagers felt provoked by Mirga's refusal to "play

the part of a gypsy." A strong and good-looking man who liked being nicely dressed, Mirga let his hair grow long, put on a game-keeper's suit, and challenged white rule in the village tavern. As Mirga's daughter sees it, "Father was never afraid. He went to the tavern as if nothing, to order a beer, he sat down, and there were drunk whites, and they watched him, and those who were angry at him tried to provoke him. And they provoked him until he began to fight."

It was one such encounter in the village tavern that seems to have led to the brutal police intervention recalled above by Mirga. His daughter's more detailed account runs as follows:

> [After a fight had erupted in the tavern] they brought a big tire from a tractor and pressed him underneath. But father didn't give up, somehow he managed to free himself, started to run, but they blocked him, and he had to stand there and fight. And then they even called the police—not two or three but the entire detachment. Sixty or eighty of them arrived. They circled us [at the upper settlement], with sub-machine guns in hands and masks on their heads. We were scared when we looked at them. They asked father to surrender, and when they saw that he wouldn't, they began to shoot.... And father stood there with an axe ... and told them that he hadn't done anything and won't give himself up for nothing. Father stood by the door, and there was a hole through which they shot him in the leg, but even then he didn't surrender. Then we went and called an ambulance, because father was bleeding, but the police officers were masked as physicians. And that's how they got him. They started to beat him already in the ambulance, even though he was wounded.

These extraordinary events are not recorded in the white annals of local history. But there seems to have been a clear pattern of rising tensions and inter-ethnic violence throughout the 1970s. Mirga's daughter supplies another illustration of a riot triggered by an altercation at the "house of culture":

> Once we wanted to go to a dance. We paid for everything, but we hadn't danced once when some drunk white boys started:

"gypsies out!" And S. [another fighter from the upper settle-
ment] was also there, and—simply, a fight. We ran ... straight
home, and when we saw that we were being pursued by many
whites, we began to scream at the Roma to get out of their
houses.... There were many, many drunk [white] boys. We
had huts there, and they began breaking windows with rocks,
and so on.... The one [Romani woman] who died recently, she
was a terrific fighter who wasn't afraid even of men.... And she
stood behind the well with a pitchfork, waiting for the white
one. She pierced him with the pitchfork, because there were
many whites. Old ones were joining young ones, and we were
not so many, because ours was a small settlement. So mothers and children had to run.... We had to escape and hide, and
only men stayed behind to guard our homes.... They [*gadji*]
kept threatening us that they will return the next day, that
they won't leave us in peace. And we ... were hiding up in the
forest, with the children, even small ones who had just been
born,... we simply didn't know when they might come for
us.... That's what they did back then. They kept threatening
us, and we kept escaping....

What we see here is clearly an unexpected situation whereby the
adaptable Roma of the model settlement targeted for integration became
embroiled in much more serious inter-ethnic conflicts than the universally
despised category III *cigáni* left behind at the creek. I dare not assign blame
for the rapid deterioration of relations, since for every Romani account of
white cruelty there is a conflicting account supplied by the villagers, but
wish merely to point out that the planned integration of Svinia's Roma engendered brutal encounters that have left no trace in the official records.[14]

The 1970s ushered in an era of escalating ethnic polarization. Whereas
old Juraj Kaleja, the founder of the Svinia settlement and the ancestor of
most of its residents, used to be treated to drinks by villagers entertained
by his feats of strength—one of which was to carry a brick tied to his penis—his "integrated" sons and grandsons found themselves increasingly
isolated from their former patrons. Godparenthood as an effective mechanism for bridging the ethnic divide came to an end with the termination of
the traditional rural economy and the former direct dependence of Roma
on white patrons.[15] The music band of the "creek people," which used to

entertain the villagers at every important event, fell victim to new tastes and rural gentrification. The village tavern, officially open to "blacks" and "whites" alike, became the centre of disputes unless the "blacks" kept to their own table in the corner, known literally as *cigánsky stol*. School, an institution that was expected to indoctrinate young citizens with the ideals of socialism, succumbed to segregationist pressures and contributed instead to the entrenchment of apartheid.

Manifestly, there were exceptions to the rising tide of mutual distrust and ethnic isolation that marked this era. There were instances of friendship and even courtship between Roma and ethnic Slovaks. But their number was exceedingly small, and few solidified into lasting bonds. For example, it happened only once during living memory that a village woman eloped with and eventually married a Rom. The man hailed from a Magyar-speaking community in southern Slovakia, and he was a skilled worker with a steady job in a Prešov factory. Still, the relationship caused a scandal. Here is how the woman's mother describes the onset of the liaison in the 1970s:

> Once she brought him home, and I recognized it right away. "Luba, you must be crazy, it is a gypsy, I saw it right away." And father says, "what do you want here?" and chased him out.... So he left and hasn't come back since. And she went after him. I told her, "Luba, you have become deranged, you want to live with a gypsy."

Luba (the name has been changed) happened to have a son from a previous failed marriage, but she left him with her mother and moved in with her "gypsy," with whom she had four more children. Once she tried to come for a visit in order to show her parents their grandchildren, but Luba's son intervened and asked her never to return with his "bastard" half-siblings. Now, some twenty-five years later, the son still lives with his grandmother, remains single, and continues to feel the stigma cast over the family by his mother's behaviour. Luba's father is dead. According to his widow, "[he] got stroke because his daughter eloped with a gypsy." Luba herself lives in Prešov and suffers from her husband's alcoholism and their children's criminal inclinations. As the grandmother puts it, "they steal;... that's already in their blood or something like that."

The deepening crisis in the 1980s

The chasm separating the two groups in all areas of life continued to widen during the 1980s. On the one hand, ethnic Slovak residents went on raising their standard of living, which allowed them to build and renovate more homes, install telephones, acquire more cars and modern appliances, and, in the realm of public services, construct a new school and civic building. New wealth derived no longer mainly from employment opportunities outside Svinia; the local agricultural cooperative attained better profitability, which translated into higher incomes for its members. By 1989, the cooperative had become the second most successful enterprise of its kind in the entire Prešov district, increasing its profit margin by more than 150 per cent (*Plénum MNV*, 22.2.1989; 236/3). On the other hand, the living conditions of the Roma continued to deteriorate. As the village chronicler pointed out at the opening of the decade, they all lived in one-room dwellings and suffered from alcoholism and poverty. Although she sought the reasons for their low standard of living in a postulated lack of ambition, discipline, and endurance, the scribe warned, "They are, however, members of our society, and if they are not helped as soon as possible to attain more cultured living conditions, worthy of socialist humanity, then we shall pay a much higher price within a few years" (*Pamätná kniha*, vol. III, p. 175).

This prophetic warning is echoed in Svinia's official annals. Whereas the "gypsy question" had occupied a marginal position in municipal council meetings during previous decades, by the early 1980s the white establishment seems to have realized that it had become a problem that overshadowed everything else. In 1980, after decades of paying mere lip service to higher-order ordinances and resolutions related to Roma, the municipal council finally recognized that its efforts in this field had brought forth "opposite results" and requested assistance from the Prešov district administration with "this most burning problem of the village" (*Plénum MNV*, 29.8.1980; 236/3). The problems felt during the 1980s were a continuation and escalation of unresolved issues from previous decades, which need not be repeated in detail. The unkempt appearance of the upper settlement and the disorderly conduct of its residents drew the ire of white neighbours who objected to heaps of garbage (23.4.1982), loose dogs (18.2.1982), and illegal migrants from other communities (*Rada MNV*, 18.3.1982; 236/5). Growing numbers of unruly and criminally inclined children and adolescents were identified as the cause of a rising tide of vandalism, thefts, break-ins, and assaults (*Plénum MNV*, 22.6.1984; 236/3). The school continued to experience problems with discipline, absenteeism and failure, which magnified as the contingent of Romani students more than doubled from 60 in 1982 to 132 in 1988 (*Rada MNV*, 12.2.1982; 236/5; *Pamätná kniha*, vol. III, p. 253). An apparently new problem specific to Romani youth appeared in the form of drug abuse (*toxikománia*) around the mid-1980s (*Pamätná kniha*, vol. III, p. 267).

The measures taken to address the escalating "gypsy questions"—pluralized since the early 1980s—were, for the most part, applications of methods introduced in previous decades. As the conduct of local Roma increasingly shifted into the realm of deviance and criminality, police assistance became more frequent and thorough (*Plénum MNV*, 24.8.1984; 236/3; ibid., 28.2.1986; ibid., 4.5.1988). Police now often cooperated with municipal and school officials in identifying and evicting unregistered residents, punishing the parents of truant children, or rounding up and destroying dogs at large. This was in addition to their involvement in more serious conflicts, samples of which were provided earlier. Segregation also endured as a preferred local answer to inter-ethnic problems, one that assumed an increasingly important role as a defence mechanism against the rising tide of Romani criminality. In 1985, the "special classes" for Romani students were delegated to a dilapidated former manor house, creating more space for the "white school" that moved into a new building soon thereafter (*Pamätná kniha*, vol. III, p. 252).[16] The daycare/kindergarten unit serving Romani children was relocated again, finding a permanent home just outside the lower settlement (*Plénum MNV*, 26.4.1989; 236/3). A canteen dispensing lunches to Romani students was set up, at some distance from the school cafeteria reserved for white customers (*Pamätná kniha*, vol. III, p. 195). Early on in the 1980s the entire upper settlement was surrounded with a high fence (*Plénum MNV*, 26.4.1985; 236/3), triggering demands from the neighbours of the lower settlement for a similar protective device (24.8.1984).

These measures brought only temporary relief, and as the crisis deepened, so did the despair of the villagers and their official representatives. Confrontations between angry citizens protesting against a growing number of perceived and genuine injuries inflicted by the Roma and municipal council members called upon for assistance rarely led to anything more than empty resolutions or invocations of higher authorities. Increasingly

Figure 3.2. The fence enclosing the upper settlement

Magda Balčáková

helpless, the council kept demanding "the involvement of other organs and institutions" (22.6.1983), especially the Prešov district authority (24.6.1987), but toward the end of the decade even the much higher levels of regional and national governments (22.2.1989).

The "higher organs" appealed to for help did respond in a number of ways, but these did not satisfy local whites. In January 1986, the Prešov district authority convened a public meeting in Svinia at which it chastised the municipal council for not attaining satisfactory results "in the realm of ... gypsy problems and coexistence" (*Plénum MNV*, 31.2.1986; 236/3). District officials discussed new relevant Communist Party policies and announced new measures to be taken to ensure their local implementation. A key element was the appointment of a field social worker who was to conduct an experimental project aimed at the acculturation (*skultúrnenie*) of Romani residents (*Pamätná kniha*, vol. III, p. 254). A member of a larger team composed of higher-level experts, the social worker was to pioneer a new approach characterized by knowledge of the "gypsy mentality," readiness to assist, and willingness to overcome prejudice (255).[17]

Rebukes from higher-order authorities did not soften the local opposition to the upper settlement. We have seen that by the early 1970s the municipal council had listened to demands for a merger of both settlements. But the plan had failed to gain endorsement from district officials and had remained in limbo for several years (*Plénum MNV*, 25.8.1982; 236/3). During the early 1980s—propelled by the expansion of the agricultural cooperative complex through the construction of a new administration building—the plan finally received approval from district authorities on the condition that the returnees would receive building lots for the construction of decent houses (20.4.1983; 22.6.1983; 26.8.1983). The chosen location was a vacant section of land adjacent to the lower settlement and bordered by the river. By 1984, five lots had been prepared for construction, and thirteen were being readied (24.8.1984). What remained to be solved was the issuance of building permits and the financing of the actual construction for which the beneficiaries were known to lack the necessary means. A year and a half later, however, construction activity was said to have been "delayed" because the Roma were "not interested in it" (28.2.1986). One more year passed by without much happening, followed by the announcement that an eight-unit apartment building was being planned as an apparent replacement for the construction of individual family homes. It concluded with the laconic observation that "We are not able to secure the solution of the gypsy question in the municipality in accordance with our desires" (22.4.1987).

A more precise outline of the solution being sought for the ubiquitous Romani housing problem was given by a representative of the Prešov district authority at the end of 1987. The construction of single-family residences was still on the drawing board, but the number had shrunk from eighteen to four. In addition, there were plans for the immediate construction of two eight-unit apartment buildings, a daycare/kindergarten facility, and presumably some shops alluded to by the phrase "necessary services" (18.12.1987). Half a year later, the two apartment blocks were almost finished, and the same district official proclaimed that although they had solved the housing shortage only partially, single-family dwellings "for gypsies [sic] are not being carried out, and are not desired [by them], even when there are building permits" (29.6.1988). Roma were to become participants in another scheme of subsidized housing, KBV (*kolektívna bytová výstavba*), which facilitated the construction of collectively occupied apartment buildings.

The last phase of the resettlement project was completed in the spring of 1989 with the actual physical move—or, rather, *expulsion*—of the residents of the upper settlement. One week before the act, the municipal council had agreed to "arrange a lecture for the gypsies [sic] about new ways of living, hygiene, the culture of eating, and so on" (*Rada MNV*, 22.3.1989; 236/5). Neither this lecture nor any other preparation for the impending move took place. According to Romani witnesses, the "liquidation of the upper gypsy settlement"—to use the official terminology—in the early morning of 1 April 1989 happened unannounced and caught them entirely off guard. Watched by police officers, they received a couple of hours to move out their belongings, which were loaded onto waiting trucks and transported to the lower settlement. Bulldozers then levelled their homes to the ground. In agreement with the principles of the settlement liquidation program, the owners were compensated for the loss of their homes with amounts ranging from 5,000 to 10,000 crowns, roughly the equivalent of two to four months' salary, though this is disputed by many. At the next municipal council meeting, the chairman reported that the task had been carried out as planned, thanks to "the understanding of higher organs" and "effective assistance" rendered by the agricultural cooperative and the police force (*Plénum MNV*, 26.4.1989; 236/3).

Although the resettlement received laudatory endorsement from the village chronicler, she admitted that there were many problems caused by construction defects—most apartments had not been completed and lacked functioning toilets, floor coverings, and paint—and tensions between the original residents and the newcomers (*Pamätná kniha*, vol. III, p. 268). The relatively spacious and comfortable apartments became a coveted commodity and a thorn in the side of those who had been bypassed. Although the district authority consented to the construction of two further apartment blocks, completed in 1990, the 32 units couldn't absorb the more than 400 people who now dwelled in the reunited community. The effectively homeless migrants from the upper settlement moved into most of the new apartments, while the resident "creek people" remained, for the most part, in the primitive huts they had occupied all along.[18]

The completion of the relocation project led to new problems for the villagers. Instead of two relatively small settlements, they now faced a rapidly growing agglomerate of undesirables which, thanks to its modern infrastructure, attracted transient Roma from other settings. Soon after the move, concerned citizens began pointing out "free movement of foreign gypsies in the municipality" (*Plénum MNV*, 21.6.1989; 236/3) and demanding that the expanded settlement be fenced in (26.4.1989). An employee of the municipal council summed up the new state of affairs with these sombre words: "the situation has worsened in [school] attendance, employment, fluctuation. They refuse to report for sterilization, and acculturation (*skultúrnenie*) hasn't occurred in all families in spite of the new apartment buildings given to them" (21.6.1989).

The post-communist era

The 1989 "Velvet Revolution" brought to power a new, western-oriented political elite that quickly transformed Czechoslovakia into a democratic country espousing the pluralistic values of western Europe and North America. The post-communist reforms led to a formal recognition of the Roma as a full-fledged ethnic minority endowed with the same cultural and political rights as their counterparts in western Europe. In spite of temporary setbacks caused by sporadic outbursts of xenophobia and jingoism, Slovakia's declaration of independence in 1993 didn't bring about any major departure from the course set in the early 1990s, and both successor states of Czechoslovakia have followed similar policies and have experienced similar difficulties in their encounters with the Romani minority (Guy 2001).

The political, social, and economic deregulation that characterized post-communist Slovakia freed the Roma from many externally imposed restrictions and policies, such as the settlement liquidation program and numerous assimilationist measures that had curbed the free expression of Romani cultural identity (Davidová 1995). Yet the same extirpation of conventions enshrined by the over-regulated communist regime also unleashed forces and tendencies that have come to pose a serious threat to the well-being of Roma. Among those particularly acutely felt in Svinia are unemployment, openly expressed racial intolerance and discrimination, and local government reluctance to pay adequate attention to the special needs of its Romani constituents. Foremost among these, the introduction of a free-market economy, combined with the abandonment of socialist conventions under which the state guaranteed employment for every able-bodied citizen, severely reduced the chances of under-skilled and under-educated Roma of retaining their jobs, let alone finding new ones. Hampered by their very real educational deficit as well as the rising tide of intolerance and ill will of the majority society, the bulk of Slovak Roma found themselves redefined as parasites and confined to rapidly deteriorating urban and rural ghettos where welfare payments often represent the only remaining link between an unwanted minority and a disinterested and hostile majority (European Roma Rights Center 1997; Guy 2001; Radičová 2001).

Let me illustrate this process of post-communist marginalization with examples from Svinia. When I arrived there for the first time in the spring of 1993, most of the integrative measures implemented during the socialist era had already been abandoned, with no replacements in sight. The subsidized "gypsy" daycare/kindergarten, which had been relocated to the margins of the lower settlement shortly before, had disappeared without a trace. Its former principal blamed the demise on the alleged reluctance of Romani parents to pay the modest fees introduced after the fall of socialism. The newly elected municipal council, freed from the interference of higher-order bodies, had laid off the social worker supervising the integration and acculturation of local Roma. The successful Romale band had been dissolved and its instruments locked up in the "house of culture." The two commissions keeping track of Roma-related problems and issues had been dissolved. The recently constructed apartment buildings in the expanded lower settlement had been left partly unfinished, and their occupants were in the process of signing an agreement with the municipal authority absolving it of any responsibility for the upkeep of the already deteriorating infrastructure. With the exception of a handful of employees of the agricultural cooperative, all local Roma had lost their jobs. Those who had worked in Prešov-based state enterprises had fallen victim to the cutbacks accompanying their privatization. The agricultural cooperative eventually transformed itself into a collective of owners-farmers, and Romani employees were replaced by family members and other villagers who had lost their jobs elsewhere. As the unemployment ratio within the Prešov region climbed to almost 25 per cent, the uneducated rural Roma everywhere paid the heaviest toll. They ended up as clients of a complex and impersonal welfare system administered out of Prešov and designed to provide an unwanted minority with the bare essentials of life.

Upon my arrival, I was struck by the rapidly growing divide between the Roma and their ethnic Slovak neighbours. Six months earlier, the country had declared independence, and members of the majority society felt optimistic about their future. The industrial city of Prešov was being transformed into a major commercial and cultural centre that its inhabitants hoped would attract western investments and tourists. Within a remarkably short period of time, the historic town centre was beautifully restored and equipped with a plethora of pensions, restaurants, and shops that compared favourably with similar establishments in western Europe. A growing number of residents were beginning to vacate the uniform apartments provided by socialist authorities in indistinguishable grey-concrete highrises situated along the perimeter of the city and to invest in spacious and at times luxurious family residences inspired by German models. Germany and other western countries also served as the inspiration for the choice of clothing, household appliances, and cars adopted by the new, forward-looking, middle class.

During the ten years that I have been involved with the Roma of Svinia, the modernization and westernization that are so visible in Prešov and other cities have made significant inroads into the countryside as well. Following trends well known to North Americans and western Europeans, attractive villages in the vicinity of Prešov have seen an influx of city-dwellers seeking a less stressful environment, inspiring, in turn, local residents to upgrade their homes instead of moving to town. Municipal authorities have had to adapt to this trend by introducing some of the services and amenities traditionally associated with city life, such as sewer lines, piped water and water treatment plants, public lighting, reliable garbage disposal, recreational facilities, and so on. Although its large number of backward Roma makes Svinia a less appealing location than other nearby villages, it has had its share of post-communist modernization. In the ten years following my arrival, the municipality has put in new, underground telephone cables that enable every household to obtain a telephone line. It has connected the entire village to a natural gas pipeline in order to encourage the installation of gas-fired central heating systems. It has introduced a dependable garbage collection system, and it is planning to hook up Svinia to the water and sewage treatment network of Prešov. These public attempts at raising the local standard of living have had their correlates in private initiatives, which include the set-up of small businesses and, above all, extensive renovations of many existing residences and the construction of around 15 new ones. Although the "gypsy problem" dampens their optimism, most local villagers are clearly planning to stay on—their often radical claims to the contrary notwithstanding.

It is the growing wealth and spreading modernity of the majority society that make the marginality and poverty of the Roma stand out so starkly. Disappointed by the meagre results of the communist-era assimilation campaign and preoccupied with their own advancement, the villagers haven't felt it necessary to try and stop, let alone reverse, the collapse of the few integrative mechanisms that prevented the Roma from sliding into complete social isolation. Thus, when I arrived on the scene a mere three years after the demise of communism, I encountered a mob of alienated and embittered outcasts who beseeched me to alert the world community to their plight (see Scheffel 1999). What ensued became a strange collaborative relationship which, against all odds, culminated in the largest and most comprehensive community development project carried out in a Slovak Romani settlement. Generously funded by the Canadian International Development Agency between 1998 and 2003, the Svinia Project, as it came to be known, was to equip rural Roma—in Svinia and, later on, a number of other settlements— with the skills required for a successful participation in the rapidly changing society that surrounds them. While this is not the place for a detailed discussion of the project and its results, a short overview helps illuminate the underlying causes of Romani marginality during the post-socialist era.

The project began with the move of my family to Svinia in the late summer of 1998. We arrived on the heels of a devastating flood that had destroyed much of the settlement. Of the 60 huts, only ten were left standing, and 253 homeless residents had to be moved into big army tents provided by the government as emergency shelter. What happened next sheds some light on the treatment of Roma by post-communist municipal and state authorities. The municipality received emergency funding from the central government in order to set up temporary housing for the 253 homeless persons. The municipality, in turn, purchased 40 used construction portables at a price of approximately $500 per unit. But although the transaction was sealed in early September and the portables arrived in the settlement soon thereafter, it wasn't until late October that the units were ready for occupancy. In the intervening six weeks, while the homeless shivered under canvas during an unseasonably cold autumn, a small crew of white workers engaged in sporadic and unpredictable repairs required to make the units habitable. When, finally, the mayor gave the signal, the homeless found themselves in cramped quarters about the same size as their former residences but without stoves, furniture, and electricity. Woodstoves and beds arrived soon thanks to donations from the European Union, the International Red Cross, and the Czech government. Electricity, however, proved more elusive. By the spring of 1999, there was still no power installed, and most residents had reverted to the proven but illegal method of wiretaps hooked up to the apartment buildings.

With 50 huts gone and only 40 units of temporary housing purchased by the municipality, the former hut-dwellers found themselves in a state of serious overcrowding. In view of regulations requiring that emergency housing provide at least three square metres of living space per person, the portables should not have accommodated more than 160 people. In reality, everybody was squeezed in, regardless of laws or regulations. Ironically, the municipality could have purchased at least seven more units with money donated by a private foundation, but instead the council voted to use the donation to compensate a handful of white "victims" whose cellars had been flooded. A fraction of the gift went to the parents of a drowned Romani girl, with the stipulation that it be given in the form of food coupons in order to prevent it from being squandered on frivolities. In the spring of 1999 the municipality received another chunk of emergency funding from the central government, earmarked for the elimination of damage caused by the flood. The council used it to pave the square between the four apartment blocks—an area of approximately 500 square metres—and to apply a new coat of asphalt on the main street of the village—a stretch of a kilometre or so that had never been flooded.

The flood of 1998 imposed unexpected challenges on the design and execution of the project that I directed. My "clients" had been traumatized by the event, and for a long time much of what we did in the settlement responded to the need of dozens of families to rebuild their shattered lives. But the flood and its aftermath also helped me understand the position rural Roma occupied in the hierarchy of priorities of local, regional, and state authorities, and opened my eyes to the technical dimension of community development. On the latter point, a particularly instructive experience was the construction of a small housing complex intended to relieve the overcrowding among the former hut-dwellers. Financed by the Dutch government, the structure came to be known as Dutch Portables, and it consisted of twelve used units akin to those provided by the municipality except that it was overarched by a single roof. The portables were transported to the settlement in the fall of 1998, and then a crew of six technicians took six months of full-time work to join them together and assemble the prefabricated roof. The installation of three shower stalls—the first ones in the entire settlement—dragged on for another five or six months, largely because the whimsical plastic water taps that the plumbers insisted on couldn't withstand normal handling. Finally, in the summer of 1999, the complex was ready for occupancy, but the mayor kept delaying its

Figure 3.3. A meeting between Canadian and Slovak officials concerned with the Svinia Project

opening in anticipation of the installation of legal electricity. For reasons that I never fully understood, this took another full year—until the late summer of 2000. This means that the completion of this modest construction project required almost two years.

The extremely slow pace at which construction took place and the shoddiness of its execution made me appreciate the circumstances under which the settlement liquidation program of the socialist era would have operated. The stories of the apartment-dwellers about incomplete furnishings and dysfunctional bathrooms suddenly began to make sense. And, indeed, when we laid bare the maze of sewer lines and septic tanks installed in the late 1980s, we discovered entire sections of pipe that had not been joined to the main sewer line and angles connecting other sections that defied not only the rules of plumbing but also the law of gravity.

Post-communist Slovak politicians acknowledge mistakes made in the past and the urgent need to pay serious attention to the many problems faced by rural Roma. Indeed, since the creation in 1995 of an inter-ministerial post charged with the task of coordinating efforts in this realm, the government has adopted three major strategies and has issued innumerable reports, edicts, and ordinances intended to help the integration of Roma into mainstream society (Scheffel 2004a). Accordingly, when I approached the first plenipotentiary for Romani affairs during the preliminary phase of the project, I was assured full support and generous financial participation by the Slovak government.[19] Yet once the project had been approved, and activities were unfolding for which government assistance would have been helpful, promises made earlier evaporated. Throughout the five years of the project the involvement of the national government was limited to rhetorical assurances and delegations dispatched to Svinia to coincide with visits of Canadian diplomats. Without fail, the delegates arrived in expensive black limousines and aroused indignation in the mud-covered residents of the settlement. Their visits never lasted more than a couple of hours.

The relationship with the municipal government proved more constructive. From the very beginning, the project operated at the invitation of the municipal council, and all major steps were discussed with it. The collaboration, though, was fraught with problems. For one, the council comprised reform-minded members of democratic parties as well as reactionary nationalists and demagogues whose views of the Roma were openly racist. Because these two factions rarely agreed on anything, our day-to-day dealings with the council were channelled through the mayor, an educated and highly motivated technocrat who was aware of the need to tackle the Romani issue with determination. The mayor accomplished things, but the precarious balance of power that he maintained exposed us to constant criticism from his numerous opponents.

The main reason why the mayor and his allies on the council backed the project was the prospect of solving the ubiquitous housing problem in the settlement. The project's mandate included cooperation with Habitat For Humanity International, the well-known American builder of affordable homes for disadvantaged groups around the world, which established its first Slovak franchise in Svinia in 2000. The intention was to assist the municipal council in gaining political and financial backing for the construction of new homes for all local Roma; Habitat undertook building up to 30 houses in the hope that the remainder would be financed by the Slovak government. The sequence in which this plan was hatched is of some significance as it reveals much about the climate in which decisions affecting the Roma are made. Fortified by the prospect of substantial national and international assistance, the council took the first public step in September 1998, a mere two months after the flood. This step saw the distribution of a mail-in ballot in which the council requested feedback on the location of the proposed housing site. The ballot allowed two choices: upgrading and expansion of the existing settlement, or relocation of all Roma to a much bigger but also more isolated site at some distance from the village. This seemingly democratic survey had one major flaw: instead of distributing the ballot to all registered voters, the council decided to limit the survey to legal residences. Thus, instead of reaching almost 750 whites and Roma, the ballot ended up in 207 households. However, because only a part of the Roma live in residences recognized as "official" by the municipality, the poll happened to reach all of Svinia's 151 ethnic Slovak households, but a mere 56—roughly one half—of the Romani ones. Predictably, of the 199 returned ballots, eighty per cent voted in favour of moving the settlement to a new, remote site.

This crass example of deciding "about us without us"—as Romani activists have dubbed post-communist paternalism—is by no means exceptional. Although the only people affected directly by the housing plan were Roma, the council made no effort to involve a single individual from the settlement in the planning process. On the contrary, all public meetings devoted to this issue were advertised in a manner that ensured that as few Roma as possible would find out about them, let alone attend.

The 1998 vote was only the start of a long and onerous process that generated much ill will and ended in a fiasco. Throughout the subsequent four years, the mayor accomplished some remarkable feats. He identified in excess of 100 owners of the parcels of land on which the future community was to be located, and by 2002 he had managed to purchase the lion's share of the twelve hectares required for the realization of the plan. This was a most impressive achievement in a region where land ownership remained poorly defined in consequence of expropriations during the communist era, and where few people were willing to participate in a scheme intended to benefit Roma. Fortunately, the mayor had big politics on his side, because as the date of Slovakia's entry into the European Union came nearer, bureaucrats in Bratislava and Brussels accelerated their previously snail-paced efforts on the "Roma front" and promised to finance the entire housing project. Astutely, the mayor and the architectural firm retained by him designed the scheme in a way that ensured that the water and sewer pipes planned for the Romani residences had to run through the white village and hence would provide its inhabitants with amenities that would have otherwise remained outside their reach. Playing up the long-standing desire of the villagers to gain access to a central water and sewer system, the mayor thus managed to present the project as a development that would contribute to the modernization of the entire village.

Although the mayor had backers among local whites, there were many who continued to oppose the resettlement scheme. Their opposition ranged from purely xenophobic and at times racist sentiments to well-grounded doubts about the mayor's assurances that the old settlement would be levelled to the ground after the completion of the new community. Skeptics doubted how this might be accomplished and predicted that Svinia would end up having two settlements again, serving as a magnet for homeless Roma from the wider district.

Although the council had approved the project on several previous occasions, yet another—final—vote was to be held in the fall of 2002. By then the atmosphere was so charged with pent-up frustrations and animosities that council members refused to cast the decisive ballot and agreed instead to leave the decision up to the next council, which was to be elected in December 2002. The results of the ensuing municipal election harked back to the communist era. After three terms in office, the reform-minded mayor was soundly defeated and replaced with a conservative member of the populist and Roma-hostile HZDS party. The same fate befell all of the reformist members of the council. One of the first acts of the new council was to terminate plans for the Romani housing development and to abrogate its cooperation with the foreign and domestic constituents of the Svinia Project.

This single vote by a bunch of bitter reactionaries and political neophytes quashed the hopes of more than 700 Roma that they might escape the squalor of the present settlement. Although the mayor-elect and her council professed a desire to "do something" about the evidently subhuman conditions prevailing in the Romani ghetto, two years into their term nothing of significance has happened to validate this election promise. On the contrary, improvements left behind by the Svinia Project have been allowed to decay or disintegrate altogether. For example, the showers installed in the Dutch Portables no longer dispense any water, because the well that used to feed them has been plugged up with debris. The Romani daycare set up by the project and absorbed into the local school district has new chairs donated by the European Union, but the flushing toilet—the only such device in the entire settlement—and the water taps for cold and hot water no longer serve any purpose since the pipes froze and broke during the winter of 2003–4. The municipality, which is responsible for the

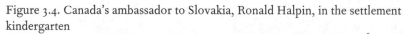

Figure 3.4. Canada's ambassador to Slovakia, Ronald Halpin, in the settlement kindergarten

physical operation of the facility, has failed to attend to the minor problem, presenting the dedicated staff with a dilemma: should they report the breakdown to public health authorities, which would then shut down the school, or should they keep quiet in the hope that the mayor will eventually spend the modest amount of time and money required for the repairs? Either way, the precarious state of the daycare demonstrates the double standard that continues to be applied by Svinia's municipal administration. It is plainly unthinkable that the village daycare/kindergarten attended by white children would be neglected in a similar way.

The situation after the 2002 municipal elections brings into focus an interesting and very important departure from the way in which the marginality of rural Roma was dealt with during the communist period. Back then, as we have seen, local authorities felt the watchful gaze of the Party and its subordinate structures at every administrative level. Of course, higher-order policies were not implemented without some degree of local resistance and sabotage. But there were mechanisms in place to ensure that core principles of the socialist modernization program were put into effect. Thus, permanent and decently rewarded employment was created for all able-bodied Romani men—and quite a few women. Levels of literacy and basic education were raised significantly. The health situation of rural

Figure 3.5. Romani students having lunch at school. Their access to the cafeteria is limited to a window in the wall

Roma improved dramatically. And although the enforcement of "law and order" within the labyrinthine environment of the settlement proved difficult, major crimes were dealt with swiftly and fairly. Today, 15 years after the collapse of the communist system, the fight against Romani marginality is conducted differently and, in many cases, less effectively. Even though Slovakia, as a newly inducted member of the European Union and a host of other bodies and associations dedicated to the furtherance of human and minority rights, has adopted legislation prohibiting discrimination of any kind, the Roma of Svinia—and many other communities—are exposed to daily injustices that would be unthinkable in advanced democratic societies. To repeat just a few particularly blatant examples, Romani students are segregated from their white colleagues at school, they are denied access to the school cafeteria and gymnasium, and they have no opportunity to study in their own language—despite constitutional guarantees. Children and adults alike lack access to clean drinking water and adequate housing, and their residency rights are openly flouted. Increasingly, they confront a discriminatory legal system that metes out disproportionate punishment for property infractions against white society while major crimes committed within the Romani community go unnoticed. For example, usury and incest are serious transgressions that can be carried on virtually openly

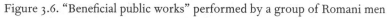
Figure 3.6. "Beneficial public works" performed by a group of Romani men

without the fear of any legal sanction, but the theft of a pig from a white farmer by a repeat offender earns a prison term of five years.

What accounts for the inadequate protection of minority and human rights in Svinia? To a large extent, the open discrimination of local Roma is the result of the democratization of Slovak society in recent years. Within a relatively short period of time, the country's public administration has been radically overhauled and, responding to demands from the European Union, decentralized. With the canon of communism left in tatters, and the formerly powerful institutions of the central government demolished or transformed into regional entities lacking any teeth, municipal authorities have emerged as the new level at which important decisions are made and enforced. The EU-inspired grassroots democracy flourishing in Slovak towns and villages today is not, however, necessarily favourably inclined toward the special needs of the Roma. In settings such as Svinia that are marked by a long history of inter-ethnic animosities and conflict, the pandering to the local *vox populi* can mean that the white (electoral) majority effectively blocks access not only to externally funded and administered modernization projects, but even to indigenous institutions such as schools and daycares, which, since the devolution of powers in the early 2000s, have come under local control (Scheffel 2004a).

During my last extended visit in the winter and spring of 2004, I had ample opportunity to observe the ongoing collapse of Svinia's Romani community. In addition to the developments mentioned above, Slovak Roma have been hit extremely hard by a wide-ranging reform of the welfare system introduced in February 2004. Ostensibly presented as a much-needed incentive for long-term welfare recipients to rejoin the labour force, the legislation has dramatically reduced social assistance and family allowance payments without, however, creating new work opportunities. With regional unemployment levels still well above 20 per cent, the Roma of Svinia and similar settlements face very bleak prospects indeed. Since a modal family of six is expected to survive on the equivalent of less than $300 per month, the low-cost apartments and huts of the ghetto have become the unavoidable destiny of all but a few residents. While their Slovak neighbours build new houses and renovate old ones, the Roma keep sinking deeper and deeper into the mud. The only exception has been a handful of money-lenders who have acquired used automobiles, cellular telephones, and other tokens of middle-class prosperity. The most unscrupulous leader of this pack has even managed to purchase a run-down house in the village, which he is now in the process of renovating.

But it would be unfair to blame the post-communist malaise exclusively on the ill will and counter-productive policies of the majority society. The social and economic collapse of Svinia's Romani community has been accelerated by its residents' inability to make use of new opportunities and to overcome the fragmentation of interests and loyalties that characterizes the local settlement. From the very beginning of my involvement, I spent more time and energy on defusing conflict between hostile family groups and their leaders than on any other aspect of the project. An early attempt to create a steering group composed of community representatives failed on the petty jealousies of those who felt left behind. Another attempt at helping a group of struggling activists set up the settlement's first properly incorporated non-governmental organization expired after the deputy chairman and his followers pulled out of the structure in order to create a rival one. The newly formed daycare/kindergarten almost collapsed because, literally, the mothers from two hostile factions disagreed about the kind of yogurt to be served for breakfast. The operation of a carpentry workshop set up in order to help people renovate their living quarters was hampered not only by the poor work morale and paltry skills of the young trainees but also by the unanimous rejection by all factions of a talented

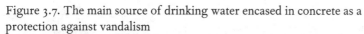

Figure 3.7. The main source of drinking water encased in concrete as a protection against vandalism

but widely disliked man as foreman. His numerous opponents—including two of his brothers—threatened to burn down the facility unless I hired a white outsider. A similar squabble erupted over the appointment of a local woman as a teacher's aide at the daycare.

The inability of local Roma to place long-term community interest above the immediate desires of individuals and families was matched by petty and not-so-petty acts of vandalism directed against innovations introduced by the project and people associated with it. A sturdy pump set up to provide safe drinking water failed to survive a single night. Subsequently, the entire contraption had to be encased in a heavy concrete coat reinforced with steel bars. A playground constructed beside the daycare building was demolished within a few weeks. Even the heavy rubber tires suspended on chains from steel rafters as a substitute for wooden swings ended up partially burnt on a trash heap. The picket fence enclosing the playground disintegrated during the first winter. It provided a handy supply of firewood. Fifty latrines built of high-grade lumber were quickly taken apart and used as additions and porches for the cramped portables. The project lost a valuable and generous partner, Heifer Project International, after two years of trying to help a dozen families establish small livestock operations. In spite of the

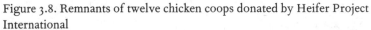

Figure 3.8. Remnants of twelve chicken coops donated by Heifer Project
International

construction of fortified and guarded chicken coops, the donated chickens
kept disappearing during nightly raids, leading, in turn, to accusations
and fights. An experiment in community gardening met a similar fate. A
solitary gardener held out for two years and managed to raise bountiful
crops of healthy carrots, onions, and potatoes. In the end, though, he too
succumbed to the jealous and violent disposition of his neighbours. By
now, the former garden has become a desolate patch of mud littered with
rubble.

A particularly telling illustration of the challenges presented by the settlement's social environment is provided by our failed experiment in community sanitation. Its centrepiece was the introduction of a regular trash
collection from each individual household, an innovation much desired by
most residents. Unlike the villagers who had access to leased metal trash
cans emptied by a garbage truck every second week, the Roma had been
excluded from this service, relying instead on a big container deposited
on the edge of the settlement and hauled away at irregular intervals. Most
people had complained about the distance they had to walk in order to
reach the collective disposal site—not more than 100 metres from the most
remote point—and had requested that the village-wide trash collection
be extended to the settlement. The mayor eventually agreed to this, and

a surprising number of residents came forward to take advantage of an arrangement subsidized by the project. Everybody willing to pay a nominal lease received a brand new metal trash can equipped with a heavy chain and padlock to prevent its theft. But when the garbage truck appeared in the settlement on its inaugural run, the crew discovered that only a handful of cans had been placed outside for pick-up. A random check revealed that many of the new clients used the receptacles as tables and rat-proof storage bins for food. Another run the following week found a few more cans outside, but the contents were frozen solid and couldn't be emptied. This kept repeating itself in spite of warnings not to dump liquid waste into the cans. Then another problem appeared as the electricity-starved occupants of the temporary portables had begun to string up home-made wiretaps between their residences and nearby apartments. The garbage truck couldn't pass under the low-slung live wires, and when their owners refused to extend the lines a little higher, the mayor lost his patience and aborted the experiment.

Notes

1. Viewed from a contemporary perspective, though, the numbers still were rather small. A census held in 1775 established 277 Romani families, with slightly more than 1,000 heads, for the entire Šariš region. The largest concentration prevailed in the historic centre of the district, Velký Šariš, which accounted for twelve families (Horváthová 1964:132). For other parts of Slovakia, see Šalamon (1992), Kollárová (1992), and Mann (2001).

2. The capital city of Budapest is not included in these figures.

3. A meeting that took place in August 1953 provides a sampling of the demands voiced by the "autonomists." Hosted by the Czechoslovak Writers' Union and attended by literati, academics, government officials, and Romani representatives from across the country, the assembly called for the recognition of a Romani nationality and for the creation of a standardized Romani language that would be preserved and taught in schools and universities. Demands were made for the participation of Roma as teachers and social workers, for the establishment of a Romani-language newspaper, and for the rejection of assimilation as the desired outcome of state intervention (Jurová 1993:35). Similar views were repeated at gatherings held throughout the early 1950s (ibid.:36–37).

4. This law was inspired by similar legislation being promulgated in the Soviet Union at the same time.

5. The numbers of Roma and Romani settlements cited for Slovakia during the 1950s are not always consistent and must be used with caution. For example, 1954 figures used by the ministry of health indicate a population of 81,931 Roma dispersed over 1,204 settlements with 11,121 dwellings (Ministerstvo zdravotníctví 1957) while 1956 figures used by another government agency postulate 1,305 settlements inhabited by approximately 95,000 Roma (Jurová 1996:404), and a throughout reliable contemporary survey puts the combined number of rural *and* urban Roma at around 80,000 (Osvetové ústredie 1956:7). The same variance prevails at the regional level. While one government source claims 50,593 Roma for all of eastern Slovakia in 1955 (ibid.:7), another government report, released in 1958, postulated a figure of 66, 371 for the same region (*Zpráva o súčasnej situácii* 1958). The warning that figures used during the early phase of socialism must be used with caution is underlined by the questionable quality of the high-profile census of itinerants carried out in February 1958 as a post-facto justification for the law banning itinerancy. It counted 43,465 Romani itinerants (*Kontrolní zpráva* 1958)—clearly a vastly inflated number.

6. As early as 1952, the ministry of the interior issued eight principles that were to be followed by all state agencies in their dealings with Roma. Based on the premise that Roma constituted an oppressed minority in need of special attention and treatment in order to overcome centuries of marginalization, the directive expected municipal and regional authorities to provide all necessary means for the attainment of full integration into mainstream society, including appropriate employment, housing, and schooling. Two of the principles prohibited all forms of discrimination in official relations and public life. Specifically, they forbade differential access to theatres, restaurants, bars, shops, and other institutions (Ministerstvo vnitra 1952).

7. Contemporary documents show that this selectivity was at least partly due to concerns about the use western propaganda could make of these islands of apparent poverty and exclusion. This is why highly visible tourist areas, such as the High Tatra resorts, were at the forefront of the settlement liquidation program (see Jurová 1996:387).

8. Post-1989 censuses introduced the western method of determining ethnicity by self-declaration, rather than designation by an external author-

ity as was the rule during the socialist era. Since many Roma adopt the view of the majority society that Romani ethnicity is something to be ashamed of, they tend to present themselves to census-takers as ethnic Slovaks or Hungarians. This tendency is responsible for the apparent shrinking of the Romani population reflected in the 1991 and 2001 census.

9. This explanation is compatible with practices mentioned in note 7. On the other hand, the informant's sister, who continues to exaggerate the integration of the secessionists, attributes the move to the villagers' concern about the safety of the site after a near-fatal road accident.

10. *Rada MNV* refers to the inner circle of the council of Svinia's municipal administration. *Plénum MNV* refers to the entire council. The material presented here and subsequently under these headings is found in the archive of the Prešov district—*okresný archív*—under the indicated file and box number. The dates refer to the day on which the council meeting was held.

11. The socialist era introduced a process of industrialization of unprecedented magnitude. Slovakia's agricultural production increased by 47 per cent between 1950 and 1960, while the proportion of rural population fell from 42 to 27 per cent (Kirschbaum 1995:235). Electric power output rose by almost 250 per cent between 1955 and 1959, enabling the electrification of 600 villages and 1,000 agricultural enterprises (*Ročenka* 1960).

12. The same year saw the assignment of seven building lots of 800 square metres each to white applicants. The lots were bigger but, at 2,400 crowns apiece, also more expensive than the ones given to the Roma (*Pamätná kniha*, Vol. II, p. 82).

13. In 1965, two tractor drivers employed by the agricultural cooperative lost their licences due to frequent drunkenness (*Rada MNV*, 27.3.1965; 236/4). This episode casts some doubt on the quality of white employees.

14. According to an oral account that remains to be verified, the neighbouring village of Lažany was home to a small Romani community until local hoodlums rolled burning tractor tires into the primitive huts and drove out their residents.

15. Old ethnic Slovaks explain their reluctance to serve as godparents to Romani children by the expansion of the population and of the demands associated with the institution.

16. The physical separation of the two buildings and bodies of students seems to have been triggered by a steady increase in the number of white children attending school in Prešov.

17. The re-education component received attention in the form of several initiatives aimed at Romani children and youth (*Plénum MNV*, 24.2.1988; 4.5.1988; 236/3). One of them saw the creation of a music and dance ensemble, called Romale, which performed at a variety of local events. One year after its birth in 1987, the ensemble won the first prize in a regional competition, which, in turn, led to its participation in the newly constituted "Disco-Romo" held in Jarovnice (*Pamätná kniha*, vol. III, pp. 255–60). Although the "Svinia experiment" received positive attention from public media, including a special program broadcast by Radio Bratislava, the reaction from Svinia's *gadje* community was overwhelmingly negative, it seems (p. 256). This led the chronicler, a teacher enthusiastically involved in the "experiment," to observe that the source of the hatred felt by the *gadji* stemmed from their ignorance about the people living right beside them. The Prešov district authority, on the other hand, rewarded Romale with the donation of eight brand new instruments in 1989 (p. 272).

18. The move brought back to the lower site not only the residents of the upper settlement but also a much smaller group of closely related families that had set up a small colony north-west of Svinia in a location known as Zabultov (see Figure 1.2).

19. The 1998 National Film Board documentary *The Gypsies of Svinia* provides a record of some of these promises.

conclusions
WHAT WENT WRONG
IN SVINIA?

How can we explain the profound marginality of Svinia's Roma? What accounts for their exclusion from the mainstream society that surrounds them and the social, material, and cultural benefits enjoyed by its members? It seems to me that in our search for plausible explanations we must concentrate on events and processes that transpired during the socialist era. After all, socialism promised to eradicate the disparities between "blacks" and "whites," and, as we have seen, it carried out a modernization campaign of unprecedented scope that was expected to tear down the barriers separating the two groups. Yet the barriers prevailed and became even more formidable precisely during this nominally egalitarian epoch. The implementation of an ideology devoted to the elimination of inequality was accompanied in Svinia by a sharp rise in inter-ethnic tensions and socio-economic disparities. What lies behind this paradox?

When communism began to make an impact in the early 1950s, eastern Slovakia was still very much a traditional society in the sense used by social scientists and historians. Poorly educated, parochial, attached to local customs and habits, and distrustful of outside interference, the white villagers of Svinia saw themselves as the rightful masters of their community. The fact that they shared it, in a way, with a bunch of *cigáni* hardly made a dent in their sense of entitlement. After all, tradition had carved out a well-defined position for the Roma, which curtailed their autonomy and made them useful to the villagers. The annals of ethnography are replete with accounts of quasi- and genuinely symbiotic relations between neighbouring groups whose members differ in economic strategy, lifestyle, and status. Describing one such setting in the Indian state of Orissa, the anthropologist Frederick Bailey sums up the relationship between the low-caste Panos and the high-caste Warriors in terms that apply equally to traditional Svinia and many similar communities:

> All those disabling prohibitions make it sound as if Panos lived a life of ghettoed isolation, but in fact they were closely, even precisely, integrated into the life of the village. This was not the integration of equal opportunity that the word suggests at the present day, but an integration that is constructed out of difference, out of specialization, out of limits set by convention on the work that a person can do and the power that he or she can exercise. It is the integration that God devised when he placed the rich man in his castle and the poor man at the gate and planned for each of them to stay there, so that there might be order in the world. (Bailey 1996:5)

Conditions such as this make cohabiting groups appear to be "ineradicably diverse in their natures" (8). But the clear-cut and internalized distinctions prevalent in such communities tend to favour an unreflective and, above all, peaceable "habitual ethnicity"which, under the right conditions, may bind the groups through a shared ethos of pragmatic tolerance that helps them avoid open conflict. The neighbours tacitly agree, so to speak, to accept each other not as equal but as worthy of non-interference.

Unlike modern-day versions of multiculturalism that compel their practitioners to regard the differences of other peoples as intrinsically worthy of respect, the pragmatic tolerance that prevailed in Svinia under traditional conditions of life was rooted in utilitarian considerations. The villagers needed "their" Roma, and the Roma needed "their" villagers. As we have seen, whether it was through entertainment, helping with household and farm chores, supplying of building material and certain tools and implements, or disposing of carcasses and other types of refuse, the Roma were integrated into the local economy and society. They may have been stigmatized and laughed at, but they were accepted, grudgingly perhaps, as a useful complement to the white reference group. In this respect the situation in Svinia was comparable to many similar settings throughout eastern Slovakia (Hübschmannová 1993).

The Roma could do little but accept their lowly status and the constant denigration that came with it. They constituted by far the weaker element in the local dyad of relationships, and their dependence on *gadje* patrons was practically total. The villagers, after all, not only supplied all their food and clothing but also controlled access to living space, welfare—to the limited extent it was available prior to socialism—and all other forms of protection. This overwhelming dependence was recognized and formalized through many symbolic markers of inequality and servitude, such as asymmetrical forms of address, the custom of kissing the hand of *gadje* benefactors, the delineation of "whites only" public space, the segregation of Roma in school, church, and cemetery, and the preference for ethnic Slovak godparents. Because the Roma had much more to lose from a breakdown in the local quasi-symbiotic relationship than their neighbours in the village, the onus was on them to cultivate the bonds that linked them with their white patrons. They "knew their place," so to speak, and their daily conduct affirmed acceptance of that place.

This traditional order came to an end in the course of the 1950s and 1960s. The 1950s saw the inception of a wide range of emancipatory movements around the globe, and it is instructive to draw some comparisons here. Post-colonial India faced the consequences of Mahatma Gandhi's *Harijan* campaign, which opened the doors for the Temple Entry Act and the official, though not factual, abolition of the discriminatory repercussions of the caste system. In 1955, Rosa Parks's refusal to give up her seat in the white section of a Montgomery bus sparked the desegregationist civil rights movement in the United States. In both cases powerful national governments clashed with local defenders of the traditional order in an attempt to impose metropolitan views of inter-ethnic relations on the hinterland. The "socialist humanism" propagated by Czechoslovak politicians and social engineers offered a similar emancipatory message, and it too pitted urban intellectuals and apparatchiks against the backwardness of the countryside. When the movers and shakers of Svinia's Roma arrived on the outskirts of the village in 1959 to claim their five plots of *deeded* "white" land, they must have caused a similar uproar as Rosa Parks and her followers or Indian untouchables demanding admission to Hindu temples. Their failure to ignite popular local protest comparable to the resistance mounted by conservative forces in the United States or India most likely derives from the fact that, unlike these two countries, Czechoslovakia was a dictatorship that imposed very strict limits on the expression of any kind of dissent. There was no need in Svinia to call in the local equivalent of the National Guard, because the villagers had learned to exercise caution in their dealings with state-level authorities. The absence of visible expressions of local resistance probably explains why the impact of the Czechoslovak "Village Entry Act"—as we may dub the settlement-elimination campaign mounted by the communists—on inter-ethnic relations in settings such as Svinia has received so little scholarly attention.

The material presented in this book demonstrates the abject failure of the socialist attempt at solving the "Gypsy problem" in Svinia. While ethnic Slovak residents prospered, built modern homes, acquired cars and washing machines, pursued higher education, and improved their job skills and incomes, the Roma stagnated in their primitive huts and fell further and further behind the *gadji*. Thirty years after the symbolic "village entry" of 1959, even the elite-minded innovators of the upper settlement found themselves dumped back and abandoned on the swampy ground of the ancestral camp. What went wrong after the first significant desegregationist move, and why did it fail to bring about a measure of success comparable with advances made in the southern United States or rural India?

The most obvious answer to this difficult question must, almost by necessity, point to the uncooperative stance of the villagers and their local administration. Although open resistance to the will of the Party was out of the question, I have described several ways in which the *gadji* sought to sabotage the emancipatory effort of their former clients and dependents. They ranged from critical and at times inflammatory remarks and demands voiced at public meetings all the way to insincere and even outright uncooperative responses of the municipal administration to requests from higher authorities for specific measures, such as providing building lots or desegregating classrooms. The villagers simply refused to surrender their monopoly on power and prestige or to restructure their relationship with the Roma. This lack of flexibility became a powerful brake on the modernization of Svinia and surely one of the sources of the numerous social problems faced by the community today. With its starkly bifurcated lines of progress, Svinia resembles many other societies around the globe that have ceased being traditional without ever becoming modern (Eisenstadt 1966:146).

The intransigence of the white establishment is nicely illustrated by an account that I have come to call "the rooster story." I heard it from an old Slovak woman who has always had a personal interest in the Roma and whose relations with them have been exceptionally good. Asked about the eating habits of local Roma, she volunteered this story as an example of their tendency to indulge in the consumption of carrion and other, in the eyes of the villagers, "distasteful stuff":

But what, even J. does it. Eight years ago, I had a rooster that died. And she took it. But I told her, "give me at least 20 crowns." And she, "I'll give you when I get some." And I told her, "if you don't give me any [right now], I will throw [the rooster] into the garbage." I came home from shopping, I looked into the garbage can whether she had taken it—and yes, she had. J. had taken it; [the rooster] was gone. They are all the same. It's only that J. puts on airs, but they are all the same.

Significantly, the woman whose conduct is being scrutinized here is Velryba, the matriarch of the money-lenders' clique who is universally acknowledged—by Roma and *gadji* alike—as the most successful local assimilationist. Her "unmasking" here as a mere pretender who "puts on airs" can be seen as an indictment against the integration-minded innovators who founded the upper settlement and as a justification for their expulsion and return to their carrion-eating cousins. After all, they are "all the same."

It would be convenient and easy to stop our search for explanations here and to conclude that Svinia's uneven development was caused by the ill will, prejudice, and perhaps even racism of the villagers. Indeed, if we accept the basic premise, as it is being promulgated by progressive-minded Slovak academics, that the pathological situation faced by many rural Roma "is the result of [their] exclusion from social networks" (Radičová 2001:279), it seems logical to make the next step and hold the white majority accountable for this sad state of affairs. But social reality is always complex, and it pays to look beyond the obvious. While the adversarial stance of the *gadji* undoubtedly contributed to the inability of the Roma to take full advantage of the socialist modernization program, other factors also played an important role. Foremost among these are elements intrinsic to the Romani community and the changes it underwent following the imposition of socialism.

The implementation of socialism in eastern Slovakia had wide-reaching consequences for the integration of Roma into rural society. As has been pointed out on many occasions, the entire system of rural interdependence collapsed very quickly (Hübschmannová 1993). Collectivization of agriculture in the course of the 1950s and 1960s deprived the majority of Roma of most of their traditional work opportunities, because the expropriation of farmers abruptly ended the need for the auxiliary jobs that they had depended on. Although socialism changed relatively little the type of work entrusted to Roma and their long-standing subordination to ethnic Slovaks, the new political and economic order did have three profound consequences. In the first place, unlike the pre-war "free-market" system in which they sold their labour in a competitive environment, socialism guaranteed employment without much attention to the quality of performance. Lacking incentives available to their Slovak co-workers, such as better jobs and pay in exchange for increased productivity and responsibility, many Roma came to view regular employment as a necessary evil, which required monotonous and often back-breaking labour and rewarded it with a constitutionally guaranteed income. Creativity, initiative, and productivity seemed to matter little in this economic environment. As long as one showed up for work and did something, the monthly pay cheque was certain to come.

Second, the new order of things introduced cash as the preferred medium of exchange, replacing foodstuffs and other natural products. While the traditional method of payment—in kind—provided a steady supply of life's necessities, the introduction of money increased the temptation to squander one's pay on liquor, tobacco, gambling, and other addictions. Thus budgeting and other forms of planning became of paramount importance. Not surprisingly, large-scale usury followed on the heels of the introduction of money into settlements (Davidová 1965:66). Third, while the nature of work performed by Roma during socialism differed little from the preceding era, the social relations in which it was embedded had changed radically. In the past, work and pay used to be associated with individual villagers and engendered highly personal networks of patronage and clientship, which had beneficial effects on the quality of inter-ethnic relations. The Roma cultivated "their" *gadji*, and the latter ensured that "their" *cigáni* didn't go unassisted in times of need. Socialism depersonalized labour by substituting the anonymous state for the visible local patron. And, as the reliance on concrete individuals gave way to a wholesale dependence on the state and its local agents, the careful cultivation of inter-ethnic bonds came to appear superfluous.

It is especially the last point, pertaining to the cultivation of relationships, that I wish to single out as a most important factor in the growing marginality of Svinia's Roma. Seduced by communist propaganda and the generosity of the new regime into believing that their former patrons had become powerless and the political conditions they represented obsolete, many, perhaps most, local Roma began to assert and practise a degree of autonomy clearly unacceptable to the white establishment. There were understandable acts of defiance, such as challenges to segregationist conventions in the local tavern, in which Romani counterparts of Rosa Parks refused to uphold discriminatory conventions. But there were also breaches of customary order that originated in apathy, laziness or outright destructiveness, and that pitted the Roma not only against their white neighbours but also against the new socialist regime. It was these infractions that contributed most significantly to the breakdown of local inter-ethnic relations.

Drawing on the work of Robert Putnam and his followers, the historian Robert Rotberg recently postulated that "Societies work best, and have always worked best, where citizens trust their fellow citizens, work cooperatively with them for common goals, and thus share a civic culture" (Rotberg 2001:1). Following Putnam, some scholars use the term "social capital" to distinguish between active civic communities with a rich social fabric based on trust and multiple bonds of cooperation, and disengaged societies comprised of apathetic, indifferent or fearful citizens linked by fragile bonds and authoritarian or opportunistic conventions. Communism, with its key postulates of human perfectability and altruism, presupposed the creation of communities with the highest degree of social capital, and Svinia was no exception. The multitude of political and civic organizations set up here during the first decade of socialism created a network of groups based on voluntarism that dedicated themselves to the generation and ongoing enhancement of local social capital. An individual's contribution to the advancement of socialism was measured largely on the basis of his or her engagement in these building blocks of civic solidarity. The Roma were conspicuously absent from Svinia's voluntary sector. I have already quoted one of the first official statements about local Roma, made in 1955, which postulates that "They know their rights very well, but they refuse to submit to civic duties" (*Pamätná kniha*, vol. II, p. 49). This alleged opportunism and disinterest in civic engagement are mentioned frequently in socialist-era scholarship (Davidová 1965), and it continues to be a vehemently argued accusation levelled at Roma by their *gadje* neighbours.

As every immigrant knows, integration into a new society is enhanced by participation in its voluntary sector. Here one is likely to establish useful contacts with people from all walks of life, and while the newcomer makes a contribution to the host community's social capital, this act of generosity also has beneficial consequences for one's own social standing. It is through these civic networks that immigrants find substitutes for professional contacts, friends, and family left behind in their country of origin. It is perhaps unreasonable to expect participation by the Roma in networks and institutions controlled by their less than welcoming white neighbours. Although there were exceptions, the majority of the villagers failed to apply the principles of "socialist humanism" in their interaction with the *cigáni*, and the latter would have been as uncomfortable attending a meeting of the local chapter of Young Atheists as they are today in the village church. But there were other ways in which Roma could have demonstrated civic engagement without seeking admission to white-controlled "clubs." Foremost among these were donations of time and labour for the purpose of advancing some community project that individual citizens pledged and then carried out in the form of so-called *brigády*. Because the socialist economy experienced a chronic shortage of workers in most sectors, *brigády* often proved indispensable for the completion of any larger construction project. In Svinia, *brigády* mounted by community-spirited volunteers made a significant contribution to the construction of the new school, the municipal building, the "house of culture," and the sidewalks along many residential streets. In addition to such big, one-time projects there were recurrent commitments, such as the annual spring clean-up or the autumn potato harvest. While a handful of Romani men participated in the construction of the "house of culture" through a less than voluntary *brigáda* mounted by the agricultural cooperative, Roma were conspicuous by their lack of participation in most of these demonstrations of civic-mindedness.

Although nowadays people tend to complain about the overtly ideological context in which *brigády* and other expressions of socialist-era voluntarism took place, we must bear in mind that they made a significant contribution to the local standard of living—especially in settings far removed from the attention of metropolitan officials. It was through collective effort that Svinia partook of the material progress that its residents had come to equate with communism. Whether it was the introduction of electricity, dependable trash collection, installation of telephone lines, support for the local soccer team, the library in the "house of culture," or the annual flower and vegetable show, the villagers saw these attainments as a reflection of their civic engagement—be it in the more direct form of *brigády* or the less direct planning, meetings, and lobbying carried out at the level of civic networks and organizations. In one way or another, they all contributed to the "cultural capital" of the community and the collective *kultúrnost'* of its residents.

Compared with the villagers, the Roma have made almost no contribution to the social and cultural capital of Svinia. As the *gadji* never tire of pointing out, they received a chance during their 1959–1989 sojourn in the "integrated" upper settlement, but they blew it. Instead of building decent homes, the innovators took satisfaction with glorified shacks. Instead of using the deeded plots for growing vegetables and raising livestock, the newcomers filled them with junk and garbage. Instead of teaching their children to attend school regularly and devote themselves to homework, they allowed them to vandalize the neighbourhood and become insolent. In the eyes of the villagers, the Roma, especially the ones allowed to leave the lower settlement, were spoiled by the communist regime.

Local *gadji* have two sayings that shed additional light on the inter-ethnic deadlock: "the Gypsy wants to eat without cooking," and "he likes to harvest without planting." This view correlates with the scavenging lifestyle pursued by many local Roma, and it is echoed in the denigration of *gadje* ways by young Roma. As I have pointed out, many Slovak habits are laughed at and rejected as unbecoming. This applies especially to precautionary measures aimed at averting some dangerous consequences, such as the wearing of glasses, hats, and mittens, abstinence from tobacco and alcohol, attendance at school and homework, or the use of toothpaste and soap as part of daily grooming. This disdain for the sissy ways of Slovaks, though, in no way prevents the critics from embracing *gadje* society and culture as the pinnacle of one's dreams and aspirations. These young people would be happy to partake of the pleasurable aspects of the dominant culture—such as residence in nice homes or the opportunity to travel—without having to expend some effort on attaining them. They desire results without the drudgery of the process that leads there.

I think that these snippets of evidence can be translated into a more general assertion. The illustrations of their socialist-era civic disengage-ment indicate a pervasive unwillingness on the part of local Roma to undertake *cultivation* beyond a minimal level required for daily survival. What I mean by this term is the desire to improve, to take care of, to deepen, and enhance one's connection with the natural as well as the social world. It encompasses growing vegetables and raising livestock; teaching children as well as nurturing relationships within and outside the family; prepar-ing meals, and constructing shelters. Any reasonably impartial observer

is bound to conclude that the majority of Svinia's Roma fail to take advantage even of the limited opportunities afforded by the environment in
which they live. They don't grow anything. They don't keep livestock of
any kind. The usual preparation of food is rudimentary and haphazard.
Clothing is neither made nor mended. Apartments and huts are barely
furnished and poorly maintained. Most adults don't take care of their
appearance. The disposal of waste, including the human kind, is almost
unregulated. Attention to the maintenance of good health is rudimentary
at best. Children's socialization is so informal that it borders on neglect.
Interest in formal education and other ways of gaining access to better
opportunities is minimal. And the cultivation of good neighbourly relations, within as well as outside the settlement, is an unknown art. This is
a careless society whose members survive by virtue of their ability to improvise, to endure unnecessary hardships, to bully each other into a social
order based on fighting prowess and impudence, and to take advantage of
the majority society's soup kitchens and other charitable institutions.

A careless society, such as the Romani enclave of Svinia, doesn't equip
its members with sufficient potential for self-reflection. Most, though certainly not all, of the disenfranchised rural Roma whom I have met during
the ten years of my involvement with Svinia have impressed me by the
strength of their conviction that the problems they face are caused by the
majority society and the racism, intolerance, or simple inhumanity of its
members. According to this ideology, the metre-thick layer of garbage that
covers the settlement derives not from the residents' lackadaisical attitude
to dirt, but rather from the determination of the municipal authority to see
the Roma disappear into trash and mud. Illiteracy is attributed to indifferent teachers rather than unmotivated parents and ill-prepared children.
Unemployment and other economic woes are blamed on the government
rather than one's inadequate skills and low work morale. Ill health is believed to be caused by unfriendly physicians and nurses rather than poor
hygiene and a dangerous lifestyle. Within this starkly polarized cosmology,
the Roma see themselves as victims of prejudice and exclusion who deserve
compensation for the wrongs they have endured. The sense of entitlement
generated by such self-perception defines begging as a natural self-defence
mechanism in a hostile world, and inactivity as the expectation of redress
that victims of oppression should receive from the majority society.

However, I don't think that the civic disengagement, carelessness,
opportunism, and disinterest in cultivation that pervade the Romani

community of Svinia have always been intrinsic to it. Oral histories, of *gadji* and Roma alike, testify to the presence of more constructive attitudes in the pre-socialist past when the parents and grandparents of today's de-skilled and disinterested generation practised rudimentary but useful crafts, took care of clothing, paid attention to the upbringing of children, raised livestock, maintained good order in the settlement, and, above all, cultivated neighbourly relations with the villagers. Interestingly, the breakdown of this traditional order began and spread from within the upwardly mobile cluster of innovators who had founded the upper settlement. It was here that the egalitarian doctrine of communism triggered a truly revolutionary transformation of the conditions that tied the Roma to the surrounding society. While this transformation created new avenues for integration—by means of education, universal employment, civic participation, and residential arrangements—it also generated false expectations of a millenarian future where the former underdogs of society would be taken care of by an omnipresent and benevolent state. In the course of accepting the new order, local Roma discarded their carefully cultivated association with the carriers of the old one, namely their former *gadje* patrons and employers. But the attained liberation was incomplete and of short duration. As the two groups began to drift further and further apart—in a paradoxical illustration of segregation through integration—it became apparent that the Roma had lost in their white neighbours a powerful acculturative influence. Having gained independence, so to speak, the Roma were released from the serf's obligation to please his master by pursuing a lifestyle acceptable to him. Now they could litter their yards, vandalize civic institutions, and defecate behind the fire station while waiting for the bus. What may have started as unavoidable acts of rebellion quickly escalated into ongoing indifference, sloth, and disengagement. The villagers retaliated by banning the "uncultured" Roma from private and, largely, public discourse. In the course of this banishment, the rebels against established order found themselves utterly isolated both socially and culturally—to the point where television serves as their only window on *gadje* society.

The work of Edward Shils (1964) reminds us that modernization is a creative process spearheaded by charismatic individuals and groups whose unique characters and personalities account for divergences and specificities in local patterns of development. The socialist modernization of Svinia aggravated traditional cleavages within the community and contributed to a breakdown of the old inter-ethnic order without generating a more satisfactory new one. Having had the opportunity to visit communities where the introduction of socialism didn't engender the degree of inter-ethnic animosity and bitterness prevalent in Svinia, I tend to agree with Shils that local manifestations of modernization are influenced by the elites that propel it. This implies that the uneven results of Svinia's moderniza-tion process could have been distributed more equitably had there been leaders, on both sides of the ethnic divide, intent on cooperation rather than disengagement.

Yet, at the same time, wherever we look in central and eastern Europe, the Roma stand out by their inability to keep pace with the surrounding society in terms of social and economic advancement. Some anthropolo-gists have argued that Roma have developed adaptive strategies that may not appear as such to outside observers, and that most of their groups con-stitute "resourceful and robust communities" (Gmelch 1986:326) equipped with skills and talents that serve them well in the post-communist transition to capitalism (Stewart 2002). We may very well find justification for these claims in certain parts of Slovakia, but the region with which I am best acquainted has few Romani communities that, by virtue of their quality of housing, educational profile, unemployment rate, or health situation, don't appear backward. Whether we call it backwardness, marginality, social ex-clusion, or lack of modernity, it is evident that rural Roma in Slovakia fail to even approach the innovative reservoir of their *gadje* neighbours.

What can be done to stop and reverse the downward spiral? What lies ahead for the thousands of "untouchables" inhabiting the ghettos of Svinia and similar communities? During my last extended visit, in the winter and spring of 2004, I didn't see much that inspired confidence in a brighter fu-ture. The winter started with the implementation of a new welfare policy aimed, ostensibly, at getting Roma off the dole and into the labour force. While the severe cutbacks in social benefits will mean grinding poverty for many, especially smaller, families, they are not likely to translate into high-er workforce participation in chronically underdeveloped regions, such as most of eastern Slovakia. Anyway, no government work-creation program is designed to help overcome some of the impediments faced by Roma in Svinia and similar settlements. Let me illustrate these with an example from my last visit when I managed to find temporary work for a handful of young men on a construction site in a small town nearby. The boys used scavenged old bicycles to commute between the settlement and their work site, and all went well until they ran into a group of white bullies who, equipped with a shotgun, were looking for rabbits along the country road. They decided that the funny bicycles presented a more interesting target, and they quickly smashed them to smithereens.

This is not an exceptional anecdote from a country that joined the European Union in the spring of 2004. Ostensibly protected by the world's most advanced human-rights legislation, the poverty-stricken Roma of eastern Slovakia are seen as a nuisance and an embarrassment, but precious little has been done by any level of government to offer constructive help (Scheffel 2004a). Still, as new EU citizens, Slovak Roma are free to travel and, under certain conditions, work in the expanded Union. Some are benefitting from this new opportunity, but most residents of backward settlements lack the necessary skills. I witnessed the departure of a foursome from Svinia who, packed into a small Škoda, embarked on an expedition that was to take them to a Spanish plantation where, as someone had told them, even illiterate Gypsies from the east could make decent money picking oranges and lemons. The men returned a few days later complaining bitterly about the maze of roads they had encountered in Germany. Unable to read maps, they had lost their way and had decided to come back to the safety of the settlement.

What, then, can be done to help these people overcome the numerous problems of their present existence? Clearly, even if work abroad were a realistic option, most local Roma regard Svinia as their rightful home where they wish to stay. But the overcrowded ghettoized settlement cannot provide the safety and comfort one should expect to find in a central European location at the beginning of the twenty-first century. The Roma must, therefore, break through the walls of the ghetto and claim their rightful place in the village proper. Such a breakthrough should occur gradually in order to avoid the problems encountered in the upper settlement, but occur it must; only co-residence can begin to heal the deep wounds inflicted on the social fabric of the community.

But, important as it may be, the gradual resettlement and integration of a handful of families is not likely to have a significant impact on the overall make-up of the entire Romani community. In order to truly tackle its profound exclusion, the national government would have to commit funds and energies of unprecedented proportions. This is unlikely to happen, because in the current political and economic climate most Slovaks are preoccupied with a desire to catch up with the "West," and higher-order politics reflect this trend. It is therefore probable that the social pathologies described in this book will prevail for a long time to come, engaging the imagination of western essayists (Gauss 2004) and stray anthropologists and demonstrating the endurance of parochial interests in the face of higher-order policies and plans.

But let me not end on such a sombre note. Positive change may be effected without large-scale projects and government programs, driven, as it were, by the collective will of the people who have decided to transform their lives. Such internally fuelled decisions, though, require the participants to assume control over their destiny, and this doesn't happen easily in any setting marked by exclusion and dependence. Describing the need for such a transformation on the Grassy Narrows Indian reserve in northern Ontario, Anastasia Shkilnyk offered words of encouragement that apply equally well to the situation in Svinia:

> Metaphorically speaking, if the external enabling conditions constitute the firewood for the renewal of a people, then the spark to light the fire has to come from within. This spark is the process by which a human being becomes conscious of the responsibility he bears for his own destiny.... As long as [local people] continue to blame others for their circumstances and decide that others are responsible for their survival, very little will change in their society. In the broadest philosophical sense, they have to come to understand that a slave is also a man who waits for someone else to come and free him. (1985:241)

It is not inconceivable that the white villagers might contribute at least encouragement and a measure of good will to such a process of renewal. After all, if they regard the *cigáni* as suffering from a "civilizatory deficit," their own extremist views and starkly ethnocentric sentiments clash with the liberal and multicultural ideology of the European Union of which they have recently become citizens, and now it is *them* who appear backward and uncultured from the vantage point of Brussels, Vienna, and even Bratislava. Sooner or later the young *gadji* of Svinia will be exposed to a new school curriculum that defines cultural diversity as an asset and preaches the principles of inter-ethnic tolerance and understanding. Then, in this not-so-distant future, we might see white schoolchildren pay a respectful visit to a modernized and habitable Romani settlement, motivated by similar reasons as their Canadian counterparts exploring an ethnic neighbourhood or an Indian reserve. They will listen to Janko the guitarist, re-learn how to dance the *czardász*, and twist their tongues around a few Romani phrases. If the acculturation of Svinia ever progresses to this point, then the cold war that has consumed it for the past fifty years may finally come to an end.

BIBLIOGRAPHY

Augustini ab Hortis, Samuel. 1995. *Cigáni v Uhorsku—Zigeuner in Ungarn.* Bratislava: Štúdio dd.

Bacíková, Eva. 1959. Kulturně výchovná práce mezi cikánským obyvatelstvem. In: *Práce mezi cikánským obyvatelstvem,* pp. 31–45. Praha: Úřad předsednictva vlády.

Bačová, Viera. 1988. Spoločenská integrácia cigánskych obyvateľov a cigánska rodina. *Slovenský národopis* 36(1): 22–34.

Bailey, Frederick G. 1996. *The Civility of Indifference: On Domesticating Ethnicity.* Ithaca: Cornell University Press.

Barany, Zoltan. 2002. *The East European Gypsies: regime change, marginality, and ethnopolitics.* Cambridge: Cambridge University Press.

Belišová, Jana. 2002. *Phurikane giľa: starodávne rómske piesne.* Bratislava: Žudro.

Crowe, David M. 1994. *A history of the gypsies of Eastern Europe and Russia.* New York: St. Martin's Press.

Davidová, Eva. 1965. *Bez kolíb a šiatrov.* Košice: Východoslovenské vydavateľstvo.

Davidová, Eva. 1995. *Romano Drom—Cesty Romú 1945–1990.* Olomouc: Univerzita Palackého.

Douglas, Mary. 1966. *Purity and danger.* London: Routledge & Kegan Paul.

Džambazovič, Roman, and Jurásková, Martina. 2002. Sociálne vylúčenie Rómov na Slovensku. In: Michal Vašečka (ed.), *Čačipen pal o Roma: Súhrnná správa o Rómoch na Slovensku,* pp. 527–564. Bratislava: IVO.

Eisenstadt, Shmuel N. 1966. *Modernization: Protest and Change.* New York: Prentice-Hall.

Ergebnisse der in Ungarn am 31. Jänner 1893 durchgeführten Zigeuner-Conscription. 1895. Ungarische Statistische Mittheilungen. Band IX. Budapest.

European Roma Rights Center. 1997. *Time of the Skinheads: Deniàl and Exclusion of Roma in Slovakia.* Budapest: ERRC.

Fedič, Vasil. 2001. *Východoslovenskí Rómovia a II. svetová vojna.* Humenné: Redos.

Gauss, Karl-Markus. 2004. *Die Hundeesser von Svinia.* Wien: Paul Zsolnay Verlag.

Gmelch, Sharon. 1986. Groups that don't want in. *Annual Review of Anthropology* 15: 307–330.

Grulich, Tomáš, and Haišman, Tomáš. 1986. Institucionální zájem o cikánské obyvatelstvo v Československu v letech 1945–1958. *Český lid* 73(2): 72–85.

Gruska, Viliam. 1988. Dotyky s rómskym etnikom. *Slovenský národopis* 36(1): 220–239.

Guy, Will. 1975. Ways of Looking at Roms: The Case of Czechoslovakia. In: F. Rehfisch (ed.), *Gypsies, Tinkers and Other Travellers.* pp. 201–229. London: Academic Press.

Guy, Will. 2001. The Czech lands and Slovakia. Another false dawn? In: W. Guy (ed.), *Between past and future: The Roma of Central and Eastern Europe*, pp. 285–323. Hatfield: University of Hertfordshire Press.

Haišman, Tomáš. 1999. Romové v Československu v letech 1945–1967. In: Helena Lisá (ed.), *Romové v České republice*, pp. 137–183. Praha: Socioklub.

Horváthová, Emília. 1964. *Cigáni na Slovensku.* Bratislava: Slovenská akadémia vied.

Hübschmannová, Milena. 1993. *Šaj pes dovakeras: Můžeme se domluvit.* Olomouc.

International Organization for Migration. 2000. *Social and economic situation of potential asylum seekers from the Slovak Republic.* Bratislava: IOM.

Janto, Juraj. 2000. Práca cirkví medzi Rómami. In: Juraj Janto (ed.), *Integrácia Rómov na Slovensku.* Special issue of *Ethnologia Actualis Slovaca* I(2): 57–73.

Jurová, Anna. 1992. Riešenie rómskej problematiky na Slovensku po druhej svetovej vojne. In: Arne Mann (ed.), *Neznámi Rómovia*, pp. 91–102. Bratislava: Ister Science Press.

Jurová, Anna. 1993. *Vývoj rómskej problematiky na Slovensku po roku 1945.* Košice: Goldpress Publishers.

Jurová, Anna. 1996. *Rómska problematika 1945–1967—dokumenty*. Praha: Ústav pro soudobé dějiny AV ČR.

Kirschbaum, Stanislav. 1995. *A History of Slovakia: The struggle for survival*. New York: St. Martin's Griffin.

Kollárová, Zuzana. 1988. K problematike cigánskej otázky na Spiši (1918–1938). *Slovenský národopis* 36(1): 137–145.

Kollárová, Zuzana. 1992. K vývoju rómskej society na Spiši do roku 1945. In: Arne Mann (ed.), *Neznámi Rómovia*, pp. 61–72. Bratislava: Ister Science Press.

Kontrolní zpráva o plnění usnesení ÚV KSČ o práci mezi cikánským obyvatelstvem v ČSR ze dne 8. dubna 1958. 1958. Praha: Central Committee of the Communist Party of Czechoslovakia [state archive of the Czech Republic, unit 289/volume 36].

Kotal, Jindřich. 1959. Nejdúležitější úkoly při převýchově cikánú. In: *Práce mezi cikánským obyvatelstvem*, pp. 58–62. Praha: Úřad předsednictva vlády.

Kováč, Milan, and Jurík, Milan. 2002. Religiozita Rómov a aktivity cirkví vo vzt'ahu k Rómom. In: Michal Vašečka (ed.), *Čačipen pal o Roma: Súhrnná správa o Rómoch na Slovensku*, pp. 127–144. Bratislava: IVO.

Lacková, Ilona. 1999. *A false dawn: My life as a Gypsy woman in Slovakia*. Hatfield: University of Hertfordshire Press and Centre de recherches tsiganes.

Lemon, Alaina. 2000. *Between Two Fires: Gypsy Performance and Romani Memory from Pushkin to Post-Socialism*. Durham, NC: Duke University Press.

Lindnerová, Vladimíra. 1993. Zájem státních institucí o cikánské obyvatelstvo v Československu v letech 1959–1989. *Český lid* 80(3): 195–205.

Lužica, René. 2001. Výskum perzekúcií Cigánov/Rómov na Slovensku v rokoch 1939–1945. *Etnologické rozpravy* 2: 23–29.

Mann, Arne. 1992. Prvé výsledky výskumu rómskeho kováčstva na Slovensku. In: Arne Mann (ed.), *Neznámi Rómovia*, pp. 103–116. Bratislava: Ister Science Press.

Mann, Arne. 1995. The Development of the Romany Family. In: *Roma People in Slovakia and in Europe*, pp. 61–67. Bratislava: Information and Documentation Centre of the Council of Europe.

Mann, Arne. 2001. Rómovia na Spiši (na základe súpisov z 18. storočia). *Etnologické rozpravy* 2: 18–22.

Middleton, John, and Tait, David (eds.). 1958. *Tribes without rulers*. London: Routledge & Kegan Paul.

Ministerstvo vnitra. 1952. *Úprava poměrů osob cikánského původu*. Praha: Central Committee of the Communist Party of Czechoslovakia [state archive of the Czech Republic, unit 289/volume 36].

Ministerstvo vnitra. 1959. Směrnice k provedení zákona č. 74/1958 Sb. o trvalém usídlení kočujících osob. In: *Práce mezi cikánským obyvatelstvem*, pp. 64–71. Praha: Úřad předsednictva vlády.

Ministerstvo vnitra. 1962. *Současný stav převýchovy cikánského obyvatelstva v Severočeském kraji—nedostatky—řešení*. Praha: Central Committee of the Communist Party of Czechoslovakia [state archive of the Czech Republic, unit 289/volume 36].

Ministerstvo zdravotnictví. 1957. *Cikánská otázka z hlediska zdravotnického*. Praha: Central Committee of the Communist Party of Czechoslovakia [state archive of the Czech Republic, unit 287/volume 36].

Ministerstvo zdravotnictví. 1959. Směrnice pro zdravotnickou práci u osob, které vedly kočovný způsob života. In: *Práce mezi cikánským obyvatelstvem*, pp. 76–80. Praha: Úřad předsednictva vlády.

Mušinka, Alexander. 2000. Projekt Svinia (Niekoľko poznámok k problematike integrácie Rómov. In: J. Janto (ed.), *Integrácia Rómov na Slovensku*. Special issue of *Ethnologia Actualis Slovaca* I(2): 75–83.

Nečas, Ctibor. 1981. *Nad osudem českých a slovenských Cikánú v letech 1939–1945*. Brno: UJEP.

Nečas, Ctibor. 1986. Evidence československých Cikánú z let 1922–1927. *Český lid* 73(2): 66–71.

Nečas, Ctibor. 1988. Pronásledování Cikánú v období slovenského státu. *Slovenský národopis* 36(1): 127–136.

Nečas, Ctibor. 1989. Štatistické výsledky o cigánskej populácii z roku 1924 na východnom Slovensku. *Historica Carpatica* 20: 213–223.

Obce a mestá v číslach. 1992. Prešov: Okresné oddelenie Slovenského štatistického úradu Prešov.

Okely, Judith. 1983. *The Traveller—Gypsies*. Cambridge: Cambridge University Press.

Osvetové ústredie. 1956. *Zpráva o prieskumu sposobu života obyvateľov cigánskeho povodu*. Praha: Central Committee of the Communist Party of Czechoslovakia [state archive of the Czech Republic, unit 298/volume 37].

Pamätná kniha obce Svinia. n.d. 3 volumes.

Přívora, Miroslav. 1959. Zdravotní stav cikánú a úkoly zdravotníkú v péči o cikány. In: *Práce mezi cikánským obyvatelstvem*, pp. 46–51. Praha: Úřad předsednictva vlády.

Radičová, Iveta. 2001. *Hic sunt Romales*. Bratislava: Interlingua.

Ringold, Dana. 2000. *Roma and the transition in Central and Eastern Europe: Trends and challenges*. Washington: The World Bank.

Ročenka mesta Bratislavy. 1960. Bratislava: Osveta.

Rotberg, Robert. 2001. Social Capital and Political Culture in Africa, America, Australasia, and Europe. In: Robert Rotberg (ed.), *Patterns of Social Capital: Stability and Change in Historical Perspective*. Cambridge: Cambridge University Press.

Šalamon, Pavel. 1988. Vplyv tlače medzivojnového obdobia na formovanie vzťahu obyvateľov k Cigánom. *Slovenský národopis* 36(1): 147–154.

Šalamon, Pavel. 1992. Cigáni v Abovskej a Turnianskej stolici v období osvietenstva. In: Arne Mann (ed.), *Neznámi Rómovia*, pp. 73–78. Bratislava: Ister Science Press.

Scheffel, David. 1999. The Untouchables of Svinia. *Human Organization* 58(1): 44–53.

Scheffel, David. 2000. The Post-Anthropological Indian: Canada's New Images of Aboriginality in the Age of Repossession. *Anthropologica* XLII(2): 175–187.

Scheffel, David. 2004a. Slovak Roma on the threshold of Europe. *Anthropology Today* 20(1): 6–12.

Scheffel, David. 2004b. The Roma of Central and Eastern Europe. *Reviews in Anthropology* 33(2): 143–161.

Senát Národního shromáždění. 1927. *Zákon o potulných cikánech*. Praha.

Shils, Edward. 1964. *Political Development in the New States*. New York: Humanities Press.

Shkilnyk, Anastasia. 1985. *A poison stronger than love: the destruction of an Ojibwa community*. New Haven, CT: Yale University Press.

Šípek, Zdeněk. 1989. Cikánské legitimace v Čechách v meziválečném období. *Český lid* 76(3): 133–137.

Šípek, Zdeněk. 1990. Cikánská otázka v prvním desetiletí ČSR. *Český lid* 77(3): 139–144.

Šípek, Zdeněk. 1991. Usazování cikánú na začátku protektorátu. *Český lid* 78(2): 85–89.

Srb, Vladimír. 1986. Koncentrace a urbanizace Cikánů v Československu. *Český lid* 73(2): 86–92.

Štatistický úrad SR. 1994. *Štatistický lexikón obcí Slovenskej republiky 1992.* Prešov: Štatistický úrad.

Štatistický úrad SR. 2001. *Sčítanie ľudu, domov a bytov 2001: základné údaje.* Prešov: Štatistický úrad.

Stewart, Michael. 1997. *The Time of the Gypsies.* Boulder, CO: Westview Press.

Stewart, Michael. 2002. Deprivation, the Roma and 'the underclass'. In: C. Hann (ed.), *Postsocialism: Ideas, ideologies and practices in Eurasia,* pp. 133–155. London: Routledge.

Tokár, Radko. 2001. Sociálna kultúra valašských Rómov na Slovensku. *Etnologické rozpravy* 2: 107–114.

United Nations Development Program. 2002. *Avoiding the dependency trap: The Roma in Central and Eastern Europe.* Regional Human Development Report. Bratislava: UNDP.

Urbancová, Viera. 1995. Samuel Augustini ab Hortis a jeho zabudnutá monografia o Cigánoch v Uhorsku. In: Samuel Augustini ab Hortis, *Cigáni v Uhorsku,* pp. 3–11.

Vašečka, Michal (ed.). 2002. *Čačipen pal o Roma: Súhrnná správa o Rómoch na Slovensku.* Bratislava: IVO.

Víšek, Petr. 1988. K některým novým aspektům společenské integrace Romů v socialistickém Československu. *Slovenský národopis* 36(1): 35–44.

Víšek, Petr. 1999. Program integrace—řešení problematiky romských obyvatel v období 1970 až 1989. In: Helena Lisá (ed.), *Romové v České republice,* pp. 184–218. Praha: Socioklub.

Zeman, Otakar. 1959. K otázkám práce mezi cikánským obyvatelstvem v ČSR. In: *Práce mezi cikánským obyvatelstvem,* pp. 5–23. Praha: Úřad předsednictva vlády.

Zpráva o súčasnej situácii na úseku riešenia občanov cigánskeho pôvodu a návrh na opatrenia vo Východoslovenskom kraji. 1958. Praha: Central Committee of the Communist Party of Czechoslovakia [state archive of the Czech Republic, unit 297/volume 37].

INDEX